CALIFORNIA ON STONE

ARNO PRESS NEW YORK

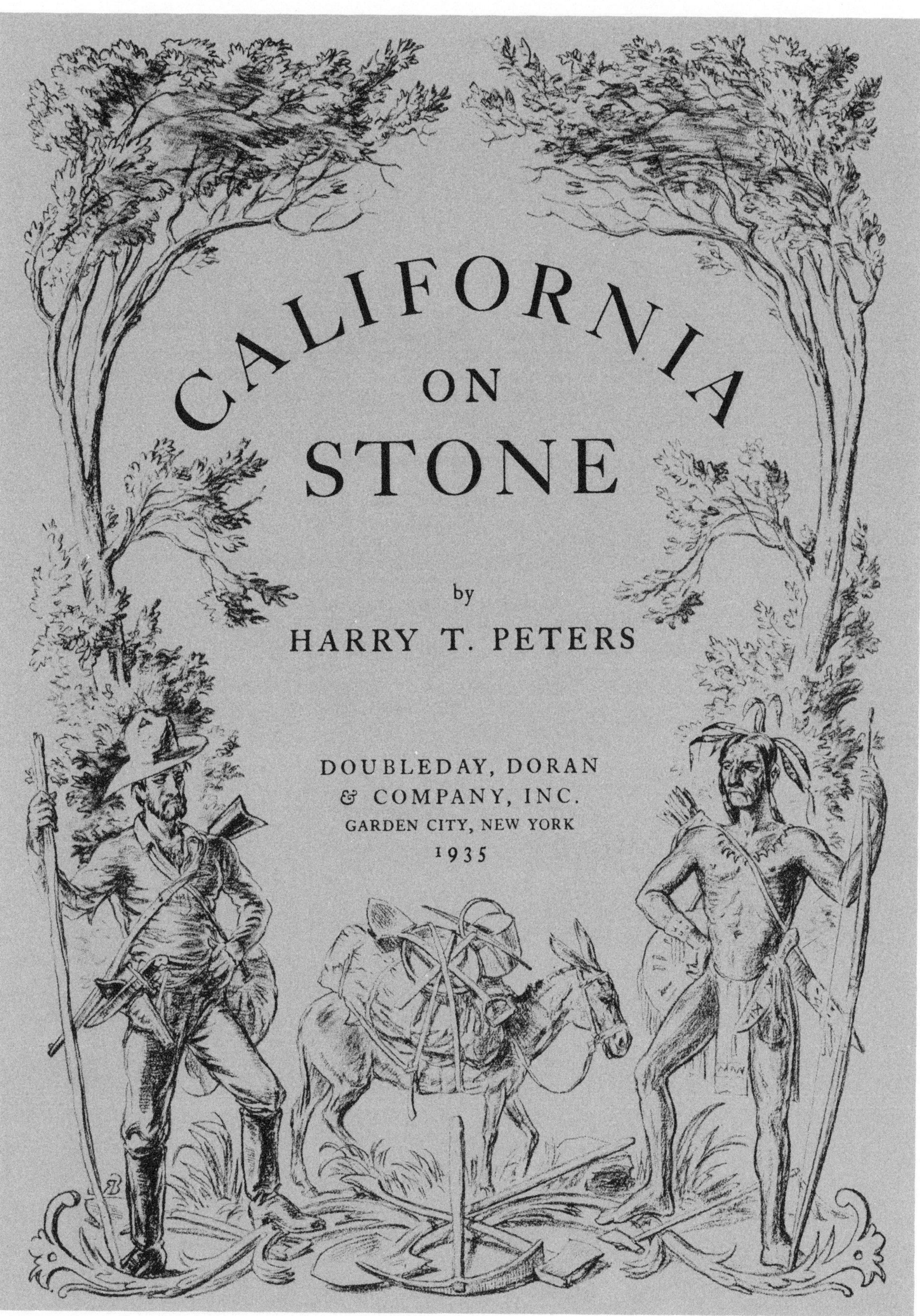
CALIFORNIA
ON
STONE
by
HARRY T. PETERS
DOUBLEDAY, DORAN
& COMPANY, INC.
GARDEN CITY, NEW YORK
1935

Editorial Supervision: Andrea Hicks
Reprint Edition 1976 by Arno Press Inc.

Manufactured in the United States of America

Library of Congress Cataloging in Publication Data

Peters, Harry Twyford, 1881-1948.
California on stone.

(America in two centuries, an inventory)
Reprint of the ed. published by
Doubleday, Doran, Garden City, N. Y.
1. Lithography—California. 2. Lithographers—California.
3. Lithographs, American. 4. Lithographs—California. 5. California in art.
I. Title. II. Series.
NE2310.C2P4 1976 769'.4'99794 75-22833
ISBN 0-405-07704-1

CONTENTS

PROLOGUE

PROLOGUE

When in 1931 the first general survey of the history of American lithography was completed and published in my volume entitled *America on Stone,* it was apparent that one of the most interesting special fields was that of lithography in California, and that a great deal of additional information on this subject remained to be ferreted out and presented in a special study. Since that time I have been able to gather bits of additional material, but if it were not for the fact that Laura Retting White, who had helped much with *America on Stone,* moved to California, this volume would never have been possible. With my collaboration from a distance, Mrs. White worked hard for several years, searching private and public collections, and interviewing students, collectors, dealers, descendants of the lithographers, and other helpful people. Therefore we are now able to explore further the great jungle of lost Americana, following the trails opened in *America on Stone* all the way to California. Here again, as in the broader survey, I am far from pretending to offer an exhaustive study of the subject: even this more limited field is inexhaustible, and I can only present what is known, as a stimulus to further collection and study. Here again, however, I feel that I am able to present enough material to satisfy collectors, and most others who may be interested in the subject, for a few years.

Now this field, for many reasons, has more mystery and fascination than any of the others. Here we find what I may call the fourth school of American lithography, combining—through the California prints made in the East, and through the migration of the lithographers themselves—the other three, and adding to these the influence of the Orient and the influences of all the other nations and all the other sorts and conditions of men that took part in the world's greatest stampede. The men who made these prints, and the traditions from which they worked, were about as heterogeneous as they could have been, and yet the peculiar and difficult circumstances under which the work was done, and the superlatively dramatic and picturesque subject matter, resulted in a body of prints, a school of lithography, even more distinct than any of the others. It is quite possible, of course—names and dates unseen—to mistake an early lithograph made in Philadelphia for an early New York or even Boston lithograph; it would be much harder to go wrong on California.

For those print collectors who may be a little rusty on their history, let us recall a few of the events in one of the most dramatic passages in the history of America and of the world. In January, 1848, a man named James W. Marshall, engaged in building a sawmill on the South Fork of the American River for John A. Sutter, picked up a flake of gold. (A biography of Sutter, a formidable colonist and a fascinating man, has recently and at last been published.) The results of this discovery, including the extension of the United States to the Pacific, the creation of the clipper ships, possibly the outcome of the Civil War, and so on indefinitely, we leave for the most part to the historians. What interests us here is that it resulted in a stampede to California from all parts of the world, in a human spectacle replete with heroism, adventure, comedy, tragedy, pathos, violence, gentleness, vulgarity, nobility, sordidness, and spectacular freaks of fortune, and in the creation of a lithographic record of this spectacle. It was America's biggest party, and as in the case of all the others, the lithographers were there to make pictures of it for the folks at home and, incidentally and unconsciously, for us, almost ninety years later.

In 1846 the white population of California was estimated at about 3,000, and by 1849 enthusiastic politicians were claiming a population of 125,000 and demanding the admission of California to the Union as a state, which came one year later. Try to imagine the rush of Argonauts pouring in from every quarter of the compass at a rate to produce such figures. (Less than five per cent. of the 125,000 were women, but these five per cent. seem to have taken pretty good care of their own.) Let us look at some of the illustrations in this volume, try to enumerate the modes of travel: mule train, clipper ship, covered wagon, horseback, foot, and so on, and try to imagine the hardships and adventures of those eager journeys around the Horn, across the Isthmus, across the plains, across the Pacific. Doesn't it strike a note of its own when a notice reads as follows: "The Great Pioneer Express runs to Volcanoville, Last Chance, Ground Hog's Glory, Hell's Delight, and Bogus Thunder"? This express missed some of the well-known stops such as Dead Man's Gulch, Sweet Revenge, Lousy Level, Git up and Git, Loafers' Retreat, Lazy Hollow, and a few more of the select towns. These were the days of famous mule trains of a hundred and fifty pack mules, with such characters as the celebrated Daniel Dancer in charge, carrying an entire town up the gulch on their backs. Then came the stage lines with their six-horse teams, racing down ravines for records, with drivers whose names were Rattlesnake Dick, Curly Dan, Hank Monk, and so on. One such driver, Jack Davis, later became one of the first of the train-robbing bandits. This road agent, like a number of his contemporaries, was far too active in his way of getting gold, but that's all part of the story. The climax was the idea of Jeff Davis, then our Secretary of War (1855). He sent for a herd of camels to help the stampede. They arrived in due order, and the files of the local papers tell tales of their first appearances in various places. They gave rise to much fiction as well as fact, and the last of them was seen as late as 1888, on the loose, on some prairie, frightening horses.

Of special interest in the transportation of the Argonauts are the clipper ships. The pictorial record of this flowering of American technical skill and adventure was made by Currier & Ives and the other lithographers in the East, but the ships themselves were created partly in order to transport the Forty-niners and their golden fleece, pictured here, and they appear again in the views of harbors of California, so they are definitely a part of this story, too. Dana's *Two Years Before the Mast* reminds us that the great sailing ships knew California and her hides long before Marshall picked up his gold flake. It was not until February 28, 1849, that a government post office was established in California and the first official mail arrived from the East; then, and not until then, was California in official communication with the outside world. Before that, one might send a letter to California unofficially, by some obliging skipper, via Cape Horn. It is to be remembered also that the great march westward, beyond the Mississippi, the building of the transcontinental railroads, and all the rest of that great pageant so sympathetically pictured by Currier & Ives and the others in the East, were largely motivated by the hunger for the same yellow metal that created the fantastic human spectacle here directly drawn on stone.

What happened, then, to these hordes of adventurers when they finally reached the Promised Land? Most of us recall the colorful pictures of all this painted in words by Bret Harte, Mark Twain, and others. For myself, there is an old log of an early clipper ship that had an imaginative first mate who painted the picture as I like to think of it. Also, I have had the privilege of hearing two of the great Forty-niners recall those days: Marcus Daly and James B. Haggin. Well can I recall how on his last birthday, after dinner, in a fine house on Fifth Avenue, Mr. Haggin told us how he sold eggs at five dollars each, and trudged with his pack of fresh food to the foothills. Lacking the spoken words of the pioneers themselves, we can turn, if we like, to the hundreds of books on the subject. (A splendid bibliography was published, two years ago, by R. E. and R. G. Cowan.)

I like best to turn to the old lithographs, made on the spot, or from sketches made on the spot, at the time, and for those who are not yet collectors, the illustrations in this volume will give some idea of the variety and interest of the story and of its setting. I have turned these pictures, and many others like them, over many times, and every time I go back to them I find something new and interesting. Keep your eye on the details; these, more perhaps than any American lithographs, are rich in them. I will point out here only an obvious, but nevertheless important, element: the beginning of what has since been called the "Yellow Peril," that cause of so much fear, strife, and legislation. In no place or time was there ever so much action, including the farcical, crowded into one place over a few crowded years. John Masefield says somewhere that to see English life as it is one must go to a hunt or a funeral, for there one will see life as Chaucer did on his way to Canterbury. It has always seemed to me that here in California of the Gold Rush one can see, not only a fascinating historical spectacle, but also some of the essence of America to this day.

It was officially declared, in the United States Census Report of 1890, that the American frontier had disappeared; the French sociologist, M. André Siegfried, recently entitled a good book *America Comes of Age;* and various other dates have been given for this moment in American biography or history. It has always seemed to me that when Marshall picked up that flake, America reached a definite turning point in her life history. Say that there and then her long, relatively happy childhood came to an end, and she entered upon the turbulence, hysterias, pains, and ecstasies of her adolescence. Pioneers had been pushing steadily westward from the beginning, but at this point they reached the Pacific; now it was not simply a new home farther west, now it was Gold, railroads, building lots, corporations—as well as adventure and freedom; now America awoke with a jolt.

However that may be, most of the Forty-niners were too busy keeping alive and on the go to record the facts and the scene at the time; and since most of the pictures were destroyed, it becomes of the utmost importance to list and record the few that we have left. And now that we have very briefly recalled the story of the Gold Rush, setting the stage, so to speak, for the arrival of the lithographer on the scene, permit me to remind the American collecting public that they must remain conscious of the time, place, and circumstances in which this body of popular art was created.

In the first place, these pictures were made under circumstances of extreme physical difficulty, and during one of history's most extraordinary cases of hysteria. When one remembers that most of the Forty-niners were almost constantly in motion, so that cities grew and withered like mushrooms, that food, clothing, health, and law and order were taken care of as best they could be during a passionate hunt for gold, and that literally everything started at scratch, it seems to me extraordinary that anyone bothered to make and sell pictures, mere pictures, at all. In the second place, even less than in the case of the Eastern lithographers were these men thinking of creating art. They were the reporters, cameramen, and newsreel men of the time and place; consciously, at least, they let art go hang; they did not even attempt the colored wall embellishments so much favored by the Eastern firms. It is interesting to note that, even so, their work surpasses in quality much of that produced in the East. Finally, it is to be remembered that these lithographs, like those made in the East, were sold at very low prices. There is hardly a record to show that any of the California lithographs of the period we are considering—1849–1880—was sold for even one dollar. Only today I received from a friend a clipping from a Boston paper of 1856 that carries an advertisement listing some of our most important Eastern lithographs for sale at six cents each. The only positive information we have about the prices of these California lithographs is contained in several letters—three to my knowledge—written on paper decorated by scenes lithographed by Britton & Rey; in these letters the writer informs his correspondent that he paid five cents for the sheet upon which he was writing. That was probably the retail price, and this illustrated letter paper was sold as picture postal cards are today in the hotels. It is perfectly fair to assume that these California lithographs were sold at the usual Eastern prices of a few cents each.

Let us take a general survey of the production as a whole. The bulk of it was produced by a few firms and alignments of firms that were right in the center of the Gold Rush. Then there are the contributions of the smaller firms and of individuals. To augment these there are those produced by the flourishing lithographic establishments of the East which were not doing business on the spot. Many of these bear the inscription: "From sketches by [So-and-so] that have been forwarded to us." The more important of these have been listed here for reference, as they really belong to *California on Stone*. Most of the important foreign contributions that add to the story and seem to have been made for California consumption have been included here, although the listing of them is not intended to be considered comprehensive, since we are concerned mainly with the American lithographer.

Even when it is thus augmented, and even when one remembers the difficulties of the time and place, the body of California lithographs of this period is rather disappointing in its volume. In 1931, when I was completing *America on Stone,* I had hopes that there might be a very large mass of unknown California material. It would now seem that there are perhaps seven hundred and fifty fairly important items. When we remember that the firm of Currier & Ives alone produced more than seven thousand different lithographs, our disappointment is natural, however irrational. Nevertheless, years of research and careful listing and study of all the more important accessible collections confirm this estimate of the volume of the surviving body of California lithographs.

It must be borne in mind that these California items have been very assiduously collected for some time, so that there seems little hope of further major discoveries. Another consideration is that everywhere in California one is reminded that their disasters, fires, and earthquakes, especially those of 1906, wiped out collections and stocks of prints. For instance, the remaining stock, and all the records, of the firm of Britton & Rey were completely destroyed in 1906.

Now this California group, leaving out of consideration at the moment the contributions to it of a few of the well-known Eastern lithographers, shows certain material differences from the Eastern groups as a whole. There are few in color; most of them remain uncolored, in black and white, and in this respect, as in their quality, they resemble the early Boston group. There are great variations in size: there were no runs of uniform stock size and of large and small folios, such as characterize the New York lithographs. Generally speaking, they are on thin (often tinted) paper of inferior quality. To a certain extent, in the case of the earlier ones, this may be explained by the facts that they were sold to be folded and mailed home, and that good paper in large quantities was probably hard to get. There seems to have been no mass production; there are few, if any, really common or plentiful groups or even single prints, and this fact cannot be attributed wholly to subsequent disasters. It is also extremely difficult to get these prints in a good state of preservation; nearly all of them show hard usage, and many are badly damaged. Large numbers are found written upon. Of course this is not always a defect, because a contemporary inscription: "We had our camp here," or something of the kind, merely makes the historical value and interest more personal.

Portrait of Joseph Britton. Reproduced by courtesy of his niece, Miss Sylvia Rey.

There are also surprising, as well as obvious, differences in subject matter. In the East, portraits of one sort or another form the second largest group; here there is an extreme dearth of these. Evidently the portrait artists did not get the gold fever; at least, there are not enough surviving portraits fairly to count.

Views and more views, scenes of all sorts, are the major portion of the output. There are practically no prints of games and sports; there are a few caricatures and a few comics. Most interesting of all, of course, are the very few of historic events. Like all lithographers, many of these did commercial work, but little of this seems important, except a few wildcat mining stock certificates, and a few business cards. A little later we find considerable work in illustrated books.

An exhaustive study of the monumental Cowan bibliography of California titles was made. Little information as to the various techniques used in the illustrations could be found. A selection of over two hundred books which might contain lithographs was compiled. Of this list, Messrs. Lingel, McDonald, and Vigilante, of the New York Public Library, graciously placed at my disposal about a hundred volumes. About thirty volumes contained lithographs. Among these were the magnificent and early plates in *Voyage Pittoresque autour du Monde*, Paris, 1882, by Louis Choris; the superb beginning in a single part of an intended series of California scenes by John W. Audubon, the leader of one of the most tragic treks of the Forty-niners; the original scenes drawn on the spot by Borthwick, Frank Marryat, McIlvaine, Cooper, and Bayard Taylor. These are but some of the high spots, taken from the books at hand. The interesting and informative set of Pacific Railroad Explorations and Surveys issued by the United States government, 1853–1856, with their fine lithographs by Sarony & Major, Hoen, Weber, Sinclair, Duval, and Ackermann, are in themselves a special field for the collector. It would take a volume to describe them. They contain many of the earliest views depicting the beginning of the West. Henry R. Wagner, in his scholarly bibliography, *The Plains and the Rockies,* gives a fine account of these reports. His notes on the artists who accompanied the various expeditions are very interesting. Then there are the folio "County Histories," some of which contain hundreds of lithographs. For those interested, the titles of these are given in the Alphabetical List. It has always been my hope that someone would assemble a bibliography of all the more important of these American books illustrated with lithographs, and I leave this field to whoever will claim it, for it is far too extensive to attempt to cover thoroughly in this volume.

Here a word might be added about another fertile field for the collector, the illustrated song and music sheet. Some of them are recorded here. The first one lithographed and published in California is reproduced. The theme song in the great push seems to have been Stephen Collins Foster's "O Susanna." Howe in *The Argonauts of '49* and Minnigerode in *The Fabulous Forties* reprint many parodies on this song. "We all sang" was a daily entry in many of the journals kept by the Pioneers. From the music houses of Atwill, Kohler, and Matthias Gray came a flood of sheet music. The Library of Congress and other public libraries are making a sincere effort to list these fugitive and rare sheets.

Portrait of Jacques Joseph Rey. Reproduced by courtesy of his daughter, Miss Sylvia Rey.

Perhaps second only to the lithographed letter sheets, which are surely the godparents of the illustrated postal card of today, the group of Mission pictures has a claim to distinction. In writing before, not having seen or studied this group, I stated with regret that the American lithographer had added only the camp meetings, the Shakers, and the Mormons to the religious gallery of the world. Perhaps this little group of Mission views is not exactly as original a contribution as those mentioned, but it is certainly different and interesting. The artist who did Paul Revere's church in Boston does not equal these California lithographers when they turned from the hurly-burly of the Gold Rush for relief and found these peaceful subjects ready and at hand.

Of course the so-called Forty-niners had little or nothing to do with these Missions, which are the most prominent feature in the early history of California. They were established long before, to propagate the Roman Catholic faith and extend the domain of Spain. In Alta California they formed a cordon extending the entire length of the coast. They were constructed in the fertile valleys, at intervals of about thirty miles. The first, at San Diego, was founded by the famous Padre Junipero Serra, in 1769. The more important of the others were Mission Dolores, Santa Clara, San José, San Juan Bautista, San Carlos, Santa Cruz, Soledad, San Antonio, San Miguel, San Luis Obispo, Santa Inez, Santa Barbara, San Buenaventura, San Fernando, San Gabriel, San Juan Capistrano, and San Luis Rey. San Gabriel in its heyday produced more than six hundred barrels of wine for export each year. San Luis Obispo is one of the most colorful in the history of the Missions. Its bands of Indian hunters were famous for their skill in killing otter and other fur-bearing animals. In its prime it had 87,000 head of cattle, 2,000 horses, 3,500 brood mares, 3,700 mules, and 72,000 sheep. These figures give some idea of the size of these Missions.

So, here again we are indebted to the American lithographer for at least a few fragmentary pictures of these most colorful bits of our not very remote past. Unfortunately the Missions were secularized, for the most part, about 1834, so our lithographers did not see them in the days of their glory. Even before that the earthquakes of 1812 had taken a very heavy toll of many of the more important buildings. As time goes on, these views must of necessity become more and more important to the historian, the illustrator, and the antiquarian, because they are part of the meager pictorial record of a very important part of California history, of a social, economic, and religious system that has long disappeared from the American scene.

Of obvious interest are the lithographs recording the activities of the Vigilantes and other groups formed to restore, or rather to create, law and order. We have certificates of membership, views of parades and hangings, and finally views of the celebrations of the establishment of regular government. There are views of the Chinese Market and the German Fest-Tag, and other curious bits recalling one of the most vivid of America's many melting pots.

Whenever possible, the stories of these lithographers have been set down fully, or rather as fully as they could be traced. In some instances descendants have been found, and the biographies are recorded here for the first time. This is in no sense a complete checklist of the work of these lithographers. Here are set down all the really important California lithographs that could be seen or collected and listed. Many of these craftsmen practised the usual prerogative and copied anything and everything they saw and liked or thought might be sold. These "borrowings" have been left out, as they add nothing to the story.

Portrait of George Holbrook Baker. Reproduced by courtesy of his daughter, Mrs. George Lilly.

Incidentally, the difficulty of the search can best be illustrated by one little fact. At the American Antiquarian Society, in Worcester, Massachusetts, where we have one of the best collections of American lithographs, the California portfolio contains only seven prints, yet one of these seven is the only known copy, and none of the important California collections has it.

Even after four more years of study, it would still seem that Britton & Rey and their associates were the most important in the field. These men and all their various associates were all in the first rank. Since the writing of *America on Stone,* much has been added to their story. Joseph Britton had started in business at 559 Hudson Street, New York, in 1847. Suddenly the gold fever seized him, and he was early on the scene of action. Like many others, as soon as the fever abated, he returned to his own vocation and began to create a new civilization in California. So far as we know, no one has a complete collection of Britton & Rey illustrated letter sheets, which form one of the most interesting and important parts of the whole group of California lithographs. In fact, no one knows of what a complete collection of these would consist. We have no records, and so we have to go on building it up from the sheets themselves. One of the surprises of the research was George H. Baker and his associates. His work was little known in the East, yet it is extremely good and of relatively large volume. It would be superfluous to discuss further, here, the various individuals who will be found recorded in the following pages. Their stories, like those of many of the Eastern lithographers, will be found rich in curious drama and in human interest. It may be that the publication of what information I have been able to gather will produce other relations of the men themselves, and more information.

As I have already said, this body of lithographs as a whole is superior in quality to almost any other body or group of American lithographs. There is distinct artistic merit in many of these prints, and the garishness and meticulous detail of much of the Eastern work are notably lacking. These men seem to have been, for all their emphasis on news values, actual artists rather than simple draftsmen and lithographers. Note especially, in these reproductions, the distinct striving for, and often attainment of, the third dimension, the distinction of planes, and the sensitive, balanced handling of detail. The complaint that many of our Eastern lithographs lack depth is a sound one; here it would be unjustified. Most curious and mysterious of all is the definitely Oriental quality of these prints. It is not only the frequent Oriental subject matter; it is the treatment, too. The English element is marked in the Boston lithographs, German and other elements in those made in New York, French influences in the Philadelphia group. Here there are perhaps touches of all these, but here, too, there is something far more arresting, something that—explain it as you will—must have crossed the Pacific.

Elsewhere I have called attention to what I like to call the individualism or sense of adventure of the American lithographers and their work. In the early days, at least, they all went their own colorful ways, taking chances, and pleasing their own private fancies and enthusiasms, as well as those of the public. Here too, of course, this exhilarating element is marked. Of course, even from the beginning, in California, the art of the lithographer was starting to give way before more commercial media, but there is no record that photography reached the Coast until well after the important part of our story is told. It is no wonder that these adventurous and footloose spirits joined the great stampede, the great adventure, and left us their own vivid record of it. It is no wonder at all, and it is our enduring gain.

THE ALPHABETICAL LIST

OF THE
ARTISTS, LITHOGRAPHERS, PUBLISHERS, AND CRAFTSMEN
WHO WORKED IN CALIFORNIA
OR ON CALIFORNIAN SUBJECTS
TOGETHER WITH NOTES
ON THEIR WORK.

INDEX TO ALPHABETICAL LIST ILLUSTRATIONS

The lithographs in the pages that follow vary so tremendously in dimensions that no attempt has been made to give exact measurements. They have been roughly classified as small, medium, and large. The papers used were also so greatly varied that description of them has been omitted.

Some titles were taken from dealers' records, and the dates and sizes of these were not always obtainable.

An asterisk before a plate number indicates that the print is reproduced here in color.

Peculiarities of spelling, abbreviation, and punctuation have been copied exactly in titles of prints, accompanying text and letters. Brackets enclose words and punctuation not appearing in titles or text. In certain instances, inconsistencies will be noted in the spelling of the proper names of lithographers and artists. This is due to the fact that spellings often vary from print to print, the individuals concerned apparently having allowed themselves a wide latitude in orthography. The dominant spelling has been followed within the text, but an exact transcription of the material on original prints has been followed in referring to them.

PLATE NUMBER	TITLE OF PRINT	REFERRED TO ON PAGE
1	"Capt. Sutter's account of the first discovery of the Gold. 13." With two vignettes: "Portrait of Mr. Marshal, taken from nature at the time when he made the discovery of gold in California" and "View of Sutter's Mill or place where the first gold has been discovered." "Lith. & Pub. by Britton & Rey, San Francisco, Cal. Entered . . . 1854"—letterhead, with text of Sutter's account.	66

PLATE NUMBER	TITLE OF PRINT	REFERRED TO ON PAGE
*2	"The Way They Come From California. N. Currier. Entered . . . 1849"—medium. (H.T.P. Checklist No. 1533.)	109
*3	"Arctic Oil Works. San Francisco, Cal. Works, Potrero. Office, 28 California St. Bosqui Eng. & Print. Co. S. F." —large, n.d.	61
4	"Bay View Race Track"—anonymous, medium, n.d. (c. 1860). *Reproduced by courtesy of the California State Library.*	41
5	"Grand Admission Celebration. Portsmouth Square Octr. 29th 1850."—anonymous, letterhead, n.d. Signature on stone, only partially decipherable: "P . . . T . . . G . . . st." *Reproduced by courtesy of the Huntington Library.*	42
6	"The Way not to Build the S. P. Railroad"—anonymous, small, n.d. *Reproduced by courtesy of the California State Library.*	43
7	"El Eco Del Pacifico, by Jaques Coo. San Francisco. (Cal.) Published by Atwill & Co. 172 Washington St. Entered . . . 1853"—music sheet.	45
8	"Chapel at Seminary Park, Alemeda Co. Cal. Erected 1871. Geo. H. Baker, lith., 408 Cal. St. S. F."—small, n.d. *Reproduced by courtesy of the Society of California Pioneers.*	51
9	"Camp Morgan, Amador Co. Cal. Advance Post, 1st Regt. 2d Brigade. National Guard of Cal." [Lithographed by George H. Baker.] Small, n.d. *Reproduced by courtesy of the Society of California Pioneers.*	51

PLATE NUMBER	TITLE OF PRINT	REFERRED TO ON PAGE
*10	"Fort Yuma. Colorado Rivr. Cala. Lith. Geo. H. Baker San Francisco"—medium, n.d.	52
11	"Independent City Guards Quick Step. Lithographed and Published by Geo. H. Baker. Sold by Dale & Co. Sac. Atwill & Co., A. Kohler, San Francisco. Gustave Amy, Marysville. J. E. Hamlin, Nevada"—music sheet, n.d. (c.1858). *Reproduced by courtesy of Mrs. George Lilly.*	44, 52, 141
12	"The Modoc War. The Massacre. Lava Beds and Advance to the Rescue. Shack Nasty Jim. Capt. Jack. Lith. Geo. H. Baker 408 California Street S. F."—small, n.d. *Reproduced by courtesy of the Society of California Pioneers.*	52
13	"San Diego Cal. Geo. H. Baker Lith. 408 California St. San Francisco"—medium, n.d. *Reproduced by courtesy of the Society of California Pioneers.*	53
14	"Yerba Buena (now San Francisco) in the Spring of 1837. Lithographed by Geo. H. Baker, from the original drawing by John J. Vioget. Copyrighted 1893"—medium. *Reproduced by courtesy of the Society of California Pioneers.*	54, 198
*15	"Puget Mill Co's Mills. Teekalet W. T. Talbot & Co. San Francisco, California. From Nature & on Stone by T. Grob. Nagel, Fishbourne & Kuchel, 529 Clay Street, San Francisco, California"—large, n.d.	127, 172
16	"Burning of Nevada City Cala. March 12th 1851. Loss $1,500,000. Pub. by W. H. Baxter of Bowers Express"—letterhead, n.d.	56
17	"May & Turnfest. San Francisco, Cala. May 7th–8th 1854. On stone by H. Steinegger. Publd. by C. F.	57, 194

PLATE NUMBER	TITLE OF PRINT	REFERRED TO ON PAGE
	Becherer. Lithy. of C. F. Becherer, California St. ab. Montgomery"—small, n.d. *Reproduced by courtesy of the Society of California Pioneers.*	
18	"1860. Fourth German May Festival. Return of the Procession at the Close of the Festival [title repeated in German]. Weaverville, Trinity County, Cal. Ambrotype taken by C. H. P. Norcross. Britton & Co. Print. C. C. Kuchel, Lith. 176 Clay St. S. Francisco. Published by Charles Schutz"—medium, n.d.*	88, 147
19	"Adventures of a Pike in California. 8. Lith. & Published by Britton & Rey Cor. Comml. & Montgy. Sts. S. Francisco"—letterhead, n.d. Seventeen vignette views: "Coming in from the Plains"; "Winter Experience"; "Disturbers of his Rest"; "Wet Diggings"; "Dry Diggings"; "Buys a Quartz Claim"; "Daming"; "Making acquaintance with the natives"; "Visits Sacramento"; "and Stockton"; "Buys a Horse"; "Other parties Claim him next day"; "Going back to the Mines"; "Dead broke"; "Sinks a deep hole"; "Makes a raise"; and "and takes th[e] Railroad for home"	66
20	"Birds Eye View of the City of Nevada, Nevada County, Cal. 1871. Drawn by Augustus Koch. Lith. Britton & Rey, S. F."—large, n.d., with twenty-three references. In margin, key to buildings, and a small view of Nevada in 1853. *Reproduced by courtesy of the Society of California Pioneers.*	81, 140
*21	"California & Oregon Stage Company. Carries Wells, Fargo & Company's Express and the U. S. Mail. View	81, 87, 194

*It was mechanically impracticable to reproduce in the plate the very faint and faded lettering of the inscriptions at the top and bottom of this print. The actual lines read as follows: [Inscription at top] "*Viertes Deutsches Mai Fest* 1860 Fourth German May Festival." [Inscription at bottom] "*Rückzug der Procession nach Beendigung des Festes.* Return of the Procession at the close of the Festival. Weaverville, Trinity County, Cal. Published by Charles Schutz."

PLATE NUMBER	TITLE OF PRINT	REFERRED TO ON PAGE
	of Mt. Shasta 14,442 ft. above the sea. On C. & O. Stage Route. F. F. Hooker, Superintendent. Bradley Barlow, J. L. Sanderson, James W. Parker, Chas. E. Huntley, Proprietors. [Signed on stone:] A. Stein. Lith. Britton & Rey, S. F."—large, n.d.	
22	"Celestial Empire in California. 14. Miners. Gamblers. Lith. & Published by Britton & Rey. Cornr. Monty. & Cal. Sts. San Francisco"—letterhead, n.d.	69
23	"A Correct View of Weaverville, Trinity Coy. Cal. A. Coquardon del. Published by Cram Rogers & Co. Lith. Britton & Rey, S. Francisco"—letterhead, n.d. *Reproduced by courtesy of the Society of California Pioneers.*	69, 106
24	"Execution of Hetherington and Brace. The Murderers of Baldwin, Randall, West and Marion. July 29th 1856. Lith. & Pub. by Britton & Rey S. F."—letterhead, n.d.	69
25	"Flume. Elevating Water Wheel. 16. Lith. & Published by Britton & Rey. San Francisco, Cal."—letterhead, n.d.	69
26	"Fort Vigilant. Rooms of the Committee Sacramento St. betn. Davis & Front. Mass Meeting Endorsing the Acts of the Vigilance Commite[e] June 14th. Daguer. by Vance. Lith. Britton & Rey"—letterhead, n.d. *Reproduced by courtesy of the Society of California Pioneers.*	69, 198
27	"Gambling in the Mines. Monte. Faro. Lith & Published by Britton & Rey. San Francisco California"—letterhead, n.d. *Reproduced by courtesy of the de Young Museum.*	70

PLATE NUMBER	TITLE OF PRINT	REFERRED TO ON PAGE
	ton, Rey & Co. S. F."—large, n.d. (Certificate dated "1878.") *Reproduced by courtesy of the Society of California Pioneers.*	
44	"Overland Mail Company. B. S. & Co. [Barlow, Sanderson & Co.] Lith. of Britton, Rey & Co."—large, n.d. (c.1860). The copy reproduced is proof before letters.	87, 89
45	Jim. Words by Bret Harte. Music by F. B. J. H. Bufford's Lith. 490 Washn. St. Boston. Published by Oliver Ditson & Co. 277 Washington St. Boston. Entered . . . 1871"—music sheet.	91
46	"Upon the Stanislow. Words by Bret Harte. Music by F—— B—— [Lithographed by J. H. Bufford.] Published by Oliver Ditson & Co. 277 Washington St. Boston. Entered . . . 1871"—music sheet.	91
47	"Wreck of Steamship Union on the Coast of Lower California, July 5th 1851. Drawn by Edwin Moody. Lithd. by J. H. Bufford 260 Washington St. Boston" —medium, n.d.	91, 164
48	Certificate of membership: "San Francisco Blues. [Signed on stone:] C. C. Kuchel. Lithographed & printed in colors by B. F. Butler, San Francisco"—small, n.d. (Certificate dated "1856.") *Reproduced by courtesy of the Society of California Pioneers.*	93, 147
49	"Defunct Ambition on the Road to Salt River, appearance and condition of the parties. Sunset. San Francisco, December, 1856. Entered . . . 1856 by Nhoj Mailliw Ettocetsew" [Lithographed by B. F. Butler]—small. *Reproduced by courtesy of the de Young Museum.*	93

PLATE NUMBER	TITLE OF PRINT	REFERRED TO ON PAGE
50	"Re-opening of Duncan's Chinese Salesroom, and display of Goods for the Second Art-Union, January 1855. B. F. Butler's Lith. San Francisco"—medium, n.d. *Reproduced by courtesy of the de Young Museum.*	96
51	"Tompson in a Quandary. San Francisco 'Local Hits' Cross Readings to be Read Downwards. Lithy. of B. F. Butler. [On stone:] San Francisco 1862. Appleton Genl. Agent 508 Montgomery St. San Francisco. Entered . . . 1862"—medium. *Reproduced by courtesy of the de Young Museum.*	96
52	"Great Fire in San Francisco. May 4th, 1850. 400 Buildings Burned! Loss $5,000,000! Pub. by W. B. Cooke & Co, Portsmouth Square"—letterhead, n.d.	99
53	"[Celebration of the 4th of July] in San Francisco Cal. the 5th July, 1852. Lith. of Cooke & Le Count"—small, n.d. *Reproduced by courtesy of the Huntington Library.*	102
54	"Stockton. June 1st 1852. J. Britton, del. Lith. & Published by Cooke & Le Count, San Francisco. Entered . . . 1852"—small. Stamped in margin: "Noisy Carrier's." *Reproduced by courtesy of the Huntington Library.*	65, 102, 175
55	"A View of the [Elephant]. Published and Sold by Cooke & Le Count, San Francisco"—letterhead, n.d., lithographed in gold. Center view of an elephant, surrounded by eight views: "The Eliza Ship for California"; "Arrival at St. F. A Monte Bank"; "Travelling about the Mines"; "Camping Out"; "Miners preparing their Fodder"; "Washing Gold in a Cradle"; "One of the few that return"; and "The End	102

PLATE NUMBER	TITLE OF PRINT	REFERRED TO ON PAGE
	of the Many" *Reproduced by courtesy of the Society of California Pioneers.*	
56	"San Francisco College . . . Drawn, designed, and lithographed at the College by J. Chittenden"—large, n.d. *Reproduced by courtesy of Roger D. Lapham.*	97
57	"Sixth Great Conflagration in San Francisco, June 22d, 1851. J. De Vere, del."—letterhead, n.d. Stamped in margin: "Noisy Carrier's Publishing Hall, 77 Long Wharf, San Francisco. Charles P. Kimball, Propr[i]etor." *Reproduced by courtesy of the Huntington Library.*	112, 175
*58	"View of San Francisco, California. Taken from Telegraph Hill, April 1850, By Wm. B. McMurtrie, Draughtsman of the U. S. Surveying Expedition. On Stone by F. Palmer, Lith. & Pub. by N. Currier, 152 Nassau St. Cor. Spruce N. Y. Entered . . . 1851" —large, with marginal key to the following places: "Clarkes Point," "Rincon Point," "Happy Valley," "Long Wharf (building)," "Pacific St. Wharf (building)," "Apollo Warehouse," "Niantic Warehouse," "Sansome St.," and "Portsmouth Square." (H. T. P. Checklist No. 3881.)	108, 163, 176
59	"View of the Mission of St. Gabriel. A. Robinson Del. [Signed on stone:] F. Swinton. Lith. of G. & W. Endicott"—small, n.d. *Reproduced by courtesy of the Society of California Pioneers.*	118, 182, 195
*60	"Sacramento City Ca. From the foot of J. Street, showing I. J. & K. Sts. with the Sierra Nevada in the Distance. Drawn Dec. 20th 1849 by G. V. Cooper. Lith. of Wm. Endicott & Co. N. York. New York, Published by Stringer & Townsend, 222 Broadway. Entered . . . 1850"—large.	105, 118, 194

13

Capt. Sutter's account of the first discovery of the Gold.

I was sitting one afternoon," said the Captain, "just after my siesta, engaged, by the bye, in writing a letter to a relation of mine at Lucern, when I was interrupted by Mr. Marshal a gentleman with whom I had frequent business transactions – bursting hurriedly into the room. From the unusual agitation in his manner I imagined that something serious had occured, and, as we involuntarely do in this part of the world, I at once glanced to see if my rifle was in its proper place. You should know that the mere appearance of Mr Marshal at that moment in the Fort, was quite enough to surprise me, as he had but two days before left me, to make some alterations in a mill for sawing pine planks, which he had just run up for me, some miles higher up the Americanos. When he had recovered himself a little, he told me that, however great my surprise might be at his unexpected reappearance, it would be much greater when I heard the intelligence he had come to bring me. 'Intelligence,' he added, which if properly profited by, would put both of us in possession of unheard-of-wealth – millions and millions of dollars, in fact.' I frankly own, when I heard this that I thought something had touched Marshall's brain, when suddenly all my misgivings were put at an end to by his flinging on the table a handful of scales of pure virgin gold. I was fairly thunderstruck and asked him to explain what all this meant, when he went on to say, that according to my instructions, he had thrown the mill-wheel out of gear, to let the whole body of the water in the dam find a passage through the tail race, which was previously to narrow to allow the watter to run of in sufficient quantity, whereby the wheel was prevented from efficiently performing its work. By this alteration the narrow channel was considerably enlarged, and a mass of sand & gravel carried of by the force of the torrent. Early in the morning after this took place, Mr Marshal was walking along the left Bank of the stream when he perceived something which he at first took for a piece of opal – a clair transparant stone, very common here – glittering on one of the spots laid bare by the sudden crumbling away of the bank. He paid no attention to this; but while he was giving directions to the workmen, having observed several similar glittering fagments, his curiosity was so far excited, that he stooped down & picked on of them up. 'Do you know,' said Mr Marshal to me,' I positively debated within myself two or three times whether I should take the trouble to bend my back to pick up one of the pieces and had decided on not doing so when further on, another glittering morsel caught my eye – the largest of the pieces now before you. I condescended to pick it up, and to my astonishment found that it was a thin scale of what appears to be pure gold'. He then gathered some twenty or thirty pieces which on examination convinced him that his suppositions were right. His first impression was, that this gold had been lost or buried there, by some early Indian tribe – perhaps some of those mysterious inhabitants of the west, of whom we have no account, but who dwelt on this continent centuries ago, and built those cities and temples, the ruins of which are scattered about thes solidary wilds. On proceeding, however, to examine the neighbouring soil, he discovered that it was more or less auriferous. This at once decided him. He mounted his horse, and rode down to me as fast as it could carry him vith the news.

At the conclusion of Mr Marshals account, and when I had convinced myself, from the specimens he had brought with him, that it was not exagerated, I felt as much excited as himself. I eagerly inquired if he had shown the Gold to the workpeople at the mill and was glad to hear that he had not spoken to a single person about it. We agreed not to mention the circumstance to any one and arranged to set off early the next day for the mill. On our arrival, just before sundown, we poket the sand about in various places, and before long succeeded in collecting between us more than an ounce of gold, mixed up with a good deal of sand. I stayed at Mr Marshall's that night, and the next day we proceeded some little distance up the south Fork, and found that gold existed along the whole course, not only in the bed of the main stream, where the had subsided but in every little dried-up creek and ravine. Indeed I think it is more plentiful in these latter places, for I myself, with nothing more than a smal knife, picked out from dry gorge, a litte way up the mountain, a solid lump of gold with weighed nearly an ounce and a half.

Notwithstanding our precautions not to be observed, as soon we came back to the mill, we noticed by the excitement of the working people that we had been dogged about, an to complet our desappointment, one of the indians who had worked at the gold mine in the neighbourhood of La Paz cried out in showing to us some specimens picked up by himself, – Oro! – Oro – Oro!!! –

PORTAIT OF Mr MARSHAL, TAKEN FROM NATURE AT THE TIME WHEN HE MADE THE DISCOVERY OF GOLD IN CALIFORNIA

VIEW OF SUTTER'S MILL OR PLACE WHERE THE FIRST GOLD HAS BEEN DISCOVERED

Lith. & Pub. by Britton & Rey San Francisco. Cal.

THE WAY THEY COME FROM CALIFORNIA.

2

A full color reproduction of this plate appears in the color section in this book.

WORKS, POTRERO. OFFICE, 28 CALIFORNIA ST.

ARCTIC OIL WORKS.

SAN FRANCISCO, CAL.

3

A full color reproduction of this plate appears in the color section in this book.

4

GRAND ADMISSION CELEBRATION.

PORTSMOUTH SQUARE OCT^R 29 1850.

5

THE WAY NOT TO BUILD THE S.P. RAILROAD.

Nº1. Tax Payers
Nº2. Rail Road Kings
Nº3. Heads of Chinese Cos.
Nº4. Chinese Laborers
Nº5. Voters in General
Nº6. White Laborers

EL ECO DEL PACIFICO,

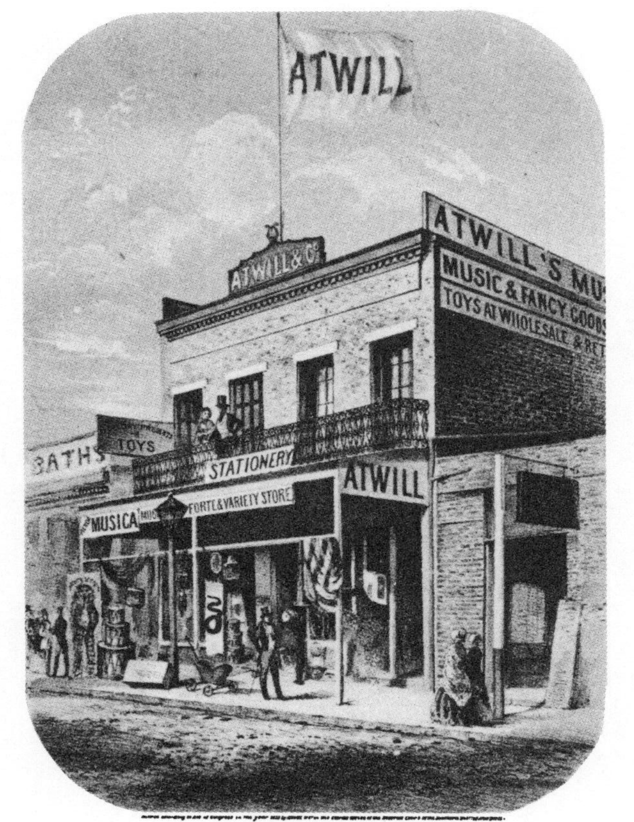

BY

JAQUES COO,

SAN FRANCISCO.(CAL.)
PUBLISHED BY ATWILL & Co 172 WASHINGTON ST.

7

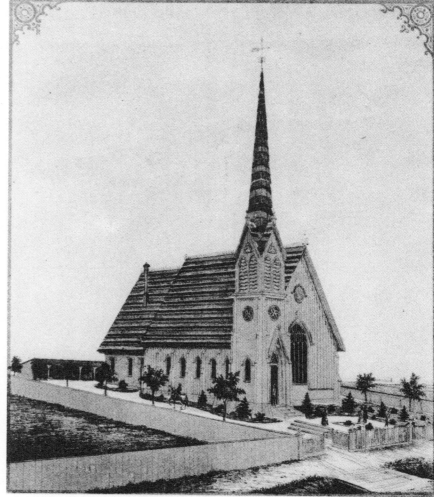

CHAPEL AT SEMINARY PARK,
Alemeda Co. Cal.
Erected 1871.

8

CAMP MORGAN, AMADOR CO. CAL.

Advance Post, 1st Regt 2d Brigade. National Guard of Cal.

Fort Yuma, Colorado River. California.

10

A full color reproduction of this plate appears in the color section in this book.

INDEPENDENT CITY GUARDS
QUICK STEP
Dedicated by the
Sacramento Union Brass Band
And played by them on the occasion of the visit of the Guards
to San Francisco Oct. 27th 1858.
Lithographed and Published by
GEO. H. BAKER.
SOLD BY
DALE & CO. SAC.
ATWILL & CO.
A. KOHLER.
SAN FRANCISCO
GUSTAVE AMY ... Marysville
J. E. HAMLIN ... Nevada

LAVA BEDS AND ADVANCE TO THE RESCUE.

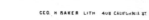

SAN DIEGO CAL.

GEO. H BAKER LITH 408 CALIFORNIA ST. SAN FRANCISCO

13

PLATE NUMBER	TITLE OF PRINT	REFERRED TO ON PAGE
61	"Chinese Life!!! Dupont Street. San-Francisco, Cal. Beutler, delt. Fishbourne & Co. Lithogrs. S. F."—letterhead, n.d. *Reproduced by courtesy of the Huntington Library.*	57, 121
62	"The Plaza, Portsmouth Square, San Francisco; as it should and as it may be, according to the plan proposed by J. J. Chauviteau, Esqre. View taken from Kearney & Merchant Streets. Gihon & Butler, Lith."—small, n.d. *Reproduced by courtesy of the California Historical Society: from the Templeton Crocker Collection.*	123
63	"Earth Quakey Times, San Francisco, Oct. 8, 1865. [Signed on stone:] E. Jump. Entered . . . 1865 by E. Jump"—medium. *Reproduced by courtesy of the Society of California Pioneers.*	131
64	"Placerville (Hangtown) El Dorado Coy. Cal. John Whitford. Published by Albert W. Bee, Placerville, 1851. San Fco. Lith. Justh & Co. Montgomery St. 253"—small, n.d. *Reproduced by courtesy of the California Historical Society.*	133
65	"View of Montgomery St. from Sacramento Wharf the Morning After the Great Fire. Lith. Justh & Co. Broadway between Dupont & Stockton St. S. F."—letterhead, n.d. Written in ink on margin: "Both of the pictures I send convey a poor idea of the fire or the ruins, as they are *far more* extensive than represented." *Reproduced by courtesy of the Society of California Pioneers.*	133
66	"The First Trial & Execution in S. Francisco on the Night of 10th of June at 2 o'clock. Del. after the nature by W. C. K. Pub. and lith. Justh, Quirot & Co. Cor.	133

PLATE NUMBER	TITLE OF PRINT	REFERRED TO ON PAGE
	Calif. & Montg. Sts. S. F."—letterhead, n.d. See Justh, Quirot & Co. in Alphabetical List for long text under the view. *Reproduced by courtesy of the Huntington Library.*	
67	"View of the Plaza of San-Francisco On the 4th of July 1851. Publ. & Lith. by Justh Quirot & Co. Calif. Corn. Montg. Sts."—small, n.d. *Reproduced by courtesy of Roger D. Lapham.*	137
68	"A California Gold Hunter Meeting a Settler. Pub. by Serrell & Perkins 75 Nassau St. N. Y. R. H. Elton 90 Nassau St, N. Y."—small, n.d.	116, 189
69	"The Independent Gold Hunter on His Way To California. I neither borrow nor lend. Kelloggs & Comstock, 150 Fulton St. New York & 136 Main St. Hartford Conn. Ensign & Thayer, 12 Exchange St. Buffalo"—small, n.d.	119, 140
70	"Knickerbocker Engine Company N. 5. San Francisco. On stone by C. C. Kuchel, 118 Montgomery St. S. F. Printed by Britton & Co."—medium, n.d. *Reproduced by courtesy of the de Young Museum.*	88, 147
71	"Virginia City, Nevada Territory. 1861. Drawn from nature by Grafton T. Brown. C. C. Kuchel, Lith. 174 Clay St. S. Francisco, Cal. Britton & Co. Print. Published by Grafton T. Brown"—medium, n.d. *Reproduced by courtesy of the de Young Museum.*	88, 90, 147
72	"Coloma, 1857. El Dorado County, California. First discovery of Gold in Cal. was made at this place early in February 1848 by Jas. Marshall & P. L. Wimmer, in the Tailrace of Sutters Sawmill, situated at the extreme lower end of the Town. The Mill was torn down in 1856.	86, 142

PLATE NUMBER	TITLE OF PRINT	REFERRED TO ON PAGE
	[Symbol, cross in small circle, with hook at top]: Place where Sutters mill stood. Drawn from nature and lith. by Kuchel & Dresel, 176 Clay St. San Francisco. Printed by Britton & Rey. Published by George Searle, Coloma. Entered . . . 1857"—medium. *Reproduced by courtesy of the Society of California Pioneers.*	
73	"Los Angeles, Los Angeles County, Cal. 1857. Drawn From Nature & on Stone by Kuchel & Dresel, 176 Clay St. S. Francisco. Printed by Britton & Rey. Published by Hellman & Bro. Entered . . . 1857"—medium. *Reproduced by courtesy of the Society of California Pioneers.*	86, 143
74	"The Mammoth Tree Grove, Calaveras County California. Sketched from nature by T. A. Ayres, 1855. Drawn on stone by Kuchel & Dresel 146 Clay St. S. F. Printed by Britton & Rey. Entered . . . 1855"—large. *Reproduced by courtesy of the de Young Museum.*	45, 86, 143
*75	"Scotts Bar and French Bar, on Scotts River, Siskiyou County, California. 1856. Published by J. M. C. Jones. Drawn from nature and on stone by Kuchel & Dresel, 176 Clay St. S. F. Printed by Britton & Rey. Entered . . . 1856"—large.	86, 145
76	"Views of the New Ditch of the Columbia & Stanislaus River Water Co. Drawn from nature by F. Holtzmann. Kuchel & Dresel's Lith. 176 Clay St. S. F. L. Nagel, Print. Published by F. Holtzmann, Columbia, Tuolumne Co. California"—medium, n.d. *Reproduced by courtesy of Roger D. Lapham.*	129, 147, 169
77	"Execution of James P. Casey & Charles Cora by the Vigilance Committee of San Francisco Thursday May	127, 152

PLATE NUMBER	TITLE OF PRINT	REFERRED TO ON PAGE
	22d 1856. Drawn by T. Grob. Printed by F. Kuhl"—letterhead, n.d. *Reproduced by courtesy of the Huntington Library.*	
78	"Monetary Panic in California!!! San Francisco February 1855. [Signed on stone:] Sv,EG. Published by Leland F. Schlesinger. Printed by F. Kuhl"—medium, n.d.	152, 187
79	"Hayes' Valley, San Francisco. C. B. Gifford, del. et lith. Printed by L. Nagel, S. F."—medium, n.d. *Reproduced by courtesy of the Society of California Pioneers.*	123, 167
80	"Lombard, North Point and Greenwich Docks, San Francisco. Ships Great Republic, Hurricane and Zenobia Discharging. On stone by H. Eastman & A. Nahl. Drawn from nature by C. B. Gifford. [L. Nagel, print.]"—medium, n.d. *Reproduced by courtesy of the Society of California Pioneers.*	115, 123, 167, 172
*81	"Private Signals of the Merchants of New York and San Francisco. Respectfully Dedicated to the Merchants of San Francisco by Charles B. Gifford. Lith. Print. in colors by L. Nagel, San Francisco. Entered . . . 1856"—large. *Reproduced by courtesy of Roger D. Lapham.*	123, 167
82	"Steamer Day in San Francisco. [Signed on stone:] E. Jump. Published by Snow & Roos, San Francisco. L. Nagel, Print. Entered . . . 1866"—medium. *Reproduced by courtesy of the Society of California Pioneers.*	131, 168, 174, 193
83	"San Juan Del Norte or Greytown. Nagel & Schwartz Lithographers, 58, Montgomery St. Sn. Franco."—	172

PLATE NUMBER	TITLE OF PRINT	REFERRED TO ON PAGE
	small, n.d. *Reproduced by courtesy of the Society of California Pioneers.*	
84	"The Mammoth Tree Grove, Calaveras Co. California, And Its Avenues. Drawn by Edward Vischer. Nagel, Fishbourne & Kuchel, Lithographers, S. F. Entered . . . 1862"—large.	169, 199
85	"San Francisco. Lith. of Geo. F. Nesbitt N. Y. [Stamped in margin:] Published by Marvin & Hitchcock, Pioneer Book Store, San Francisco. Thompson & Hitchcock, Managers and Agents of Egory's California Express, 149 Pearl St. Cor. Wall St. N. Y."—small, n.d. Written in ink in margin: "February 1860." *Reproduced by courtesy of Dr. William J. Haber.*	174
86	"Honest Voters Trying to Elect Their Officers, in front of the house. Ballot Box Stuffers, Electing Their Men, behind the house. Noisy Carriers 64. & 66. Long Wharf"—small, n.d. *Reproduced by courtesy of the Society of California Pioneers.*	175
87	"View of San Francisco, from Telegraph Hill. [Signed on stone:] Moody del. from a sketch by Swan. Lith. of Peirce & Pollard. San Francisco Published by Cooke & Le Count"—letterhead, n.d. (c.1850).	103, 164, 176
88	"Celebration of Washington's Birth Day San Francisco Feby. 23d 1852 Pub. by Cooke & Le Count. Lith. & Pub. by Pollard & Britton"—letterhead, n.d. *Reproduced by courtesy of the Huntington Library.*	103, 179
89	"Columbia January, 1852. G. H. Goddard del. Pollard & Britton's Lith. Merchant Str. S. F. Entered . . . 1852"—letterhead. With letter written July 28, 1852.	124, 180

PLATE NUMBER	TITLE OF PRINT	REFERRED TO ON PAGE
	Reproduced by courtesy of the American Antiquarian Society.	
90	"Sonora January, 1852. Pollard & Brittons Lith. Merchant Str. S. F. Entered . . . 1852 by G. H. Goddard. [Stamped on margin:] Noisy Carriers Publishing Hall 77 Long Wharf San Francisco Charles P. Kimball Propr[i]etor"—letterhead. *Reproduced by courtesy of the Huntington Library.*	124, 175, 181
91	"John Smith. Published by Lovegrove & Murray Sacramento City. Lith. of Pollard & Peregoy San Francisco"—letterhead, n.d. Nine views: "Mr. John Smith takes final leave of Mrs. John Smith"; "John Smith, being short of Cash, turns porter to the Elephant House"; "John Smith has struck a Lead"; "John Smith having made a pile leaves for Sacramento on a bust"; "John Smith bets his pile on the Jack"; "John Smith dead broke"; "John Smith resolves to reform"; "Fortune favors John Smith & he invests his dust in a 'Ranch'"; and "John Smith arrives safe home with his pile." *Reproduced by courtesy of the Society of California Pioneers.*	179
92	"A Company of prospecting miners. Lith. by Quirot, S. F."—letterhead, n.d. *Reproduced by courtesy of the de Young Museum.*	137
93	"The California Pioneers a Song respectfully inscribed to Mrs. J. Emerson Sweetser. Words & Music by Dr. M. A. Richter. Lith & del. by Quirot & Co., cornr. Califa. & Montgomery Sts. S-F. Published & Sold by Atwill & Co. in San-Francisco. N.B. The First Piece of Music Pubd. in Cala. Entered . . . 1852"—music sheet. *Reproduced by courtesy of the New York Public Library.*	44, 137

PLATE NUMBER	TITLE OF PRINT	REFERRED TO ON PAGE
	ness. [Signed on stone:] A. N. Published by A. Rosenfield"—letterhead, n.d. With text describing disaster. *Reproduced by courtesy of Dr. William J. Haber.*	
101	"San Francisco in November 1849. New York. Geo. P. Putnam. Bayard Taylor. Lith. of Sarony & Major. N.Y."—small, n.d. *Reproduced by courtesy of the California Historical Society, from the Templeton Crocker Collection.*	185, 196
*102	"San Francisco 1849. Drawn on the spot by Henry Firks for W. H. Jones Esq. of San Francisco, U. C. On stone by Ibbotson. T. Sinclair's Lith, 101 Chestnut St. Phila. Entered . . . 1849 by G. T. Devereaux for W. H. Jones"—large, with forty-five marginal references. *Reproduced by courtesy of the Robert Fridenberg Galleries, New York.*	120, 130, 191
*103	"A View of Sutter's Mill & Culloma Valley. On the south fork of the American Line [River], Alta California. Respectfully dedicated to Capt. John A. Sutter, by his obedient servant, John T. Little. Lith. of Sarony & Major, New York"—large, n.d. *Reproduced by courtesy of Yale University, from the Mabel Brady Garvan Collection.*	186
104	"Mission Dolores San Francisco. A. Schwartz Lithographer 51 Montgomery Str. Sn. Franco."—medium, n.d. *Reproduced by courtesy of the Society of California Pioneers.*	188
*105	"Sutter's Fort, Sacramento, California 1847. Lith. Snyder & Black No. 87 Fulton Street, New York"—large, n.d.	193

PLATE NUMBER	TITLE OF PRINT	REFERRED TO ON PAGE
106	"The Apollo Warehouses, San Francisco, California. Sun Lithographic Establishment. 128 Fulton St. N.Y."—small, n.d.	195
107	"The Heathen Chinee. Words by 'Bret Harte.' Music by Chas. Towner. To my friend C. H. Harris, Carl Pretzel Der leedle Vanderer. Lith. by A. Vallendar & Co. Published by S. Brainard's Sons. Cleveland. Entered . . . 1870"—music sheet.	197
108	"Overland Mail Company. Bradley Barlow & J. L. Sanderson, Proprietors. View of Uncompahgre Mountain 14,400 Ft. above the Sea on Overland Stage Route. [Signed on stone:] Holdertine. Woodward, Tiernan & Hale. St. Louis"—large, n.d.	87, 129, 204
109	"The only correct & fully complete Map of San Francisco. Compiled from the Original Map & the recent Surveys, Containing all the latest extensions & improvements, New streets, alleys, places, wharfs & Division of Wards. Respectfully dedicated to the City Authorities. By Alex: Zakreski, 1853. Drawn & Lith by Alex: Zakreski, Cor Washington & Montgomery Streets, at his Topographical Office"—small, n.d. *Reproduced by courtesy of Edwin Grabhorn.*	205
110	"View of the Procession in Celebration of the Admission of California, Oct. 29th, 1850, Crossing the Plaza of San Francisco. J. Prendergast del. On stone by Coquardon Lith. of Zakreski & Hartman"—medium, n.d. *Reproduced by courtesy of the Robert Fridenberg Galleries, New York.*	106, 181, 205
111	"San-Francisco, Vue prise d'un point élevé du côté Sud. (Californie) 45. Dessine et Lithog. par L. Le Breton. Paris, Imp. par Auguste Bry, 149, r. du Bac. Paris, E.	157

PLATE NUMBER	TITLE OF PRINT	REFERRED TO ON PAGE
	Savary et Cie. edit. 10 Place du Louvre. London, Published by E. Gambart et Co."—small, n.d. *Reproduced by courtesy of the Robert Fridenberg Galleries, New York.*	
112	"Bay-View-Park Galop. Composed by P. R. Nicholls, San-Francisco. Dedicated to W. F. Williamson, C. B. Gifford, Del. L. Nagel, Print."—music sheet, n.d.	123, 166

THE ALPHABETICAL LIST

ACKERMANN, JAMES NEW YORK

1845–1846 304 Broadway
1848–1849 120 Fulton Street
1851–1855 379 Broadway
1855–1859 377 Broadway

As I said in *America on Stone,* James Ackermann should not be confused with the very well known London firm of Ackermann & Company. The two had no connection.

Several California items done by Ackermann have turned up:

"Belle of The Prairie Quickstep. Composed and Dedicated to Miss S. B. of California by A. Patrone, late leader of the Band of the U. S. Flag Ship Savannah. Transcribed and Published by 'Californe' New York, James C. Jollie, 300 Broadway. Ackermann's Lith. 379 Broadway, N. Y."—music sheet, n.d. The view shows a girl in riding habit holding a revolver and standing by a horse; a dead deer lies close by. In the distance is seen a covered wagon train. Jollie was a music publisher, at this address in the early fifties.

"Map of That Portion of The Boundary Between the United States and Mexico From The Pacific Coast To The Junction of The Gila and Colorado Rivers. Surveyed under the direction of Hon. John B. Weller, U. S. Commissioner. Ackermann Lith. N.Y. Entered . . . 1855"—medium.

"Sketch of General Riley's Route through the Mining Districts July and August, 1849. Copied from the original sketch by Lt. Derby in the Office of the 10th Military Dept. by J. McH. Hollingsworth, Asst. Ackermann's Lithogr., 379 Broadway, N.Y."—medium, n.d. This map shows the coast from San Francisco to Monterey and the mining regions lying to the east.

A series of ten botanical plates, all 1853, small, from "Report Of A Geological Reconnaisance In California: Made in Connection with the Expedition to Survey Routes in California, to Connect with the Surveys of Routes for a Railroad from the Mississippi River to the Pacific Ocean, under the Command of Lieut. R. S. Williamson, Corps Top. Eng'rs, in 1853. By William P. Blake, Geologist and Mineralogist of the Expedition. New York: H. Bailliere, 290 Broadway":

"Fagonia Californica"; "Dalea Emoryi"; "Cercidium Floridum"; "Strombocarpa Pubescens"; "Trichoptilium Incisum"; "Eremiastrum Belliodes"; "Asclepias Subulata"; "Chorizanthe Fimbriata"; "Quercus Crassipocula"; "Bouteloua Polystachya"

Three large folded sheets of maps at the back of the book are:

"Map of the Geological Section of the Sierra Nevada At The Tejon Pass"

"Map of the Geological Section Along The Tejon Ravine From The Tulare Valley And The Tejon Depot Camp To Taheechaypah Prairie"—and—"Map of the Geological Section of the Sierra Nevada At The Canada De Las Uvas." Two maps on one sheet.

"Map of the Geological Section From The Colorado River To The Pacific Ocean 1853 Constructed from observations in the vicinity of the route from the mouth of the Gila river Over the Colorado Desert and the Peninsula Sierra to San Diego via Carrizo Creek, Vallecitos, San Felip, Warner's Pass, Santa Isabel and San Pasquale"

ACKERMANN & COMPANY — LONDON

Published the 1851 view of San Francisco lithographed in London by Hanhart (*q.v.*). Not the same firm as James Ackermann, of New York.

ANONYMOUS

The anonymous section is small, containing about thirty-five lithographs of the period, but they fall into classifications representative of the entire California output. Of these thirty-five, there are twenty-one views, four letterheads, three political cartoons, a broadside, and one unknown as to subject, the title having come from a dealer's records. The one sporting print among them constitutes exactly one third of the discovered California lithographs in that field, and it will be noted that there are no portraits. Four are book illustrations.

Even within this very small group the interest in the old Spanish missions crops out strongly, three of the views and letterheads and two of the four book illustrations having them as subject. The period of greatest influence of these missions was well past by the time the Forty-niners arrived, but they captured the imagination of the men from all over the world, just as they still do today. They seem to be, both historically and architecturally, America's unique contribution in the way of religious buildings.

In the remaining views and letterheads we find the typical fire scene, with a map showing the damage done, a shipwreck, and a celebration with parading Forty-niners and Chinese coolies.

Among the views and letterheads, there are two bird's-eye views and a panorama—popular forms of depicting cities and countrysides among the Californians, due perhaps to the fact that the artist had little difficulty in finding a good-sized hill from which to work. San Francisco, particularly, throughout the whole production came in for an amazing share of these aërial views—an easily understandable fact to anyone who has seen its "roller coaster" topography. This may also account for the astonishing grasp these men had of perspective, which I have mentioned in the Prologue. An artist could hardly live in a country where the first object to meet his eye might be ten or fifteen miles away without something of that feeling of distance being absorbed into his mind and coming out again in his work. They must have developed far-seeing eyes—and consequently when we look at the pictures they have left us, we too actually feel the space that they saw.

"Auburn Hotel, Auburn Station, Placer Co. California. J. J. Smith, Prop."—small, n.d. This view of the hotel shows a locomotive, and a six-horse wagon team.

"Avalon, Santa Catalina Island Cal."—large, n.d.

"Battle at Kennedy's Farm During the Encampment of the Second Brigade, C. M. October 14, 1863"—medium, n.d. Shows a company of infantry drawn up in squares, and troops of cavalry dashing about in a sham battle.

"Bay View Race Track"—medium, n.d. (c. 1860). This is one of three sporting prints which turned up. The track also figures in Nagel's "Bay-View-Park Galop." Murdoch's "Lady Vernon" shows another San Francisco track, Pioneer Course. PLATE 4

"Birds Eye View of San Francisco. 1852"—medium.

"Birds Eye View of San Francisco. 1854"—large.

"City Hall, San Francisco"—small, n.d.

"Coming Events Cast their Shadows Before 'Keep your seat Horace, We'll get you there on time' "—medium, n.d. A very interesting six-horse stage coach. In the coach is Horace Greeley, an excellent portrait; on the box seat are two figures—one driving, the other unquestionably a portrait of Frémont. One of the really interesting prints in the development of California into statehood.

"David S. Terry, Democratic Candidate for Presidential Elector. Blood Will Tell! [Signed on stone:] G. B."—small, n.d. A political broadside showing the gravestone of Senator Broderick; a vignette of the Broderick-Terry duel being visioned by a distressed angel; below is an account, from the Stockton *Independent,* of the duel and of political conditions at the time.

PLATE 5 "Grand Admission Celebration. Portsmouth Square Octr. 29th 1850"—letter-head, n.d. This is possibly the same as Zakreski & Hartman's "View of the Procession." The indecipherable signature on the stone, "P . . . T . . . G . . .st, may be the "J. Prendergast, del." of that print.

"Harbor of San Francisco, Upper California"—small, n.d.

"Los Angeles in 1854 (Looking Eastward)"—small, n.d.

"Mission Dolores"—letterhead, n.d.

"The Mission of Santa Barbara, at present in charge of Rev. Father J. J. O'Keefe, Santa Barbara, California. Founded Dec. 4th, 1776. Present building completed 1822"—small, n.d.

"North Beach from Russian Hill, San Francisco. 1862"—size unknown, n.d.

"Old Mission R. C. Church, founded October 8th, 1776. San Francisco's Centennial. [Signed on stone:] K"—small, n.d.

"Panorama of San Francisco, 1859–1860"—small, n.d.

"Rail Road. Monoply. Mr. Crocker's Kindergarten. (J.-B.)"—medium, n.d. Spelled out on blocks piled upon one another. To left are two boys with dunce hats; to right is Mr. Crocker with stick pointing to block A; bottom foreground are all the school children. A cartoon from the *Wasp*.

"Ranch Near French Camp, San Joaquin Co.—Cottage Farm, Merced Co. Home And Farm Of D. K. Woodbridge, Ceres, Stanislaus Co. Cal."—medium, n.d.

"Residence and Ranch of J. L. Beecher, Oneil Tp. San Joaquin County, California"—medium, n.d.

"Rubio Canyon Falls, Mt. Lowe, Cal."—large, n.d.

"San Diego, California"—medium, n.d. (c.1850).

"San Francisco from Goat Island. 1855"—size unknown, n.d.

"San Francisco. Showing California Street from Montgomery"—small, n.d.

"Six Months in California"—size unknown, n.d.

"View of Sutter's Fort, Sacramento 1847"—medium, n.d.

"View of the Conflagration from Telegraph Hill San Francisco, Night of May 3d, 1851"—and—"Map of the Burnt District of San Francisco. Showing the Extent of the Fire"—letterhead, with two views, n.d. Fishbourne issued a map with the same title, but they differ.

"The Way not to Build the S. P. Railroad"—small, n.d. A cartoon, giving in "balloons" the opinions of groups of taxpayers, railroad kings, Chinese coolies, white laborers, and voters in general. PLATE 6

"Wilberforce University, San Francisco"—small, n.d.

"Wreck & Burning of the Steamer Independence on the Island Margarita, Feby. 16th, 1853. 150 lives lost. From the sketch of Mr. Cross"—letterhead, n.d. Probably the same as No. 2 on Britton & Rey's "Disasters of 60 Days."

Four plates in the "U. S. Postal Rail Road Expedition & Survey; U. S. War Dept., Reports of Explorations and Surveys, To Ascertain the Most Practicable and Economical Route for a Railroad from the Mississippi River to the Pacific Ocean," Washington, 1855–1856:

"Benecia. U. S. Military Post"; "Mission Church of San Xavier Del Bac"; "Mission of San Diego"; and "Valley of the Gila & Sierra De Las Estrellas from the Maricopa Wells"

ANTHONY & BAKER — SAN FRANCISCO

This may have been one of George H. Baker's alignments. Most of the firm's production consisted of woodcuts and engravings, the following being their only lithograph that has turned up:

"Michigan Bar. Lithograph View by Anthony & Baker. San Francisco. Sun Print."—medium, n.d. In lower margin: "Located on the banks of the Consumnes River, twenty-seven miles east of Sacramento City. Mining was commenced in this place in the fall of 1850, by a company of men from Michigan, who successfully worked a portion of the Bar, and named it after their state."

ARMSTRONG, THOMAS — SAN FRANCISCO

1850 woodcut engraver, Montgomery Street near Bush
1856–1857 wood engraver, 153 Sansome Street

The only lithograph of his I have seen is "View of the City and Harbor of San Francisco, California, Oct. 31, 1849. Drawn and engraved by Thomas Armstrong. Copyright by A. Rosenfield, 1867"—small.

ATWILL (JOSEPH F.), *ET AL.* — NEW YORK AND SAN FRANCISCO

Joseph F. Atwill:
1833 137 Broadway, New York
1834–1847 201 Broadway
1849 300 Broadway

J. F. Atwill & Company:
1850 158 Washington Street, San Francisco
1851–1852 Post Office Bldg., Clay Street
1852 music store, 212 Clay Street
1852–1853 music dealer, Plaza
1854 music store, 172 Washington Street
1856–1858 music, 172 Washington Street

Atwill & Company:
1852–1853 music store, Post Office Bldg., Plaza
1853 172 Washington Street
1856–1857 music, 172 Washington Street

In New York, Atwill was chiefly a music publisher and dealer. In San Francisco, he published or sold, sometimes both, the following:

PLATE 11 Baker's "Independent City Guards Quick Step"; Butler's "The Grand Plaza"; "The Lumber Merchant"; "San Francisco Quadrilles"; "Testimonial Loving
PLATE 93 Cup"; Quirot & Company's "California Pioneers"; and Sarony & Major's "View of San Francisco, 1851"

The above is correct view of Yerba Buena, now San Francisco, in 1837.

YERBA BUENA (NOW SAN FRANCISCO) **IN THE SPRING OF 1837.**

Lithographed by Geo. H. Baker. From the original drawing by John J. Vioget

Jacob P. Leese. built the first house.

FROM NATURE & ON STONE BY T. GROB

NAGEL, FISHBOURNE & KUCHEL, 599 CLAY ST., SAN FRANCISCO, CAL

PUGET MILL C^{o}S MILLS.

TEEKALET W.T.

W. C. Talbot & Co

SAN FRANCISCO, CALIFORNIA.

15

A full color reproduction of this plate appears in the color section in this book.

Pub. by W.H. Baxter of **BOWERS** Express

BURNING OF NEVADA CITY CAL.ª MARCH 12.th 1851 LOSS $ 1,500,000.

16

May & Turnfest

San Francisco, Cal.ª May 7th & 8th 1854.

17

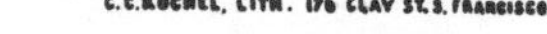

AMBROTYPE TAKEN BY C.H.P. NORCROSS. BRITTON & CO PRINT C.C.KUCHEL, LITH. 176 CLAY ST. S.FRANCISCO.

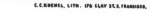

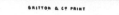

ADVENTURES OF A PIKE IN CALIFORNIA.
8.
GROCERIES
NO CREDIT
Coming in from the Plains.
Winter Experience.
Disturbers of his Rest
Wet Diggings.
Dry Diggings
Buys a Quartz Claim
Making acquaintance with the natives
Daming
Visits Sacramento
Buys a Horse
and Stockton
Going back to the Mines
Other parties Claim him next day.
Dead broke
Sinks a deep hole
Makes a rais
and takes th Railroad for home

Lith: & Published by Britton & Rey Cor. Comm! & Montg.y Sts. S. Francisco.

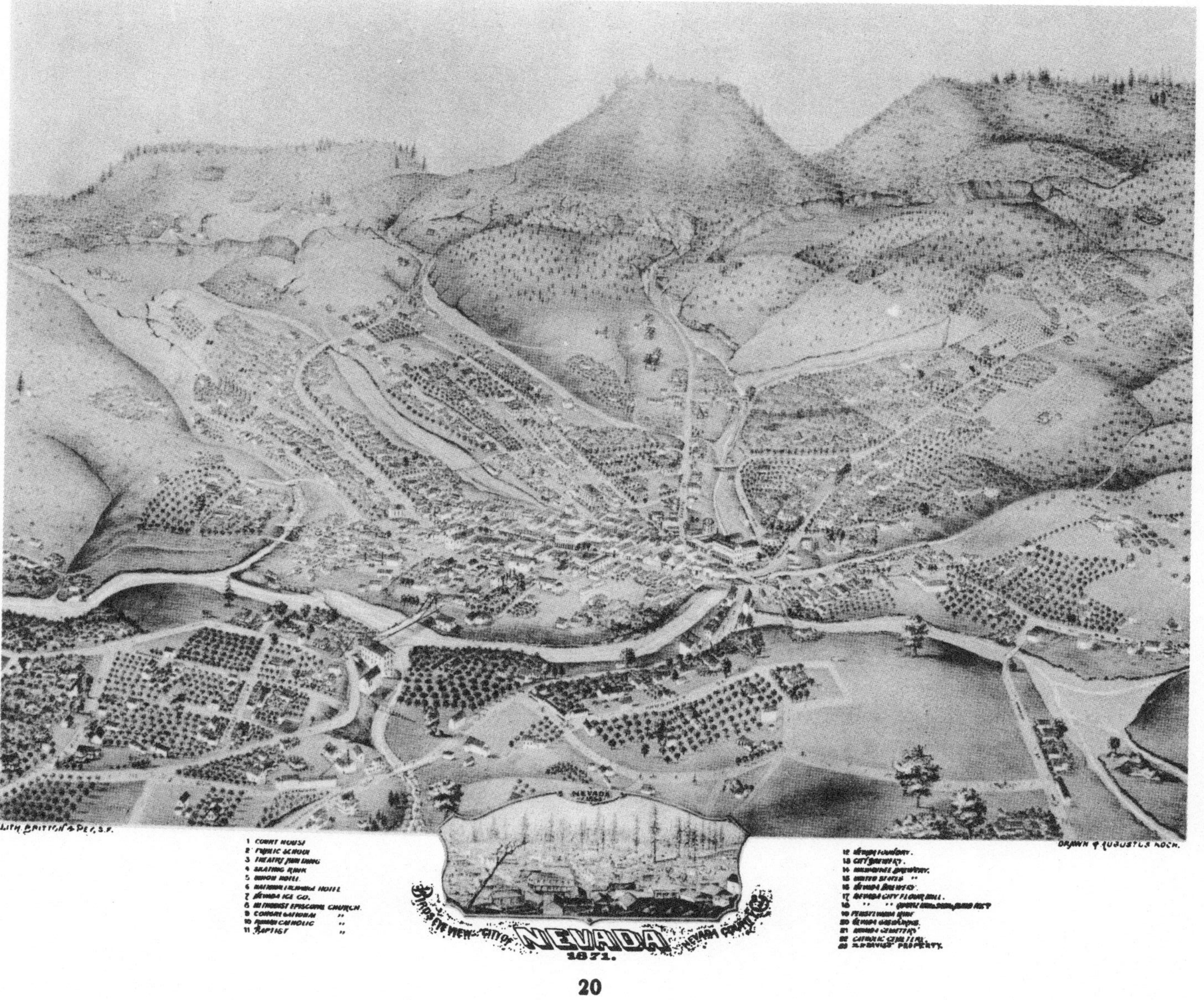
LITH. BRITTON & REY, S.F.
DRAWN BY AUGUSTUS KOCH.
BIRDS EYE VIEW CITY OF NEVADA NEVADA COUNTY, CAL.
1871.
1 COURT HOUSE
2 PUBLIC SCHOOL
3 THEATRE BUILDING
4 SKATING RINK
5 UNION HOTEL.
6 NATIONAL EXCHANGE HOTEL
7 NEVADA ICE CO.
8 METHODIST EPISCOPAL CHURCH.
9 CONGREGATIONAL ,,
10 ROMAN CATHOLIC ,,
11 BAPTIST ,,
12 NEVADA FOUNDRY.
13 CITY BREWERY.
14 MILWAUKEE BREWERY.
15 UNITED STATES ,,
16 NEVADA BREWERY.
17 NEVADA CITY FLOUR MILL.
20 NEVADA GAS WORKS.
22 CATHOLIC CEMETERY.

LITH. BRITTON & REY S.F.

BRADLEY BARLOW.
J. L. SANDERSON.
JAMES W. PARKER.
CHAS C. HUNTLEY.
} PROPRIETORS.

CALIFORNIA & OREGON STAGE COMPANY.

E. F. HOOKER
SUPERINTENDENT.

CARRIES WELLS, FARGO & CO.S EXPRESS AND THE U.S. MAIL.

VIEW OF MOUNT SHASTA 14.442 FT ABOVE THE SEA - ON C.& O. STAGE ROUTE.

21

A full color reproduction of this plate appears in the color section in this book.

Lith. & Published by BRITTON & REY. GAMBLERS Corn.r Mont.y & Co.l St. San Francisco.

A. Coquardon del. *Lith. Britton & Rey S.Francisco*

A CORRECT VIEW OF WEAVERVILLE, TRINITY CO.Y CAL.

PUPLISHED BY CRAM ROGERS & CO.

Lith & Pub by Britton & Rey S.F.

EXECUTION OF HETHERINGTON AND BRACE

The Murderers of Baldwin Randall, West and Marion. July 25th 1856.

Atwill also published a music sheet which shows the Atwill & Company store at 172 Washington Street, where they dealt not only in music, but in "fancy goods, stationery, holiday presents & toys," and various other things. This music sheet is reproduced.

"El Eco Del Pacifico, by Jaques Coo. San Francisco. (Cal.) Published by Atwill & Co. 172 Washington St. Entered . . . 1853" PLATE 7

"Atwill & Co.'s Fancy Goods. Emporium 172 Washington St. San Francisco" —small, n.d.

AUDUBON, JOHN WOODHOUSE NEW YORK

In 1852 he wrote and published the "Illustrated Notes of an Expedition Through Mexico and California," listed under Nagel & Weingaertner. Audubon was born in Henderson, Kentucky, November 30, 1812, and died in New York, February 21, 1862. He was the son of the great ornithologist, J. J. Audubon. Audubon was an artist of note. He left a journal describing one of the most tragic trips undertaken by any of the gold hunters. This journal was published in 1906. It contains a biography by his daughter, Maria R. Audubon. It was Audubon's intention to publish his drawings in ten parts, but owing to distractions in his family life only one part was completed. The journal is illustrated with sketches of San Francisco and the gold-mining country. From the fine artistic quality of the plates in Part One it seems a great pity that the work was never finished. The one part issued was made in a small quantity and presented to friends. It has become very rare. The hardest blow to Audubon was the loss of about two hundred paintings and water colors depicting his trip. These he entrusted to a friend to bring back. They were lost at sea in the wreck of the steamer *Central America*.

AYRES, THOMAS A. SAN FRANCISCO

Ayres was the artist of Kuchel & Dresel's "The Golden Gate," "Mammoth Tree Grove," and "The Yo-Semite Falls" (reproduced in *America on Stone* as Plate 22). He also drew Nahl's "General View of the Great Yo-Semite Valley." PLATE 74

The following four small lithotints by Ayres are dated as 1854 by the de Young Museum:

"Benecia and Mont Diablo from Straits of Carquinez"

"Entrance to the Golden Gate off Point Lobos"

"North Beach from Meiggs Wharf"

"View from Telegraph Hill looking Towards Sausalito"

Ayres evidently worked mostly in crayon. There were ten of his drawings exhibited in New York City in the early part of 1930. The list follows:

"Entrance To The Bay of San Francisco"—This was probably the original for Kuchel & Dresel's "The Golden Gate"

"The Mammoth Tree Grove. The Hotel, 1855"

"Relief Valley Near The Summit of the Sierra Nevada Head Waters of the Stanislaus River, California, (1856)"—The valley takes its name from being the scene of the relief of a portion of the Donner party in 1847.

"Scene From Above Sullivans Crossing, Tuolumne Co., Cal."

"Scene from The Summit of Telegraph Hill Looking Towards Saucilito. (1856)"—The drawing shows a view of San Francisco Bay from the Golden Gate to San Pablo Bay, including the long docks and waterfront buildings of San Francisco.

"Sonoro from the South. Morning. 1853"

"Sutter's Fort, from Flora's Garden, looking Southwest"

"Tejon Indian Reservation. Old adobe House of Lieut. Beal. (1854)"

"Tejon Pass from The Indian Reservation Land of Tulase (Tulare) Valley (1854)"

"View of The Castle Rocks at the Head of S. Fork. Stanislaus River, Cal. (1855)"

These drawings, made on the spot, have artistic merit and place Ayres in the front rank of the draftsmen of the period. They were from the Drum Collection, which included many fine California lithographs.

BAINBRIDGE, HENRY — SAN FRANCISCO

See Sarony & Major's "View of San Francisco, 1851," and Napoleon Sarony's "View of Sacramento City."

There is a "Henry Bainbridge, Clerk" listed in the city directory for 1852, but whether this is the same one, I do not know.

BAKER (GEORGE HOLBROOK), *ET AL.*

SACRAMENTO AND SAN FRANCISCO

1854–1857	Barber & Baker, Sacramento
1857–1862	George H. Baker, Sacramento
1862–1866	George H. Baker, San Francisco
1866	522 Montgomery Street
1867	430 Montgomery Street; also Baker & Tepper, same address
1868	428 Montgomery Street
1869	430 Montgomery Street; also Baker & Bawden, job printers, same address
1870–1873	408 California Street
c.1876	103 Montgomery Street
1880	329 Sansome Street

PROLOGUE

George Holbrook Baker was born March 9, 1827, in East Medway, Mass., at the home of his maternal grandfather, who was an organ builder and bell founder. Baker years later in San Francisco made a lithograph of the Holbrook home, showing a typical New England farmhouse with the adjacent small organ factory. He came of English stock, some of his ancestors having arrived in America as early as 1630, and men from both sides of his family fought in the American Revolution. His mother was a music teacher and a singer of some note, and from her he inherited his artistic talent. His father's people lived in Dedham, Mass., and Baker lived both there and in Boston during his youth.

He was sent to New York and apprenticed to a commercial artist named Smith for whom he worked for three years for the customary bare living. At the end of that time, Smith put him to drawing maps so exclusively that Baker got bored with his work and left. He then became a student at the National Academy of Design, where he was studying at the time the Gold Rush fever broke out. While there he won many prizes for his work.

All during his youth and up to the time he left for the West, Baker did much sketching and painting, especially in the White Mountains. The love Baker had in these days for the mountains and all of nature stayed with him all his life, as is shown in much of the work he later did in California.

When Baker was twenty-two years old, an art student in New York, the great emigration to the gold fields of California was under way and Baker decided to go West. He joined a party of twelve men under Captain Edward

A. Paul of Boston. This little group of men left Boston on January 8, 1849, for New Orleans and Vera Cruz, Mexico. Baker in a letter to his family said "it was my desire to go by way of Mexico, as presenting a more interesting and adventuresome route in preference to a long dreary voyage on the ocean, which to me appeared little preferable to six months in prison." Baker got his wish for "an adventuresome" trip. When nearly across Mexico the party was set upon by a band of Mexicans, and in the ensuing battle "pistols were used on both sides and stones thrown about quite freely." One man was killed and two were wounded, one of whom later died after the party had arrived at Mazatlan. From Mazatlan the remainder of the party embarked for San Francisco, where they arrived in May, 1849. A full account of this trip is given in letters from Baker to his family which were printed in *The Quarterly of the Society of California Pioneers,* San Francisco, December, 1930. Baker's diary from the time of his arrival in San Francisco to August 17, 1850, has also been printed in the society's quarterly for March, 1931.

Like almost everybody else who landed in San Francisco in those days, Baker headed immediately for the gold mines. There he stayed only a few days, for, making but a measly $17 a day, he decided he could profit more in business. He returned to San Francisco and set himself up in business with merchandise which had been sent out to him by his family. Just what this merchandise was, I do not know, but it may have included bells. Baker's daughter, Mrs. George Lilly, now living in San Francisco, writes in one of the issues of the quarterly:

> The Holbrooks were organ builders and bell founders, the first bell founders in America. Two of the bells at the Santa Barbara Mission, one large and one small one, are Holbrook bells, as is also one of those at the San Gabriel Mission.

For the next few years we find Baker entering into one business venture after another, sometimes alone, sometimes in the quickly formed and easily dissolved partnerships that existed in those fluent and affluent days. Baker and his current partner would set out to sell Eastern goods in some mining section; then the partner would perhaps have a recurrence of the gold fever and desert the goods for pick, pan, and shovel. Baker himself admits he was often tempted to go looking for the "elephant" once more, but his first attempt remained his last, and he went on with his merchandising, sometimes making money, often losing.

At one time he organized "Bakers Express," a mail service from San Francisco to the Feather River mines. In his diary he records the adventures of his first 290-mile trip with the mail, made on mule back, and with discouraging results financially. In the diary his accounts are often closed with the remark, "so wags the world"; and one entry closes, "I fear I shall yet believe in the total depravity of all mankind"—this after he had been badly "done" by several dishonest local agents.

During these years Baker traveled all through the mining country, with frequent trips to Sacramento and San Francisco. Busy as he was, he did not neglect his pencil and sketch pad. He speaks in his diaries of snatching time out to relax and sketch; the evidence remains in his lithograph and wood-cut views of the mining towns.

In 1852, Baker went up the river to Sacramento, where he lived for the next ten years. At first he was in the general merchandising business there with General Wynn. About 1854 he went into business with a man named Barber, and the firm of Barber & Baker turned out many woodcut views of California, some of which are found as book illustrations.

In 1856, he was publishing and editing the *Granite Journal* and the *Spirit of the Age*. He presumably carried on at the same time his activities in the firm of Barber & Baker, in which, incidentally, Baker was the artist and Barber the woodcutter.

Later—the exact date is not known—Baker set up independently as a lithographer, still in Sacramento. During the time he lived in Sacramento, Baker was a bosom chum of George Henry Goddard, but curiously enough none of the work by Goddard which I have seen was lithographed by Baker. After the great flood of 1862 in Sacramento, Baker decided to move to San Francisco, where he went into the lithographing business and lived until his death in January, 1906, just before the great earthquake and fire.

Baker was married in 1854 in Sacramento, and his two sons and one daughter were all born there. His daughter, Mrs. Lilly, was born in 1860 on the day that the first Pony Express came through to Sacramento bringing news that Eugénie had been proclaimed Empress in Paris—consequently, she was named Eugénie. She tells us that Baker was a man of constant activity, keeping voluminous diaries, writing many letters to his family whenever he traveled, writing numerous articles about his travels which were published in Eastern papers—and, of course, all the time sketching. Mrs. Lilly says that her father could never sit down without reaching for paper and pencil with which to draw quick sketches. She spoke particularly of the delight and the rapidity with which he could transform a few scrawly lines into a tree—and these trees are often an identifying feature of Baker's unsigned work. The photograph of Baker reproduced in the Prologue was loaned by his daughter.

Baker once went on a sketching trip through the mining district with a man named Butler, but whether this was Benjamin F. Butler, the lithographer, or W. C. Butler, the woodcutter, I do not know. Whichever one it was, Mrs. Lilly says that "he was a rough, rude sort of fellow,"—a characterization no doubt applicable to many of our worthy Forty-niners. The rough-and-ready humor in many of Benjamin F. Butler's cartoons leads me to suspect him as Baker's companion on this trip.

In September, 1873, Baker went to Yosemite with J. M. Hutchings, making many sketches of the valley with the idea of publishing them in a series to be called "G. H. Baker's Scenery of the Pacific Coast." As I understand it, this series was never issued in its entirety, but the Yosemite views and many others of various parts of the state were supposedly parts of the intended series.

As a lithographer Baker worked independently, not forming associations with various others, as so many other lithographers of the time did. The only exception to this appears in 1867 in an advertisement of "Baker & Tepper, General Lithographic Printers, 430 Montgomery Street, San Francisco." It was apparently a most temporary partnership, for although Baker continues at that address it is always as "Geo. H. Baker, Lith."

The only lithograph on which the Barber & Baker imprint appears is Fishbourne's "Map of the Mining Region."

A list of Baker's work follows:

Advertising posters, all "Lith. by George H. Baker," for R. F. Osborn & Co.; Henley's Indian Queen Hair Restorative; L. & M. Sachs & Co.; W. & I. Steinhart & Co.; Feinhausen & Gerichten; Goodwin & Co.; American Exchange Hotel; G. Rosenberg & Co.; E. H. Jones & Co.; and Russ House.

Two advertising cards: one, "George H. Baker, Practical Lithographer, 430 Montgomery Street (U. S. Treasury Bldg.) San Francisco. Special attention given to orders for bonds, certificates of stock, checks, drafts, notes, &c," the other, "Lithography in all its branches, engraving, designing, ornamental printing. George H. Baker, Practical Lithographer, 408 California Street, San Francisco"

"Benecia and Straits of Carquinez from the Southeast. Benecia & Harbor from the Northwest"—letterhead, n.d.

"A Birds-Eye View of Sacramento 'The City of the Plain.' Drawn, Designed & Published by George H. Baker. Sac. 1857. Lithography of Britton & Rey. San Francisco. Entered . . . 1857"—large; with border of twenty-eight views of public buildings, Sutter's Fort in 1846, the Embarcadero of Sacramento in 1849, and the seal of the city of Sacramento. A well-drawn bird's-eye view.

"Camp Colton. Encampment of Amador Battalion. 1871"—small, n.d.

"Camp Morgan, Amador Co. Cal. Advanced post, 1st. Regt. 2d Brigade. National Guard of Cal."—small, n.d. PLATE 9

"Centennial Celebration, San Francisco, 1876"—medium, n.d.

Certificate of membership in the "National Guard"—medium, n.d.

Certificate of membership in the "Society of California Pioneers"—small, n.d.

"Chapel at Seminary Park, Alemeda Co. Cal. Erected 1871"—small, n.d. PLATE 8
This is a nicely drawn little view of the chapel that once stood on the present site of Mills College for Women. The chapel was evidently short-lived, for a note in ink on the margin of the print says it was "totally destroyed by gale wind, Oct. 12th, 1871."

"Cliff House & Seal Rocks"—small, n.d.

"Commercial Hotel. John Kelly, Jr. Manager. Charges, $2 per Day"—small, n.d.

Five scenes, all small, n.d., showing the damage done by the earthquake of October 21st, 1868:

"Coffee & Risdon's Building, Market St., S. F."; "More & Hesleps Flour Mill, Haywards. Loss $12,000"; "Rosenbaum's Store & Rail-road House, Clay St. S.F."; "San Leandro Courthouse, Alameda Co."; "View of the town of Haywards, Alameda Co., Cal. The Center of the Great Earthquake Shock"

These earthquake views appear without Baker's imprint, but Mrs. Lilly has identified them as his.

"East Medway, Mass. 1850"—small, n.d. This is a view of Baker's birthplace.

"Falls of the Tuolumne"—medium, n.d.

PLATE 10 "Fort Yuma. Colorado Rivr. Cala."—medium, n.d. This view of the hottest town in the United States shows a party of emigrants crossing the Colorado River on a crude ferry. On the far bank stands the old Spanish prison, still to be seen today. Among the goods already landed on the near shore is a cannon, which Mrs. Lilly tells us is one of those salvaged from the Civil War and laboriously transported across the country to California.

"G. H. Baker's Scenery of the Pacific Coast"—medium, n.d. This was the frontispiece for Baker's intended series of views.

"Golden Gate and San Francisco Bay on the 100th Anniversary of American Independence. 1776. 1876"—large, n.d.

PLATE 11 "Independent City Guards Quick Step. Dedicated by the Sacramento Union Brass Band, and played by them on the occasion of the visit of the Guards to San Francisco, Oct. 27th, 1858. Sold by Dale & Co. Sac. Atwill & Co., A. Kohler, San Francisco. Gustave Amy, Marysville. J. E. Hamlin, Nevada" —a music sheet, n.d.

"Lake Tahoe & Western Summit from Zephyr Co., California"—small, n.d.

"Map No. 3 of Salt Marsh & Tide lands situate in the City & County of San Francisco. To be sold at Public Auction . . . Sale to commence Friday, Nov. 26th, 1869"—small, n.d.

"Map of Pueblo Lands of San Jose . . . July, 1866"—medium, n.d.

"Military of San Francisco. National Guard of California. Lithographed & Published by George H. Baker, 408 California St. San Francisco"—large, n.d. Showing "Commander-in-Chief: His Excellency, Gov. H. H. Haight; Ad'j't Gen'l: Thos. N. Cazneau; Ass't Ad'j't Gen'l: Maze Edwards; Gen'l Staff: John B. Frisbie; Albert S. Evans; Cutler McAlister; Jona. Letterman; Aids: Wm. Doolan; H. Linden; C. H. King; John Scott; R. H. Lloyd. Officers Of Second Brigade." Across the bottom of the plate are 32 officers and men, each in the full-dress uniform of his company.

PLATE 12 "The Modoc War. The Massacre. Lava Beds and Advance to the Rescue. Shack Nasty Jim. Capt. Jack"—small, n.d. In 1872 the Modoc Indians refused to go to the U. S. Reservation at Klamath in southern Oregon and went instead to the near-by Lava Beds. General Canby was sent to confer with them in April, 1873, and was treacherously killed. War then followed between the government and the Modocs, led by Captain Jack. In the end the band had to surrender and Captain Jack was executed. In the Baker lithograph "The Massacre" shows the killing of General Canby; "Lava Beds and Advance to the Rescue" depicts the battle between the Indians and the soldiers; "Shack Nasty Jim" and "Capt. Jack" are portraits of two of the Indian chiefs.

"Pioneer Stage Company from Sacramento to Virginia (City), Carrying the Great Overland Mail & Wells, Fargo & Company's Express. This route affords a fine view of Lake Bigler or Tahoe, running for twenty miles along its shores"—medium, n.d.

"Port of San Francisco, June 1, 1849. From the original drawing by George H. Baker made at date expressly for the New York Tribune and published in that paper's issue of Aug. 28th, 1849"—medium, n.d. Note below view reads: "About 200 vessels were then detained here their crews leaving for the mines on arrival in port. Only a portion of these can be shown here. The view is from Rincon Hill looking N.W. showing San Francisco Bay Mt. Tamalpais Angel Island and the hills of Marin in the extreme distance. In the mean distance lies the embryo city flanked by Telegraph and Russian Hills Population estimated at 2000 all adults with very few women Many living in tents."

"Pumpkin Buttes, near Fort Reno, Dacotah"—small, n.d.

"San Diego, Cal."—medium, n.d. PLATE 13

"Sentinel Rock and Three Brothers. Merced Riv."—medium, n.d.

"South Dome, Liberty Gap & Nevada Fall, Yosemite"—medium, n.d.

Stock certificate of the "Occident Gold and Silver Mining Company"—small, n.d.

"Synagogue of Congregation Emanu-el. Erected in San Francisco, 5627"—large, n.d.

"A View of the Town and Harbour of San Francisco. Drawn by George H. Baker, Artist. Published by H. Mansfield, New Haven, Conn."—small, n.d. A scarce view.

"Washington Grammar School. Erected 1861. Promoted to High School, 101 Pupils"—small, n.d.

PLATE 14 "Yerba Buena (now San Francisco) in the Spring of 1837. From the original drawing by John J. Vioget. Copyrighted 1893"—medium. A reprint of the Britton & Rey view by this title (*q.v.*).

"Yosemite Fall, 2634 Feet High, Yosemite Valley, Mariposa Co., Cal."—medium, n.d.

"Yosemite Valley, Mariposa Co. Cal. Altitude 4000 Ft. Above the Sea. View Looking West from Indian Trail"—medium, n.d.

BALDWIN — UNKNOWN

"Grand Gulf City, California"—medium, (c.1860).

BANCROFT (A. L.) & COMPANY — SAN FRANCISCO

1872 721 Market Street
Later Unknown

See Gray & Gifford. Lithographs of Bancroft's are:

"Bancroft Map Of The Bay Counties 1890. Lithograph by Bancroft & Co."—large.

"Bird's Eye View Of Healdsburg Cal. 1876. Lithograph by A. L. Bancroft"—medium. Five small views beneath.

"Bird's Eye View Of Los Angeles, Cal."—"Bird's Eye View of Wilmington, Cal."—and "Bird's Eye View of Santa Monica, Cal. Entered . . . 1876"—large. Three views on one sheet.

"Birds Eye View Of San Diego, Cal. 1876. Lithograph by A. L. Bancroft & Co."—large, n.d.

"Birds Eye View of Santa Monica, Los Angeles County, Cal. From a sketch by E. S. Glover"—small, n.d.

"G. W. McNear's Warehouses & Docks, Port Costa, California"—small, n.d.

"Official guide map of city and county of San Francisco, compiled from official maps in surveyor's office. San Francisco. A. L. Bancroft & co. 1873"—large.

"Official Map of Sutter County, California . . . Approved . . . May 1873"—large, n.d.

"State House. 1849. San Jose. L. Goodrich, Delt."—very small, n.d. San Jose was the capital of California from December, 1849, to May, 1851.

Stock certificate, small, n.d. of the "Monumental Mining Company"

"View of Los Angeles from the East. Brooklyn Heights in the foreground. Pacific Ocean and Santa Monica mountains in the background. Drawn by E. S. Glover. Published by the Brooklyn Land & Building Co., Los Angeles, Cal. Entered . . . 1877"—medium.

"View of New Tacoma and Mount Rainer, Puget Sound, Washington Territory. Terminus of the Northern Pacific Railroad. Drawn & Published by E. S. Glover, Portland, Oregon. Entered . . . 1878"—medium.

Lithographed the plates in "California-Album. Herausgegeben von C. J. Brick. Im Selbstverlage des Verfassers. San Francisco: Druck von Rosenthal & Roesch. 1883."

Also lithographed the plates in "History of the Catholic Church in California. By W. Gleeson, M.A. San Francisco: Printed For The Author, By A. L. Bancroft and Company, 1872":

"Father John Salva Tierra, S.I. Apostle of Lower California"

"Hernando Cortes. Conqueror of Mexico"

"Charles The Fifth"

"Female Indian of California making baskets"

"Cleaning grass seed. San Joaquin Valley. California."

"Copy of An accurate Map of California. Drawn by the Society of Jesuits, and Dedicated to the King of Spain. 1757"

"Father Junipero Serra, O.S.F. Apostle of Upper California"

"Mission of Santa Barbara. From a drawing by Vischer"—probably one of the Mission views in Vischer's "Pictorial of California" (*q.v.*)

"View of the Port of Monterey in 1842"

"Le R. P. Narciso Duran. Préfet apostolique des Franciscains Espagnols Missionnaires dans la Nouvelle California"

"Ancient Work, Liberty Township, Ross County, Ohio. (Eight miles S.E. from Chillicothe)"

"Newark Works, Licking County, Ohio"

"Fort Ancient, East bank of the Little Miami River, 33 miles above Cincinnati"

BANNISTER, ALFRED UNKNOWN

See Britton & Rey's "Map of Tulare County."

BARLOW, BENJAMIN W. UNKNOWN

Drew Britton & Rey's "Map of the City of Benicia," and drew and published D'Avignon's "Map of the City of Benecia." (The name of the city appears spelled both ways.)

BAXTER, W. H. NEVADA CITY, CALIFORNIA

PLATE 16 "Burning of Nevada City Cala. March 12th, 1851. Loss $1,500,000. Pub. by W. H. Baxter of Bowers Express"—letterhead, n.d. A typical flamboyant scene of a fire in a mining town. The copy reproduced has the names of the buildings written across them in faded ink, as is often found in these letterheads.

BEAUMONT, EDOUARD DE PARIS, FRANCE

Born at Lanion, France, 1821. Painter and lithographer.

"Croquis Du Jour. 1. Mines D'Or. De La Californie. 'Faut-il être dindon, pour croire de pareils canards!' Chez Aubert Pl. de la Bourse. Imp. Aubert & Cie."—small, n.d.

"A La Campagne. Au Bord De La Seine. 'Voyons, Melle. Josephine, montez sur notre canot le Cormoran, il est en partance pour San-Francisco, en droite ligne, avec relâche à l'ile St. Denis!' Chez Aubert & Cie. Pl. de la Bourse, 29 Paris. Imp. de Me. Ve. Aubert r. de l'Abbaye, 5 Paris"—small, n.d.

"Fariboles. En Route Pour La Californie. 'Tiens je distinque encore mon pauvre Adolphe sur le rivage, doit-il être dèsolè dans ce moment-ci, ah! grand Dieu, voila qu'il prend la taille à une pêcheuse de crabbes, plus souvent que je lui rapporterai des millions à ce monstre là!' Chez Aubert & Cie. Pl. de la Bourse 29 Paris. Imp. de Me. Ve. Aubert, r. de l'Abbaye, Paris"—small, n.d.

"Au Bal Masque. 'Est y laid, ce sauvage là! N'en dis pas d'mal, Nini, c'est un Californien.' Chez Aubert Pl. de la Bourse. Imp. Aubert & Cie."—small, n.d.

"Au Bal Masque. Californien. 'Un mossieu qui a du succes.' Chez Aubert, Pl. de la Bourse. Imp Aubert & Cie."—small, n.d.

"Fariboles. 'Jeunes fidèles de la Paroisse Notre Dame de Lorette partant en pèlerinage pour la Californie.' Chez Aubert & Cie. Pl. de la Bourse 29. Paris. Imp. de Me. Ve. Aubert, 5 r. de l'Abbaye Paris"—small, n.d.

BECHERER, C. F. SAN FRANCISCO

c.1854 California near Montgomery Street

One most interesting print by Becherer has turned up:

"May & Turnfest. San Francisco, Cala. May 7th–8th 1854. On stone by H. Steinegger. Publd. by C. F. Becherer. Lithy. of C.F. Becherer, California St. ab. Montgomery"—small, n.d. This festival of an early German turnverein was held on the site where, in 1850, J. C. Russ had gone far into the wilderness bordering San Francisco to build a home. In 1856 it became known as Russ' Gardens and was for many years a famous amusement park. The spot that was then wilderness is now at Harrison and Sixth streets, in the midst of San Francisco's "South of Market" industrial section. PLATE 17

BEUCH UNKNOWN

"Beuch Del." appears on the "Leland's Map of Marysville" listed under W. B. Cooke & Company.

BEUTLER UNKNOWN

This name I have seen once only, as the artist of Fishbourne & Company's "Chinese Life!!!" I do not know whether this was really Benjamin F. Butler, but it seems likely. PLATE 61

BIEN, JULIUS NEW YORK

1850	12 Avenue B
1851–1852	90 Fulton Street
1853–1854	47 Gold Street and 97 Fulton Street
1854–1856	90 Fulton Street
1856–1857	107 Fulton Street
1858–1859	58 Fulton Street
1860	60 Fulton Street
1861–1863	18 Broadway
1864–1868	24 Vesey Street

Bien, whose work is covered in *America on Stone,** will always be remembered chiefly as the first great scientific cartographer in the United States. Soon after his arrival in 1849 in this country from Germany, where he was born, he became interested in improving the quality of maps, and thanks to

*Pp. 93–94, *America on Stone,* by Harry T. Peters. Doubleday, Doran & Co., 1931.

President Pierce and his administration, he was soon making maps of the new surveys in the West.

Five of these are:

"Map of public surveys in California to accompany report of surveyor gen'l. 1862. New York, J. Bien, Entered . . . 1863"—large.

"Map of Routes For a Pacific Railroad, compiled to accompany the report of Hon. Jefferson Davis, Secretary of War, in the offices of P.R.R. Survey, 1855. Scale, 1 to 6,000,000. Lith. by J. Bien, N. Y."—large, n.d. A note on the map signed by Gen. G. K. Warren, says it is only a hurried compilation to exhibit the relations of the different routes.

"Map of the County of Los Angeles. Entered . . . 1877"—very large. This was seen at the reconstructed Mission of San Juan Capistrano, where it hangs on a wall in one of the old common rooms.

"State of California. 1876. Compiled from the official records of the general land office and other sources by C. Roeser. New York, photo. lith. & print by J. Bien, Entered . . . 1876"—large.

"U.S. Coast Survey. City of San Francisco and Its Vicinity. Entered . . . 1859" —large.

A California view of Bien's is "Central City, Looking Up Spring Gulch. Entered . . . 1866"—small.

Bien also made many lithographs for Pacific railroad reports.

BINGHAM, DODD & COMPANY HARTFORD, CONN.

Lithographed the plates in "The Oldest and The Newest Empire: China And The United States. By William Speer, D.D. Chicago, Ill. Jones, Junkin & Co. 1870." Some of the plates depict the Chinese in California.

Bingham & Dodd, of Hartford, are mentioned in *America on Stone*.

BIXBY, M. SAN FRANCISCO

Appears only as the publisher of Wagner & McGuigan's "Map of the City of San Francisco."

BLAKE, WILLIAM P. NEW YORK

Author and artist of the "Report Of A Geological Reconnaissance In California: Made in Connection with the Expedition to Survey Routes in

California, to Connect with the Surveys of Routes for a Railroad from the Mississippi River to the Pacific Ocean, under the Command of Lieut. R. S. Williamson, Corps Top. Eng'rs, in 1853. By William P. Blake, Geologist and Mineralogist of the Expedition. New York: H. Bailliere, 290 Broadway."

Blake also published a separate edition. In this issue, he says that the lithograph plates (which form one of the attractions of the work) were printed directly from the original stones, and that the original issues were transfers.

See James Ackermann, A. Hoen & Company, Sarony, Major & Knapp, and Thomas S. Sinclair.

BLUNT, SIMON F. UNKNOWN

A United States Navy man who drew some of the plates listed under W. H. Dougal. Also see Curtis B. Graham.

BOGARDUS, JOHN P. SAN FRANCISCO

c.1850	unknown
1854	solicitor, Excelsior Printing office, 151 Clay Street
1856–1857	advertising solicitor, 151 Clay Street
1858	solicitor, 151 Clay Street

Bogardus published C. J. Pollard's "San Francisco, from Rincon Point," and "View of San Francisco, February 1850." Bogardus was probably a man with vision, and owing to this and to his advertising sense these pioneer views were made.

BÖHM, G. UNKNOWN

See Lewis & Böhm.

BOOSEY, W. LONDON

Drew on stone one of the M. & N. Hanhart's "View of the Town and Harbour of San Francisco."

BORTHWICK, J. D. LONDON

See Quirot & Company's "View of Mokelumne Hill"—listed under Justh, Quirot, *et al.*

Borthwick was the author and artist of "Three Years in California.

Published by William Blackwood and Sons, Edinburgh and London. 1857." The eight plates by Borthwick were lithographed by M. & N. Hanhart:

"Our Camp On Weaver Creek"; "Monté In The Mines"; "Faro"; "A 'Flume' On The Yuba River"; "Chinese Camp In The Mines"; "Bull & Bear Fight"—four vignettes; "A Ball In The Mines"; and "Shaw's Flats"

BOSQUI (EDWARD) & COMPANY SAN FRANCISCO

1852–1853	Edward A., clerk, 185 Kearny Street
1854–1857	Edward A., bookkeeper and clerk at Palmer, Cook & Co., Union Street
1858	Edward A., clerk, res., Union & Taylor streets
1859 on	Clay and Leidesdorff Streets

(Bosqui was mentioned in *America on Stone* erroneously as "T. Bosqui.")

Edward Bosqui was born in 1833 in Montreal, of French descent. He was a poor boy, and when about seventeen years old decided to go to California. He went by way of Panama, where, like a good many others who headed for the Gold Rush in those wild days, he became stranded. He worked his way up through Mexico, a hazardous trip, but young Bosqui survived the many hardships, learning meanwhile to speak Spanish like a native

He arrived in San Francisco in the latter part of 1850, and his first job was as cashier of the first bank to be established there. Afterwards he served as General Frémont's private secretary.

He first went into the printing business in 1859 at Clay and Leidesdorff Streets, and stayed at that location for thirty-nine years. Bosqui did bookbinding, as well as printing and lithography—in fact, lithography seems to have been a minor part of his work. He printed the *Evening Bulletin* in the early days of its existence, and did a great deal of commercial label work.

Bosqui was a handsome man, highly cultivated, speaking both French and Spanish. He was one of the founders of the Bohemian Club, the School of Design, and the Art Association of San Francisco. He also belonged to the Vigilantes. His daughter, Mrs. Archie Treat, now living near San Francisco, has in her possession a book Bosqui wrote and printed about his early experiences going to and in California. He died in 1917.

Besides the few prints listed below, the only lithographic work of Bosqui's

FLUME

Lith. & Published by BRITTON & REY. ELEVATING WATER WHEEL San Francisco Cal.

FORT VIGILANT

Rooms of the Committee Sacramento St. betn. Davis & Front

Daguer[re] by Vance.

Lith. Britton & Rey.

MASS MEETING

Endorsing the Acts of the Vigilance Committe

June 14th

GAMBLING IN THE MINES

MONTE

Lith & Published by BRITTON & REY. FARO San Francisco California

R. E. Ogilby del. Lith. Britton & Rey San Francisco

Grass Valley, Nevada County
CALIFORNIA.

28

Cambridge Park Course Boston
Union Course. L.I.
LADY VERNON.
SAN FRANCISCO, CAL.
August 1855.
Pioneer Course. San Francisco.
Pioneer Course. San Francisco.

FROM NATURE BY J. M. LAPHAM. LITH. BRITTON & REY SAN FRANCISCO

MAMMOTH ARBOR VITAE.

STANDING ON THE HEAD WATERS OF THE STANISLAUS & SAN ANTOINE RIVERS, IN CALAVERAS COUNTY, CALIFORNIA. DIAMETRE 31 FEET AT THE BASE; CIRCUMFERENCE 96 FEET - HEIGHT 290 FT. - 3000 YEAR

MINERS COAT OF ARMS

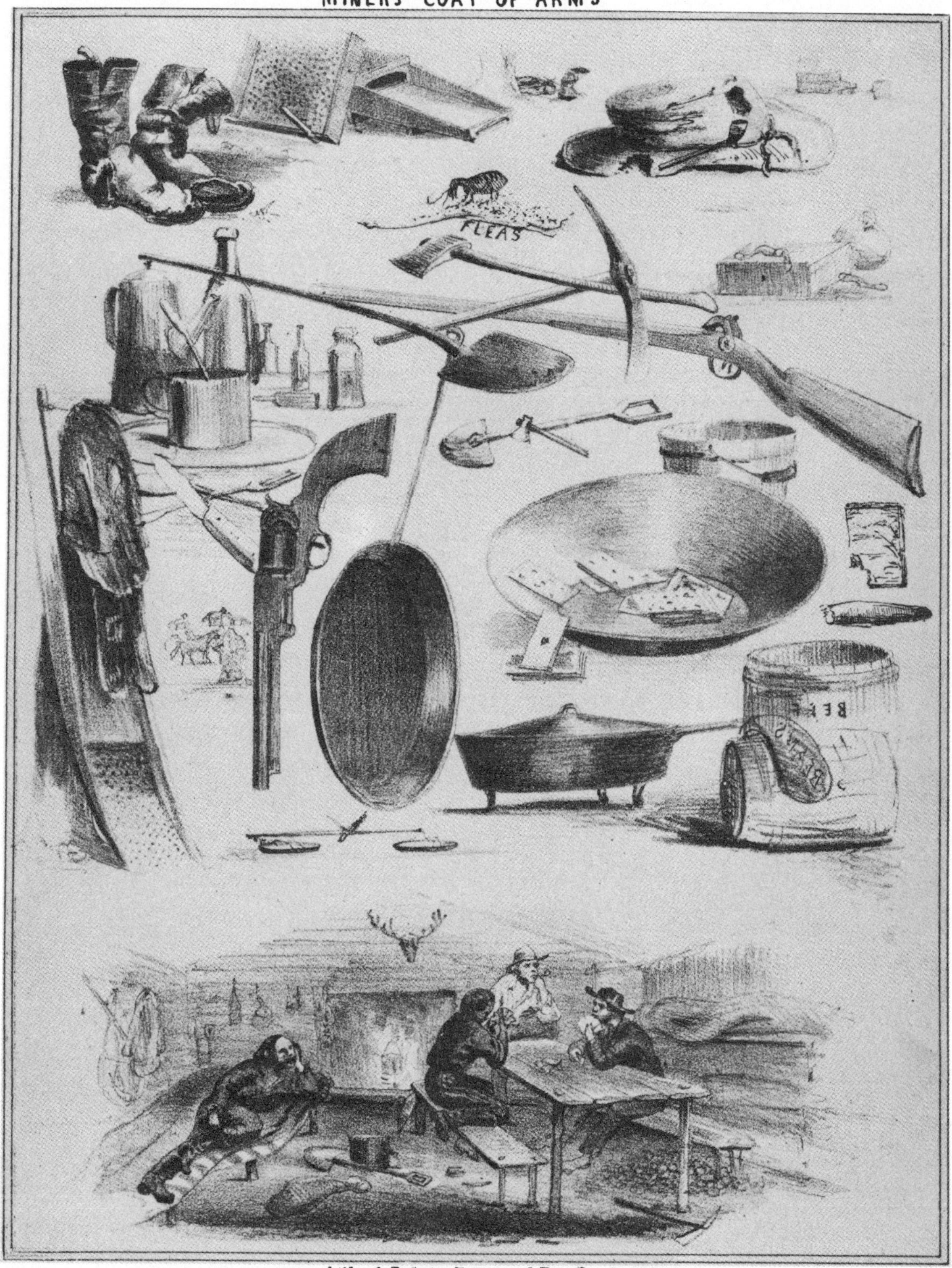

Lith. & Pub. by Britton & Rey San Francisco

Lith. Britton & Rey

Miners' Ten Commandments.

A NEW *VERSE*-ION, INCLUDING A PREAMBLE, BY-LAWS AND DECREE.

BY CADEX ORION.

PREAMBLE.

Away "deown east" there dwelt a man,
E'en over in the State of Maine,
Who had enough of tall pine trees
Himself and wife to well maintain.

But years rolled by, and children came
Around the little fire side,
And claimed a right to eat and drink,
Nor could such wants well be denied.

The pine trees grew, and children too—
Though in their manner far apart:
The trees grew *thin*, the children *thick*,
And thus from Maine were doomed to part.

"Old Zenas" to his wife did say—
"I'll move you all to Michigan,
And California I will seek,
And dig until a richer man."

Across the Plains he bent his steps
And passed large droves of Buffalo,
Wild Horses, Turkies, very fine,
And Tigers, Jackalls, Indians too.

At times he hadn't *nary* piece
Of meat whereby to feed upon,
Nor any water for his thirst—
And thus he saw the *old lion*.

At last his clothes in tatters hung
About his sore and weary form—
His "harp of hopes" was soon uns rung
And fancied nigh the gathering storm.

He mourned his lot, and often wept
To think he ever took the *jaunt*—
And then he'd rave, and swear he b'leaved
He's soon to see the *Elephant*!

And thus "Uncle Zenas" soliloquised:—"I onct lived in peace and prosperity away deown in the State of Maine, and owned tew ceows, ten oxen and three shoats—besides dear Polly, and Ike, and Jake, and Tabitha, and Sarah Ann Eliza, Jane, together with the darling babe that was named *Rachel*, because she lifted up her voice and *wept* when I kissed her and departed for Californy! Y-as, 'tis even I, 'Old Zenas,' that's neow in Californy, and haint struck a single *pocket* nor *crevice* yet, and I've travelled e'en a' most as fur as 'tis tew hum. And here the road forks! Wonder which of these onlikely roads nears off tew Hangtown? Helloa! I'm blazed ef here aint jest the sarkumstance I'm looking for, by golly! A guide board, sartin as preachin! No taint, nether—coz the fingers are pintin up, and it reads—

"*Behold, a new verse-ion of the Miners' Ten Commandments, By-Laws and Decree.*"

Which reads as follows:

BY-LAWS.

One claim thou may'st own, and there drive your stake,
And coyote and crevice 'till you make or you break;
Always find the *bed-rock*, keep at work and pump out—
Do anything rather than be running about.

If the gold isn't there, keep cool and don't swear,
Nor either get tight, and say you don't care;
Nor practice the art of "salting" your claim—
For by such a practice you'll get a hard name.

Climb out, *very cool*, with pick, pan and shovel
And don't seek the cabin and pore over a novel—
But mark a new claim, and pitch in again,
And never have doubts of striking a vein.

Should you strike a rich pocket, a crevice or lead
Don't drink quite a barrel on the fortunate deed
But pocket your dust and go whistling away,
Content to enjoy it at some future day.

Should you venture your luck in daming the rivers,
And work in the water, getting *colds, coughs and shivers*,
Let "old rye" alone, and with wisdom of thought,
Sell out if you can, and bless him who bought.

Wend your way to dry diggings, purchase sluice-box or tom,
And a claim, too, if rich—judge of those you buy from—
Hire eight or ten "Coolies"—come the *cooly* at once,
Thus showing the people you are not quite a dunce.

By "Johnny Celestial" make two dollars per day,
On the labor of each, you see, that will pay;
Whereas, if you hire Uncle Sam's sturdy son,
You would pay more for labor, and hardly make one.

And lastly, thus reads the Decree:

FIRSTLY—It is decreed unto all the people of California, that ye do observe all that is herein written, that ye avoid some of the shoals and quicksands of this life, and especially during your sojourn in California, where a lesson or a warning cannot be given too soon. California is one vast amphitheatre—containing an assemblage of human beings from every land and every clime. All classes, all colors, and all conditions, are each day before your gaze, and soon they are associated more or less with you all. And now, my Disciples, this is why I publish this Decree, and give you this warning that ye may be prepared to meet the tempters.

SECONDLY—It is decreed, O ye Miners, that I first publish unto you, the decree; as ye are the most numerous of any of the tribes of California; And I pray you will hearken unto me with an attentive ear, that ye may be profited thereby. Ye are indeed mighty, and the wise men and the counsellors of ten have sought thy abode to teach ye wisdom and understanding.

THIRDLY—And thus it is decreed that thou shalt not labor to thine discomfiture and bodily pain. Thou shalt labor as becometh good Disciples and shall not exceed ten hours each day. Thy food shalt consist of that which is most wholesome and nourishing, and thy raiment shall be of woollen and of firm texture, and each week shalt thou cleanse thine apparel.

FOURTHLY—In default of the same, thy brother miners shalt take thee down even unto Feather River, and cleanse thee—apparel, body and all together, until thou wilt lend thine own exertions to do it thyself.

FIFTHLY—If vermin infest thee or thy blankets, thou shalt be banished from the cabin, thee and thy raiment until thou shalt rid thyself of thine unwelcome visitors. And on the day—yea, the hour—in which it shall appear that thou art ridden of all plagues—then in solemn possession shalt thou be marched with thy brother miners back even unto the cabin, and all feast sumptuously.

SIXTHLY—It is decreed that thou shalt not be made servants one to another, only as each serves the other in his turn. Neither shalt thou forsake thy brother miner while on the couch of sickness and pain, but shall carefully watch over him, and administer unto every necessary want, until he shall be able to arise again and proclaim himself well of his malady.

SEVENTHLY—It is also decreed, that thou, O Miner, who hath a family in a distant country, shall, whenever in thy power, remit the avails of thy labor to keep them in food and raiment during thy sojourn here. Thou shalt not neglect thy wife and children and go after strange women, who, with a syren's tongue and winning smiles, would lure thee to her snares of shame and degradation, and rob thee of thine honor, thy virtue and thy gold; and at last would despise and curse thee, and turn thee away empty handed. Beware, lest thou art overtaken in thy secret wanderings, and lose thy life, and thy friends mourn thy untimely fate.

EIGHTHLY—And it is also decreed, that thou, O young man, who hast left thy father's house to sojourn in the land of California—even in the mines thereof—thou too, I pray, take heed. Remember the counsel of thy mother and sisters, and forget not thy solemn pledges of affection. Nor shalt thou forget to pen an epistle each mail to thy kindred, that they may know how fares the wanderer, and when he is to return. Neither shalt thou forget that young and comely maiden who gave to you her warm and trusting affections, while you vowed to remain true, and never forget that starry night just on the eve of thy departure. Remember all these promises, that in thy after life thou mayst be blessed with future generations likened unto thee.

NINTHLY—It is decreed, that thou, O Bachelors, shalt be banished for a season, working out thy salvation here in the mountains, even among the eternal snows of the Sierra Nevada, and here remain until you come to the sage conclusion that there is a more congenial atmosphere by the side of the gentler sex. If such is the result of thy experience, thou mayst take up thy bed and walk, leaving thy tools for others of thy kind. Ever after thy works shall be judged, and when a certain period of time shall expire, and thou hast not employed the time profitably, and obeyed the Scriptures, wherein it reads—"Multiply and replenish the earth"—if you have failed in this, thou shalt again and forever serve among the snows of the Sierras. Therefore, ye bachelor miners, take warning.

TENTH AND LAST DECREE—FOR THE PEOPLE.—It is now lastly decreed, that thou Californians all male and female, who comest hither to better thy fortunes—thou art commanded to pay special attention to this Decree. Thou—a certain class—journeyed hither to repair thy ruined circumstances, to pay off old debts which have hung like a heavy weight over the horizon of thy future happiness. Thou hast come hither willing to brave the storms and tempests, both of nature's warring elements and also the "party feuds" and "political gusts" that often lend violent commotion to this golden land. Thou, O Politician who in thy Atlantic home didst crave office, and thy ambitious desires were not gratified—thou who labored so energetically for the *good* of the people (and thyself, too)—thou who wert beaten by the political opponent, thou comest hither to retrieve thy fortunes, to build up thy high minded hopes, to court Dame Fortune's smiles once more, and to raise up unto thyself a great name. But beware, thou lofty aspirant of fame; there are those here who art long before thee, who have their wires laid, and now have wealth on their side. Take heed; be wise; do thou go to one Bryant, and there select a pick, pan and shovel and sojourn for a while in the mountains, for there thou wilt have an equal chance among thy fellow laborers. And thou, O Speculator, from Gotham, thinkest thou that in California, even in San Francisco thou canst succeed, and have built up thy broken fortunes by thy schemes and thy small capital? Thou, too, beware, for in San Francisco there are speculators congregated from all countries, even of the shrewdest kind, and have studied and practiced all manner of devices. Take heed, therefore, and invest thy small capital in miners' supplies, and flee to the mountains, or to some inland village, and there be content with health, good water and fair profits.

And thou, pilgrims to the Eureka State, tarry not at the Bay, but pierce the Northern wilds and the mountain scenery; rush for pure air, health, wealth, and plenty of labor. Despair not in the hour of thy afflictions, but brave the storm manfully, and soon thou art safe. And thou fair maidens, daughters of Eve, who hast braved the hardships and dangers of a voyage to our golden shores, and thou heroines and pioneer mothers, we greet thee.—thrice welcome are ye all. Thou whom in memory were cherished—thou whom we so much wished for, who art so highly prised and cherished in every land—thou art indeed here.—And thou aged, though single maidens, thou art here too; nor wilt thou remain in single blessedness long, for thou wilt not meet with so many fair competitors to bear away the prizes from you, but will soon be heard exclaiming, Eureka! Eureka!

And now, each and every one, take heed of this my decree; and all of ye my Disciples, shall say at the last—We have followed thy precepts, and verily we have found our reward

I have seen are the ten illustrations in a book, "Grapes and Grapevines of California," which he also wrote.

"Arctic Oil Works. San Francisco, Cal. Works, Potrero. Office, 28 California St. Bosqui Eng. & Print. Co. S. F."—large, n.d. PLATE 3

"Hotel Del Monte. Monterey, California. Jules Tavernier, del."—medium, n.d.

Stock certificate of the "Fairfax Mining Company"—small, n.d.

"View of San Francisco, formerly Yerba Buena, in 1846–7. Before the Discovery of Gold. Executed by the Bosqui Eng. & Print. Co. Copyrighted. Designed & copied from views taken at the time & published by Capt. W. Swasey, a continuous resident since 1845"—medium, n.d. This is an extremely rare and fine view. In the foreground, in the Bay, are the U.S.S. "Portsmouth," transports "Loo Choo," "Susan Drew," and "Thomas H. Perkins," and the merchantman "Vandalia." Has 40 marginal references.

BOWEN, JOHN T. NEW YORK AND PHILADELPHIA

Lithographed the plates in "Illustrations Of The Birds of California, Texas, Oregon, British And Russian America. By John Cassin. Philadelphia: J. B. Lippincott & Co. 1862." Bowen's work is listed in *America on Stone.*

BOYD UNKNOWN

"Clear The Way! or Song of the Wagon Road. Music Composed and Dedicated to the Pioneers of the Great Pacific Rail Road. By Stephen C. Massett. San Francisco, Cal. 1856. Published by the Author. Boyd, del."—music sheet, n.d. At top of sheet is the following quotation: "Men of thought be up and stirring Night and day!" The view shows a steam engine headed for California, with three Indians in the foreground. Boyd is given as artist and probably drew the composition on stone.

BRADY, JOHN B. SAN FRANCISCO

1850 draftsman, City Hall
1851 unknown
1852 civil engineer, 61 Sacramento Street

Appears as the artist of Butler's "Official Map of the City of San Francisco"—the only work of his I have seen.

BRANDARD, J. LONDON

Brandard lithographed the eight plates in the London edition of "Mountains and Molehills," by Frank Marryat (*q.v.*):

"High and Dry"; "The Bar of a Gambling Saloon"; "The Winter of 1849"; "A Fireman's Funeral"; "Crossing the Isthmus"; "Chagres River"; "Where the Gold Comes From"; and "Horse Market—Sonora."

BRITTON & REY, *ET AL.* SAN FRANCISCO

Joseph Britton:

1847 559 Hudson Street, New York

Pollard & Britton:

1852 Merchant Street, San Francisco

Joseph Britton:

1852 139 Montgomery Street

Britton & Rey (Jacques Joseph):

1852–1853 Montgomery & California Streets

1854–1858 Montgomery & Commercial Streets (one year listed as "Est. 1851")

Britton & Company (Joseph Britton, Henry Steinegger, and X. Van De Casteele):

1859–1864 Montgomery & Commercial Streets

1864–1865 533 Commercial Street

1866 (Joseph Britton and Henry Steinegger), 533 Commercial Street

Britton, Rey & O'Brien:

1859–1861 plumbers and gasfitters

Rey, Jacques J:

1862–1864 with John Drouihat & Company, manufacturers of billiard tables

1865 Lithographer with Britton & Company

1866 office with Britton & Company

Britton, Rey & Company: (Henry Steinegger)

1867 533 Commercial Street

1868–1880 Commercial & Leidesdorff Streets

(The names of Britton and Rey were erroneously given in *America on Stone* as "James" Britton and "Jacob" Rey.)

The firm of Britton & Rey was undoubtedly the largest producer of lithographs in California. The two men were the Currier & Ives of the West, resembling that famous combination not only in the volume of their production but in their personal relationship as well.

PROLOGUE

Joseph Britton was a Yorkshire Englishman, born in 1825. At ten years of age he came to America and lived in New York until he was twenty-four. As a young man he apparently worked there as a lithographer, for in 1847 there was issued a music sheet, "The Shepard's Cottage," from J. Britton at 559 Hudson Street. In 1849 the lure of the California Gold Rush struck him and he joined the George Gordon party, the first gold seekers to make the journey by way of Lake Nicaragua. He went directly to the gold fields and prospected until he became discouraged by his lack of success and returned to San Francisco. There, in 1852, he formed a partnership with C. J. Pollard, and a few lithographs from this firm have been found. (They will be found listed under Pollard.) The association was of short life, however, for in the same year we find him setting up business as a lithographer with J. J. Rey.

PROLOGUE

Jacques Joseph Rey was born in Bouxviller, Alsace, in 1820. As a young man he studied art and lithography. His daughter has in her possession a lovely little portrait which Rey painted of his European teacher, unfortunately unknown. About 1850 he went by way of Panama to California, where, contrary to the custom of those days, he did not seek a fortune in the mines. Just what he did at first is not definitely known, but 1852 finds him entering into partnership with Joseph Britton. Three years later he married Britton's sister, thus cementing a friendship and partnership which accounts for some of the most notable lithography done in California from the first to the last of our story.

Joseph Britton remained a bachelor all his life. He lived always with the Rey family, and Rey's daughters tell us that throughout the long association of these two men, in business and in family life, they were the most amiable friends. In their lithographic business Rey has been spoken of as the artist of the firm, and Britton the business man, although he, too, could sketch.

Rey was a cultured Frenchman with strong artistic instincts, both in music and graphic arts. He sang well and understood the piano. As a young man he traveled in Russia with a nobleman, acting as companion, secretary, and interpreter.

The Rey home in San Francisco was a beautiful place overlooking the Bay. There were three daughters and one son in the family, and, according to one who knew them all well, the house was a gathering place for artistic society for many years. His daughters have inherited his charm, and one, Mrs. Marie

Sander, his artistic ability as well. Their present home in Berkeley contains many beautiful landscapes she has painted. Another daughter, Mrs. Hermione Sproule, is interested in music and community enterprises, and Miss Sylvia Rey is the historian of the family. All are enthusiastic and highly successful gardeners, and a visit to their home is a delightful experience not soon forgotten. They very kindly loaned us the photographs of Joseph Britton and J. J. Rey which are reproduced in the Prologue.

Many of the lovely and cherished possessions of the Rey family were destroyed or lost in the fire of 1906. Most of the family silver was irremediably damaged. They tell an amusing anecdote concerning an odd spoon which was in their silver chest in the days before the fire. It was monogrammed "C P" and for years it had puzzled them as to its origin and history. It was a lovely, fragile piece of silver, and they often commented on its mysterious acquisition. Then at one time they were entertaining as their house guest "Charlie" Parsons, and on the first evening of his stay with them, when they went in to dinner, the first object on the table that caught the guest's eye was the spoon. "Why," he exclaimed, "there is one of my mother's spoons." It then turned out that the spoon had been carried in a lunch basket many years before in New York on one of the numerous picnic sketching trips taken by young Joseph Britton and Charles Parsons,* who needs no introduction here.

Both Britton and Rey were public-spirited citizens, and streets in San Francisco have been named after them. Of the two, Britton took the more active part in public life. Perhaps an editorial, published in the San Francisco *Star* at the time of his death in 1901, will best tell the story:

> We "unlock" the forms of The Star to note the death, on Thursday night, of Joseph Britton, one of San Francisco's best known and best men, at the ripe age of seventy-six. He came to California in '49, and was engaged in business here since '52, in which year he formed a copartnership with the late J. J. Rey, his brother-in-law. He co-operated with A. S. Hallidie, Henry L. Davis, and James Moffitt in building the first cable railroad in the world [the Clay Street cable car line, still running in San Francisco]. He was interested in a number of enterprises, and amassed a fortune by honorable methods. He was a man who ever took an interest in public affairs, though he never sought and many times declined public office. In the early sixties, and again in 1870, he

*His life was outlined in *Currier & Ives: Printmakers to the American People,* Vol. I.

was persuaded to accept the office of Supervisor, where he distinguished himself by his rugged honesty and determined policy. He was ever against political bossism, and a non-partisan in local affairs. He was one of the Freeholders elected to frame the Charter and was made chairman of the Board. His nephew, V. J. A. Rey—the son of his old partner—is, we believe, his nearest surviving relative here. His death is a public loss.

Another obituary notice says: "No man in San Francisco possessed the civic spirit in greater degree or has exercised it more intelligently." It was also stated that "he early became conspicuous in the ranks of the Vigilantes." One who knew him has said that he was a typical Englishman, bluff, honest and outspoken.

Britton and Rey both had large interests in real estate in and around San Francisco, and in addition owned shares in various mining firms, most of which came to nothing. According to Rey's grandson, many of their shares in these mining companies were acquired in lieu of payment for lithographic work. One of their curious side ventures was into the plumbing and gas-fitting business, in 1859, as the firm of Britton, Rey & O'Brien. At another time they became interested in a flying machine which was backed by Fred Marriott, the enterprising publisher of the San Francisco *News Letter*. Needless to say, nothing came of this, but it is one more demonstration of the wide interests of these two forward-looking pioneers.

After Rey's death and Britton's retirement from active participation in the business, it was carried on by Rey's son, Valentine J. A. Rey, until 1906, when it was taken over by Carlisle & Company. Britton Rey, the grandson, still maintains an office under the name of Britton & Rey, although he does no lithographic work. In the same building are several lithographic and photo-engraving firms which were originally offshoots of the old company. The building is located on Leidesdorff Street, which in the sixties and seventies was often referred to as "Pauper's Alley," because it was there that discouraged miners, returned "broke" from the Comstock Lode and other mining sections, gathered to talk over their experiences.

Joseph Britton:

"J. Britton, Del." appears on Cooke & Le Count's "Birds Eye View of San Francisco," "Stockton," and "View of Sacramento City." **PLATE 54**

Also see Pollard & Britton, listed under C. J. Pollard, *et al.*

Britton & Rey:

Since such a large part of Britton & Rey's work consisted of letterheads, I am listing them first, separately from their other prints. They led all the other lithographers in the quantity of letterheads they produced—just how many, we do not know. Some were numbered as parts of a series, as will be seen on some of the titles, the highest we have found being number 24. Not all of this series have come to light—but including those that have, and others not so numbered, here is a list of over fifty. There must have been many more, and it is to be hoped that they will turn up, for surely there was no more unique contribution made by the California lithographers than these:

PLATE 19 "Adventures of a Pike in California. 8"—n.d. Seventeen vignette views:

"Coming in from the Plains"; "Winter Experience"; "Disturbers of his Rest"; "Wet Diggings"; "Dry Diggings"; "Buys a Quartz Claim"; "Daming"; "Making acquaintance with the natives"; "Visits Sacramento"; "and Stockton"; "Buys a Horse"; "Other parties Claim him next day"; "Going back to the Mines"; "Dead broke"; "Sinks a deep hole"; "Makes a raise"; and "And takes th[e] Railroad for Home"

"Bar Room in the Mines"—and—"Long Tom"—n.d.

"Birds Eye View of San Francisco. Entered . . . 1856"

PLATE 1 "Capt. Sutter's account of the first discovery of the Gold. 13. Entered . . . 1854"—with text of Sutter's account, and two vignettes:

"Portrait of Mr. Marshal, taken from nature at the time when he made the discovery of gold in California"; and "View of Sutter's Mill or place where the first gold has been discovered"

(For information about Captain Sutter, see the note under Snyder & Black's "Sutter's Fort.") This scarce letterhead represents the beginning of our story. When James Marshall (his name appears spelled with both single and double "l"—but he signed it the latter way) stumbled over a nugget of gold at Sutter's Mill one afternoon, it started the growth of the California depicted by the lithographers. This letterhead gives us one of the very few contemporary portraits of Marshall. The text of Sutter's account on the letterhead is reproduced, and the reader is warned again that the orthography is transcribed exactly as it appears on the lithograph itself. In this connection it is amusing to note this sign, which is tacked on a door at the reconstructed Sutter's Fort in Sacramento: "Sutter was well educated in French, German and

Spanish, but his English spelling and grammar are admittedly deficient." The account follows:

> "I was sitting one afternoon," said the Captain, "just after my siesta, engaged, by-the-bye, in writing a letter to a relation of mine at Lucern, when I was interrupted by Mr. Marshal a gentleman with whom I had frequent business transactions—bursting into the room. From the unusual agitation in his manner I imagined that something serious had occured, and, as we involuntarily do in this part of the world, I at once glanced to see if my rifle was in its proper place. You should know that the mere appearance of Mr. Marshal at that moment in the Fort, was quite enough to surprise me, as he had but two days before left the place to make some alterations in a mill for sawing pine planks, which he had just run up for me some miles higher up the Americanos. When he had recovered himself a little, he told me that, however great my surprise might be at his unexpected reappearance, it would be much greater when I heard the intelligence he had come to bring me. 'Intelligence,' he added, 'which if properly profited by, would put both of us in possession of unheard-of-wealth—millions and millions of dollars, in fact.' I frankly own, when I heard this that I thought something had touched Marshall's brain, when suddenly all my misgivings were put at an end to by his flinging on the table a handful of scales of pure virgin gold. I was fairly thunderstruck and asked him to explain what all this meant, when he went on to say, that according to my instructions, he had thrown the mill-wheel out of gear, to let the whole body of the water in the dam find a passage through the tail race, which was previously to narrow to allow the watter to run of in sufficient quantity, whereby the wheel was prevented from efficiently performing its work. By this alteration the narrow channel was considerably enlarged, and a mass of sand & gravel carried of by the force of the torrent. Early in the morning after this took place, Mr. Marshal was walking along the left Bank of the stream when he perceived something which he at first took for a piece of opal—a clair transparant stone, very common here—glittering on one of the spots laid bare by the sudden crumbling away of the bank. He paid no attention to this, but while he was giving directions to the workmen, having observed several similar glittering fagments, his curiosity was so far excited,

that he stooped down & picked on of them up. 'Do you know,' said Mr. Marshal to me, 'I positively debatted within myself two or three times whether I should take the trouble to bend my back to pick up one of the pieces and had decided on not doing so when further on, another glittering morsel caught my eye—the largest of the pieces now before you. I condescended to pick it up, and to my astonishment found that it was a thin scale of what appears to be pure gold.' He then gathered some twenty or thirty pieces which on examination convinced him that his suppositions were right. His first impression was, that this gold had been lost or buried there, by some early Indian tribe—perhaps some of those mysterious inhabitants of the west, of whom we have no account, but who dwelt on this continent centuries ago, and built those cities and temples, the ruins of which are scattered about thes solidary wilds. On proceeding, however, to examine the neighbouring soil, he discovered that it was more or less auriferous. This at once decided him. He mounted his horse, and rode down to me as fast as it could carry him with the news.

At the conclusion of Mr. Marshals account, and when I had convinced myself, from the specimens he had brought with him, that it was not exagerated, I felt as much excited as himself. I eagerly inquired if he had shown the Gold to the work people at the mill and was glad to hear that he had not spoken to a single person about it. We agreed not to mention the circumstance to any one and arranged to set off early the next day for the mill. On our arrival, just before sundown, we poket the sand about in various places, and before long succeeded in collecting between us more than an ounce of gold, mixed up with a good deal of sand. I stayed at Mr. Marshall's that night, and the next day we proceeded some little distance up the south Fork, and found that gold existed along the whole course, not only in the bed of the main stream, where the [omission] had subsided but in every little dried-up creek and ravine. Indeed I think it is more plentiful in these latter places, for I myself, with nothing more than a smal knife, picked out from dry gorge, a little way up the mountain, a solid lump of gold wich weighed nearly an ounce and a half.

Notwithstanding our precautions not to be observed, as soon as we came back to the mill, we noticed by the excitement of the working people that we had been dogged about, an to complet our disappointment, one of the indians who had worked at the gold mine in the neighbourhood of La Paz cried out in showing us some specimens picked up by himself,—Oro!—Oro—Oro!!!"

"Celestial Empire in California. 14."—n.d., two views: "Miners"; and "Gamblers" PLATE 22

"A Correct View of Weaverville, Trinity Coy. Cal. A. Coquardon, del. Published by Cram Rogers & Co."—n.d. PLATE 23

"Day & Night of a Miner's Life. 24"—n.d., four vignette views.

"Disasters of 60 Days"—n.d., with five views:

"Wreck of Steamship Tennessee, Indian Cove, March 6th, 1853"

"Wreck & Burning of the Steamship Independence; Island Margarita. Feby. 16th, 1853. 150 lives lost"

"Collapse of Flue on Board Jenny Lind of San Francisquito, April 11th, 1853. 50 lives lost"

"Wreck of Propellor Steamship Lewis, Duxbury Reef, April 9th, 1853"

"Explosion of R. K. Page Nicolous; Feather River, March 21st, 1853"

"Dividing the Pile"—and—"Hard Road to Travel. 7"—n.d.

"Execution of Casey & Cora, by the San Francisco Vigilance Committee, May 22nd, 1856. Taken from Cor. Davis & Commercial"—n.d.

"Execution of Hetherington and Brace. The Murderers of Baldwin, Randall, West and Marion. July 29th, 1856"—n.d. PLATE 24

"Explosion of the American Eagle on the San Joaquin River 25 Miles below Stockton Oct. 8, 1853"—and—"Explosion of the Steamer Stockton on Suisson Bay Oct. 18, 1853"—n.d.

"A Fight with a Grizzly. 18"—n.d., with four views:

"Surprise & First Shot"; "Getting to close quarters"; "The death struggle"; and "The rescue"

"Flume"—and—"Elevating Water Wheel. 16"—n.d. PLATE 25

"Fort Vigilant. Daguer. by Vance"—n.d., with two views: PLATE 26

"Rooms of the Committee Sacramento St. betn. Davis & Front"; and "Mass Meeting Endorsing the Acts of the Vigilance Committe[e] June 14th". (On fourth fold of letter paper is printed the Constitution of the

Vigilance Committee, adopted May 15th, 1856.) Also issued with: "Noisy Carrier's Book & Stationery Co." in place of "Daguer. by Vance."

PLATE 27 "Gambling in the Mines. 4"—n.d., two views:
"Monte"; and "Faro"

PLATE 28 "Grass Valley, Nevada County, California. R. E. Ogilby, del."—n.d.

"Life in the Mines. 6"—n.d., four views:
"Slap Jacks"; "Rush for new diggings"; "Tree'd"; and "Nooning"

"The Miners. No. 3"—n.d.

"The Miners. No. 4"—n.d. Shows a group of miners panwashing, with two small views of "Sutter's Fort" and "Mokelumne Hill." (This print, with identical title, was also issued by Quirot & Company.)

PLATE 31 "The Miners Coat of Arms. 2"—n.d.

PLATE 32 "Miners' Ten Commandments. A new verse-ion, including a preamble, by-laws and decree, by Cadez Orion"—n.d. Besides the text of the ten commandments, this lithograph has three views at the top, one showing a miner standing on the back of an elephant holding a spade in one hand and in the other two stone tablets for the on-looking miners to read.

The elephant crops up frequently in pictures of the Gold Rush days. It undoubtedly stood as a symbol to the Forty-niners. One version has it that in those days gold was found in such quantities as had never before been dreamed of, and the elephant, as the largest existing animal, was used as its symbol. Newcomers were asked if they "had come to see the elephant"—that is, had come to look for gold. An opposing version has it that the elephant stood for failure to find gold "in them thar hills." The text of the commandments follows:

Miners' Ten Commandments.* A New Verse-ion, Including a Preamble, By-Laws and Decree. By Cadez Orion.

Preamble.

Away "deown east" there dwelt a man,
E'en over in the State of Maine,
Who had enough of tall pine trees
Himself and wife to well maintain.

*An earlier Miners' Ten Commandments, with woodcut illustrations, was issued about 1855 by James Hutchings.

But years rolled by, and children came
  Around the little fire side,
And claimed a right to eat and drink,
  Nor could such wants well be denied.

The pine trees grew, and children too—
  Though in their manner far apart;
The trees grew thin, the children thick,
  And thus from Maine were doomed to part.

"Old Zenas" to his wife did say—
  "I'll move you all to Michigan,
And California I will seek,
  And dig until a richer man."

Across the Plains he bent his steps,
  And passed large droves of Buffalo,
Wild Horses, Turkies, very fine,
  And Tigers, Jackals, Indians too.

At times he hadn't nary piece
  Of meat whereby to feed upon,
Nor any water for his thirst—
  And thus he saw the old lion.

At last his clothes in tatters hung
  About his sore and weary form—
His "harp of hopes" was soon unstrung
  And fancied nigh the gathering storm.

He mourned his lot, and often wept
  To think he ever took the jaunt—
And then he'd rave, and swear he b'leaved
  He's soon to see the Elephant!

And thus "Uncle Zenas" soliloquized:—"I onct lived in peace and prosperity away deown in the State of Maine, and owned tew ceows, ten oxen and three shoats—besides dear Polly, and Ike, and Jake, and

Tabitha, and Sarah Ann Eliza Jane, together with the darling babe that was named Rachel, because she lifted up her voice and wept when I kissed her and departed for Californy! Y-as, 'tis even I, 'Old Zenas,' that's neow in Californy, and haint struck a single pocket nor crevice yet, and I've travelled e'en a'most as fur as 'tis tew hum. And here the road forks! Wonder which of these onlikely roads nears off tew Hangtown? Helloa! I'm blazed ef here aint jest the sarkumstance I'm looking for, by golly! A guide board, sartin as preachin! No taint, nether—coz the fingers are pintin up, and it reads—

"Behold, a new verse-ion of the
Miners' Ten Commandments, By-Laws
and Decree."

Which reads as follows:

By-Laws.

One claim thou may'st own, and there drive your stake,
And coyote and crevice 'till you make or you break;
Always find the bed-rock, keep at work and pump out—
Do anything rather than be running about.

If the gold isn't there, keep cool and don't swear;
Nor either get tight, and say you don't care;
Nor practice the art of "salting" your claim—
For by such a practice you'll get a hard name.

Climb out, very cool, with pick, pan and shovel,
And don't seek the cabin and pore over a novel—
But mark a new claim, and pitch in again,
And never have doubts of striking a vein.

Should you strike a rich pocket, a crevice or lead,
Don't drink quite a barrel on the fortunate deed;
But pocket your dust and go whistling away,
Content to enjoy it at some future day.

Should you venture your luck in daming the rivers,
And work in the water, getting colds, coughs and shivers,

Let "old rye" alone, and with wisdom of thought,
Sell out if you can, and bless him who bought.

Wend your way to dry diggings, purchase sluice-box or tom,
And a claim, too, if rich—judge of those you buy from—
Hire eight or ten "Coolies"—come the cooly at once,
Thus showing the people you are not quite a dunce.

By "Johnny Celestial"* make two dollars per day,
On the labor of each, you see, that will pay;
Whereas, if you hire Uncle Sam's sturdy son,
You will pay more for labor, and hardly make one.

And lastly, thus reads the Decree:

FIRSTLY—It is decreed unto all the people of California, that ye do observe all that is herein written, that ye avoid some of the shoals and quicksands of this life, and especially during your sojourn in California, where a lesson or a warning cannot be given too soon. California is one vast amphitheatre—containing an assemblage of human beings from every land and every clime. All classes, all colors, and all conditions, are each day before your gaze, and soon they are associated more or less with you all. And now, my Disciples, this is why I publish this Decree, and give you this warning, that ye may be prepared to meet the tempters.

SECONDLY—It is decreed, O ye Miners, that I first publish unto you, the decree; as ye are the most numerous of any of the tribes of California; And I pray you will hearken unto me with an attentive ear, that ye may be profited thereby. Ye are indeed mighty, and the wise men and the counsellors of ten have sought thy abode to teach ye wisdom and understanding.

THIRDLY—And thus it is decreed that thou shalt not labor to thine discomfiture and bodily pain. Thou shalt labor as becometh good Disciples, and shall not exceed ten hours each day. Thy food shall consist of that which is most wholesome and nourishing, and thy raiment shall be of woollen and of firm texture, and each week shalt thou cleanse thine apparel.

*"Johnny Celestial" was evidently a Forty-niner's nickname for the Chinese. See Britton & Rey's letterhead, "The Celestial Empire in California," Plate 22.

FOURTHLY—In default of the same, thy brother miners shalt take thee down even unto Feather River, and cleanse thee—apparel, body and all together, until thou wilt lend thine own exertions to do it thyself.

FIFTHLY—If vermin infest thee or thy blankets, thou shalt be banished from the cabin, thee and thy raiment, until thou shalt rid thyself of thine unwelcome visitors. And on the day—yea, the hour—in which it shall appear that thou art ridden of all plagues—then in solemn possession shalt thou be marched with thy brother miners back even unto the cabin, and all feast sumptuously.

SIXTHLY—It is decreed that thou shalt not be made servants one to another, only as each serves the other in his turn. Neither shalt thou forsake thy brother miner while on the couch of sickness and pain, but shall carefully watch over him, and administer unto every necessary want, until he shall be able to arise again, and proclaim himself well of his malady.

SEVENTHLY—It is also decreed, that thou, O Miner, who hath a family in a distant country, shall, whenever in thy power, remit the avails of thy labor to keep them in food and raiment during thy sojourn here. Thou shalt not neglect thy wife and children and go after strange women, who, with a syren's tongue and winning smiles, would lure thee to her snares of shame and degradation, and rob thee of thine honor, thy virtue and thy gold; and at last would despise and curse thee, and turn thee away empty handed. Beware, lest thou art overtaken in thy secret wanderings, and lose thy life, and thy friends mourn thy untimely fate.

EIGHTHLY—And it is also decreed, that thou, O young man, who hast left thy father's house to sojourn in the land of California—even in the mines thereof—thou too, I pray, take heed. Remember the counsel of thy mother and sisters, and forget not thy solemn pledges of affection. Nor shalt thou forget to pen an epistle each mail to thy kindred, that they may know how fares the wanderer, and when he is to return. Neither shalt thou forget that young and comely maiden who gave you her warm and trusting affections, while you vowed to remain true, and never forget that starry night just on the eve of thy departure. Remember all these promises, that in thy after life thou mayst be blessed with future generations likened unto thee.

NINTHLY—It is decreed, that thou, O Bachelors, shalt be banished for a season, working out thy salvation here in the mountains, even among the eternal snows of the Sierra Nevada, and here remain until you come to the sage conclusion that there is a more congenial atmosphere by the side of the gentler sex. If such is the result of thy experience, thou mayst take up thy bed and walk, leaving thy tools for others of thy kind. Ever after thy works shall be judged, and when a certain period of time shall expire, and thou has not employed the time profitably, and obeyed the Scriptures, wherein it reads—"Multiply and replenish the earth"—if you have failed in this, thou shalt again and forever serve among the snows of the Sierras. Therefore, ye bachelor miners, take warning.

TENTH AND LAST DECREE—FOR THE PEOPLE—It is now lastly decreed, that thou, Californians all, male and female, who comest here to better thy fortunes—thou art commanded to pay special attention to this Decree. Thou—a certain class—journeyed hither to repair thy ruined circumstances, to pay off old debts which have hung like a heavy weight over the horison of thy future happiness. Thou hast come hither willing to brave the storm and tempests, both of nature's warring elements and also the "party feuds" and "political gusts" that often lend violent commotion to this golden land. Thou, O Politician, who in thy Atlantic home didst crave office, and thy ambitious desires were not gratified—thou who labored so energetically for the good of the people (and thyself, too)—thou who wert beaten by the political opponent, thou comest hither to retrieve thy fortunes, to build up thy high minded hopes, to court Dame Fortune's smiles once more, and to raise up unto thyself a great name. But beware, thou lofty aspirant of fame; there are those here who art long before thee, who have their wires laid, and now have wealth on their side. Take heed; be wise; do thou go to one Bryant, and there select a pick, pan and shovel, and sojourn for a while in the mountains, for there thou wilt have an equal chance among thy fellow laborers. And thou, O Speculator, from Gotham, thinkest thou that in California, even in San Francisco thou canst succeed, and have built up thy broken fortunes by thy schemes and thy small capital? Thou, too, beware, for in San Francisco there are speculators congregated from all countries, even of the shrewdest kind, and have studied and practiced all manner of devices. Take heed, therefore, and invest thy small capital in miners' supplies, and flee to the mountains, or to some inland village, and there be content with health, good water and fair profits.

And thou, pilgrims to the Eureka State, tarry not at the Bay, but pierce the Northern wilds and the mountain scenery; rush for pure air, health, wealth, and plenty of labor. Despair not in the hour of thy afflictions, but brave the storm manfully, and soon thou art safe. And thou fair maidens, daughters of Eve, who hast braved the hardships and dangers of a voyage to our golden shores, and thou heroines and pioneer mothers, we greet thee,—thrice welcome are ye all. Thou whom in memory were cherished—thou whom we so much wished for, who art so highly prized and cherished in every land—thou art indeed here. And thou aged, though single maidens, thou art here too; nor wilt thou remain in single blessedness long, for thou wilt not meet with so many fair competitors to bear away the prizes from you, but will soon be heard exclaiming, Eureka! Eureka!

And now, each and every one, take heed of this my decree; and all of ye, my Disciples, shall say at the last—We have followed thy precepts, and verily we have found our reward.

PLATE 33 "Miners Weighing Their Gold"—and—"The Dream of a Prospecting Miner. 17"—n.d. This was also issued by Quirot & Company.

PLATE 34 "The Mining Business in Four Pictures. 9"—n.d.:
"Going into it"; "Making something"; "Making nothing"; and "Going out of it"

PLATE 35 "20"—n.d., an untitled letterhead with four mining scenes; also issued by Quirot & Company. Both issues bear as a signature on the stone a Greek beta (β).

PLATE 36 "Past & Present of California. 11"—n.d. Here again, among several vignette views, the elephant turns up.

"Petaluma, Sonoma Cy. Cal. October 1855. L. W. Worth, del."—n.d.

"A Prospecting Party"—n.d., four views:
"Starting"; "Not even the colour"; "The end of the mule"; and "Returning"

PLATE 37 "San Francisco, 1854"—n.d. Identical with Sarony & Company's "San Francisco in 1854." This view was subsequently issued by Britton & Rey at least four times under other titles. Twice certain portions of the city were

MINERS WEIGHING THEIR GOLD.

THE DREAM OF A PROSPECTING MINER.

Lith. & Published by Britton & Rey corner Montgomery & California Sts S. Francisco.

THF MINING BUSINESS IN FOUR PICTURES. 9.

GOING IN TO IT.
MAKING SOMETHING.
MAKING NOTHING.
GOING OUT OF IT.

Lith & Published by Britton & Rey. corner of Montgomery & Commercial Sts. S.F.

20.

Lith. of Britton & Rey California St. corn. Montgomery St. S-Francisco.

Past & Present of California.

Lith. & Pub. by Britton & Rey S. Francisco.

Lith. of Britton & Rey Cor. Montg'y & Comm'l Sts

SAN FRANCISCO, 1854.

Friday April 28th 1854.

Dear Mother:

The above picture is a very good view of the city at the present time: The entrance to San Francisco bay, from the Pacific Ocean, is represented in the left of the picture. It is about five miles from the city to the "Golden Gate," at which place preparations are now being made for erecting a strong Fortification. From the middle of the picture, to the right, the front half of the city (nearest the bay) is all made ground, and when the buildings were erected the water flowed beneath them, they being on "Piles". Two inches directly under figure 1 is Telegraph hill; Two-and-a half inches under figure 2 is Mr. Meiggs's wharf (twelve hundred feet in length); Three inches beneath figure 3 is Grace Church (Episcopal); Three-and-a-quarter inches below figure 4 is about the place where I board; Three and a half inches under figure 5 is the Methodist Church; Three inches beneath figure 6 is the City Hall; Two-inches-and three quarter below figure 7 is Montgomery block, one of the largest buildings in the United states; Three inches underneath figure 8 is the Post Office; Two inches and three quarters be-neath figure 9 is the United States Mint for California, which is now coining $150,000 per day; Two inches and five eights below figure 10 is near the locality of Le Count & Strong's Bookstore (in which I now am); Two inches and a quarter be-neath figure 11 is the United States Marine Hospital, on Rincon Point; and three inches below figure 12 is the new Rassette House. The island below figure 6 is called "Yerba Buena" (Good Herb); to the right of which the upper part of "Mont Diablo" can be seen. The bay is about seven miles wide. The distance from the foreground to the water is about one mile and a half, and the distance from Meiggs's wharf to Rincon Point is near two miles, more or less. On the other side of Telegraph hill are some of our largest shipping warehouses. This year a new grade for the streets has been established, and in some places it is thirty feet from the front door to the pavement. There are thirteen Fire-engine companies in the city, and the city is well provided with Reservoirs. On the City Hall there is a large bell, which strikes the alarm in case of fire; a man is constantly on the lookout from the roof of the building. A Ferry boat leaves the City four times per day for Oakland; which is situated on the opposite side of the bay, and directly under figure 10. The population at the present time is nearly fifty thousand, although some persons think it is more. Of the buildings now in the course of erection, nine out of ten are being built of brick. Altogether, it is a great city! Walton

15.

SUNDAY MORNING

Lith & Published by BRITTON & REY — LOG CABIN — San Francisco Cal.

SUNDRY AMUSEMENTS IN THE MINES.

A SUNDAYS AMUSEMENTS.

A DAILY PLEASURE.

OCCUPATION FOR RAINY DAYS.

A PLEASANT SURPRISE.

Lith. & Published by Britton & Rey

FROM NEW·YORK DIRECT

LITH. & PUB^D BY BRITTON & REY

FAMILY AND FIRE·SIDE

SAN FRANCISCO

blocked in with swirling clouds of smoke and flame to depict the 1854 and 1855 conflagrations. The letter reproduced reads as follows:

Friday April 28th 1854

Dear Mother:

The above picture is a very good view of the city at the present time. The entrance to San Francisco bay, from the Pacific Ocean, is represented in the left of the picture. It is about five miles from the city to the "Golden Gate," at which place preparations are now being made for erecting a strong Fortification. From the middle of the picture, to the right, the front half of the city (nearest the bay) is all made ground, and when the buildings were erected the water flowed beneath them, they being on "Piles." Two inches directly under figure 1 is Telegraph Hill; Two-and-a-half inches under figure 2 is Mr. Meigg's Wharf (twelve hundred feet in length); Three inches beneath figure 3 is Grace Church (Episcopal); Three-and-a-quarter inches below figure 4 is about the place where I board; Three and a half inches under figure 5 is the Methodist Church; Three inches beneath figure 6 is the City Hall; Two-inches-and three quarters below figure 7 is the Montgomery block, one of the largest buildings in the United States; Three inches underneath figure 8 is the Post Office; Two inches and three quarters beneath figure 9 is the United States Mint for California, which is now coining $150,000 per day; Two inches and five eights below figure 10 is near the locality of Le Count & Strong's Bookstore (in which I now am); Two inches and a quarter beneath figure 11 is the United States Marine Hospital, on Rincon Point; and three inches below figure 12 is the new Rassette House. The island below figure 6 is called "Yerba Buena" (Good Herb), to the right of which the upper part of "Mont Diablo" can be seen. The bay is about seven miles wide. The distance from the foreground to the water is about one mile and a half, and the distance from Meigg's Wharf to Rincon Point is near two miles, more or less. On the other side of Telegraph Hill are some of our largest shipping warehouses. This year a new grade for the streets has been established, and in some places it is thirty feet from *the front door to the pavement*. There are thirteen Fire engine companies in the city, and the city is well provided with Resorvoirs. On the City Hall there is a large bell, which strikes the alarm in case of fire; a man is constantly on the lookout from the roof of the building. A Ferry Boat leaves the City four times a day for Oakland; which is situated on the opposite side of the bay, and directly under figure 10. The population at the present time is nearly fifty thousand, although some persons think it is more. Of the buildings now in the course of erection, nine out of ten are being built by brick. Altogether it is a great city!

Walton.

"San Francisco, 1854. Fire of July 11th"—n.d.

"San Francisco, 1858"—and—"San Francisco, 1849 & 1850. From Telegraph Hill"—n.d. The first is identical with the 1854 view.

"San Francisco, Cal. Burning of St. Charles and Hillman's Hotel on the Morning of Feby. 18th, 1855"—n.d.

"San Francisco Upper California"—n.d. Issued by Quirot & Company as "San Francisco Upper California, in November 1851."

"Scenes in a Miner's Life. 23"—n.d., six views:

"Night in the log cabin"; "Camping out"; "Going to work"; "Hole gives out"; "New diggings struck"; and "Next day"

"Sonora from the North. G. H. Goddard, del. Published by G. S. Wells, Sonora, May 1853. Entered . . . 1853 by G. S. Wells"

"Sonora, Jany. 1853. George H. Goddard, del."—n.d.

"Springfield, Tuolumne County. G. H. Goddard, del. Published by G. S. Wells, Sonora May 1853. Entered . . . 1853 by G. H. Wells."

PLATE 41 "St. Mary's Church. San Francisco Cal."—n.d. This old church still stands, having been one of the very few buildings in its district to escape the fire of 1906.

PLATE 38 "Sunday Morning"—and—"Log Cabin. 15"—n.d. Two views on one sheet.

PLATE 39 "Sundry Amusements in the Mines. 23"—n.d., four views:

"A Sunday's Amusements"; "A Daily Pleasure"; "Occupation for Rainy days"; and "A Pleasant Surprise" Has same series number as "Scenes in a Miner's Life."

"Surrender of the Prisoners James P. Casey and Charles Cora to the Vigilance Committee, Sunday, May 18th, 1856. 2500 citizens under arms, & a reserve of 2500, ready, at a moment's notice. From cor. Dupont & Broadway"—n.d.

"Tremendous Conflagration of Columbia, July 10th, 1854"—n.d.

"Two Roads in California. 3"—n.d. (c.1856), eight views:

"Jones & Brown Landing"; "Brown stick to it"; "Getting ahead"; "Industry's reward"; "Jones don't like hard work"; "Trys a fast way to make money"; "Wommen and Wine"; and "Ruin in the Gutter"

"View of Goodyears Bar, Sierra Co. Cal. Drawn by W. B. M. Pub. by S. W. Langton & Bro., Downieville, Sierra Coy. California"—n.d. W. B. M. is William B. Monmonier. PLATE 42

"View of Montecristo, Scooper's Ranch in the Foreground. Drawn & published by Wm. B. Monmonier. Montecristo Aug. 1st, 1856"—n.d.

"View of Montgomery St., Oroville"—and—"Court House & Theatre Block, Oroville, Cala. Published by Garham & Lockwood. Post office Literary Depot, Oroville. April 1858"—n.d.

"What! Jim! Come home tight again? No, I ain't tight. I've been knocket of my horse and robbed, and after robbing me, they put me on my horse again and cut his head of!"—n.d.

"What We Want in California. 12"—n.d., two views: PLATE 40

"From New-York Direct"; and "Family and Fire-side"

"The Winter in California. 21"—n.d.

"The Winter of 1852 & 3"—n.d. Identical with "The Winter in California."

"The Wreck of the Yankee Blade, as She appeared on the evening of October 1st, 1854. From a drawing made upon the spot by one of the passengers, A. T. Harrison"—n.d.

Britton & Rey's lithographs other than letterheads are the following:

"Assassination of James King of Wm. by James P. Casey. San Francisco, May 14th, 1856"—small, n.d. A broadside with an account of the event and four views: "Assassination," "Funeral of Jas. King," "Surrender of the Jail," and "Execution."

It was the assassination of James King of Wm. by James P. Casey that brought about the 1856 reorganization of the Vigilance Committee. His curious name, by which he was always known, he adopted at sixteen to distinguish himself from another James King with whom he was frequently confused.

Born in the District of Columbia in 1822, he went to California at the beginning of the Gold Rush period and for several years was in the banking business at Sacramento and in San Francisco. In 1855, upon the failure of Adams & Company, with which he was associated, he became the editor of the *Daily Evening Bulletin*. He started at once to write brilliant and scathing editorials on the corruption, political and otherwise, which was then rife throughout the city and state.

At the time Charles Cora murdered United States Marshal William H. Richardson, who had accused him of ballot-box stuffing, the citizens were in a state of high indignation, and it needed only Cora's acquittal by a "fixed jury" to arouse talk of the Vigilantes. For several months after this trial, James King of Wm. continued to pour forth his anger over the outcome of the trial, until the forces of the underworld decided he was too dangerous an influence for their comfort.

On May 14, 1856, King wrote an article attacking James P. Casey, mentioning that Casey had served a term in Sing Sing prison before coming to California. Casey seized upon resentment of this mention as an excuse to waylay King on a foggy street and shoot him down, with no chance to defend himself. Casey immediately surrendered himself at the jail, where he was held in safety for the six days before James King of Wm. finally died. His shooting of King, however, aroused the citizens of San Francisco to such a fury that at first an assembled mob wished to lynch him. Certain leaders quelled this stormy gathering, but the tense feelings resulted in the reorganization of the Vigilance Committee of 1851. A few days after King died, Charles Cora and James P. Casey were tried and hanged by the Committee. Their execution is shown in the Kuhl letterhead reproduced as Plate 77.

"At the Play. Respectfully inscribed to the Wealth, Enterprise & Beauty of California by their faithful Friend, F. Marriott, July 1879. [Signed on stone:] G. G. Gariboldi, Decor. Entered . . . 1879"—large. On a separate sheet, a key to the portraits and "Short Sketches of Some of the Notables in the Drama of 'Life in California.'" F. Marriott was the proprietor of the San Francisco *News Letter*.

"Birds Eye View of Los Angeles, Los Angeles County, Cal. 1871. Drawn by Augustus Koch"—large, n.d. (eleven border views).

"Birdseye View of Nevada City, Nevada County, Cal. Revised June 1st, 1885, by A. S. Chase. Entered . . . 1883"—large (seven border views).

"Birdseye View of San Francisco and Surrounding Country. Drawn by G. H. Goddard. Published by Snow & Roos. Entered . . . 1868"—large. Published also in 1875 by Snow & May. Republished in 1880 by Snow & Company.

"Birds Eye View of the City of Nevada, Nevada County, Cal. 1871. Drawn by Augustus Koch"—large, n.d., with twenty-three references in margin, key to buildings, and a small view of Nevada in 1853. PLATE 20

"Birds Eye View of the City of Oakland and Vicinity. Drawn by Augustus Koch"—large, n.d. (c.1870).

"Birds Eye View of the City of Petaluma, Sonoma County, California. 1871. Drawn by Augustus Koch"—large, n.d.

"Birds Eye View of the City of San Francisco. Drawn by G. H. Goddard. Entered . . . 1868"—large.

"Birds Eye View of Woodland, Yolo County. 1871. Drawn by Augustus Koch"—large, n.d.

"Buena Vista Vinicultural Society's Vineyards and Vaults, Sonoma, Sonoma County, California"—large, n.d.

"The California Powder Works. Santa Cruz County, California. Office in San Francisco"—medium, n.d.

"California State Normal School. San Jose"—size unknown, n.d.

"California & Oregon Stage Company. Carries Wells, Fargo & Company's Express and the U. S. Mail. View of Mt. Shasta 14,442 ft. above the sea. On C. & O. Stage Route. F. F. Hooker, Superintendent. Bradley Barlow, J. L. Sanderson, James W. Parker, Chas. E. Huntley, Proprietors"—large, n.d. (c.1872). See Britton, Rey & Company's "Overland Mail Company" and the note under Britton & Company's "California Stage Company." PLATE 21

"Calvary Presbyterian Church, San Francisco. Revd. Wm. A. Scott, D. D., Pastor. On stone by A. Wenderoth"—medium, n.d.

"The Catalpa. The Rescuers and the Rescued"—large, n.d.

Certificate of membership in the "Committee of Vigilance of San Francisco. Designed & drawn on stone by Chas. Nahl"—large, n.d. (c.1856). (Reproduced in *America on Stone*.) One copy of this was seen lithographed on silk.

Certificate of membership in the "Committee of Vigilance of San Francisco. Reorganized 15th May, 1856, for the mutual protection of life & property. This is to Certify that No. — is a Member of the Committee of Vigilance of the City of San Francisco and is in the Military Organization thereof"—medium, n.d. The small vignette shows the soldiers marching. This is probably from the same stone as the above. There are minor changes in the composition and the wording.

"Charles Crocker"—small, n.d.

"Charles de Young, M. H. de Young, I. S. Kallock and I. M. Kallock"—small, n.d. (c.1880). The principals in a noted murder trial. Charles de Young, editor of the *Chronicle,* was slain by I. M. Kallock because of a fancied insult to his father.

A check: "Adams & Company, Bankers. For Le Count & Strong"—n.d. (check was dated 1853).

"Diploma Awarded by the Alameda County Agricultural Society"—medium, n.d. Eight small scenes surrounding border showing different modes of life on a farm.

"Forrest Hill, Placer County"—small, n.d.

"1879. Fourteenth Industrial Exhibition of the Mechanics Institute of San Francisco, Cal. Awards This Diploma to . . ."—medium, n.d.

"Grammar School Certificate"—medium, n.d. (certificate filled in "1866").

"Haverley's Theatre. California. Bush Street. San Francisco. Haverley's Spectacular Company in the great Pageantry Drama of Michael Strogoff. Published by the 'Wasp' Publishing Co. S.F. [signed on stone]: Keller"—medium folio, colored, n.d. Portrait at top circle; six panel inserts of scenes from the play, *Michael Strogoff.*

"Hotel Del Monte, Monterey, Cal. The Famous Seaside Resort of the Pacific Coast. Published by the San Francisco *News Letter*"—small, n.d.

"Index Map of the City of San Francisco. Assessor's office 1867"—large, n.d.

"Interior View of the Mechanics Institute Pavillion Ninth Industrial Exhibition. A. D. 1874"—large, n.d.

PLATE 29 "Lady Vernon. San Francisco, Cala., August 1855 . . . Painted by John Murdoch. Entered . . . 1855"—large. See Murdoch.

"Long Beach, California"—large oval, n.d.

"Los Angeles, Cal. S. F. Cook, del. Copyright by A. J. Hatch & Co. San Francisco. Entered . . . 1888"—large.

"Mammoth Arbor Vitæ. Standing on the head waters of the Stanislaus & San Antoine Rivers, in Calaveras County, California. From nature by J. M. Lapham. Entered . . . 1853"—large. An identical view, "drawn by A. K. Kipp," was issued by "J. H. Daniels Lith. Boston. Entered . . . 1861." PLATE 30

"Map Exhibiting The Salt Marsh Tide And Submerged Lands Disposed Of By The State Of California. Entered . . . 1875"—large.

"Map of San Francisco, Compiled from Latest Surveys & Containing all late Extensions & Divisions of Wards"—small, n.d. (c.1852).

"Map of San Francisco from the latest surveys. Engraved expressly for the San Francisco directory. 1873. San Francisco. Entered . . . 1873"—medium.

"Map of the City of Benicia. Founded by Mariano G. Vallejo, Thomas O. Larkin and Robert Semple, 1847. Surveyed and Drawn by Benjamin W. Barlow"—large, n.d.

"Map of the Mining Region of California 1855"—small, n.d.

"Map of the New Republic"—small, n.d. A map of Lower California and the western coast of Mexico.

"Map of the State of California. Compiled from U. S. land & coast surveys, [etc.] By George H. Goddard. Entered . . . 1857"—large.

"Map of Tulare County, State of California. Made by Alfred Bannister, C. E. In accordance with an order of the Honorable Board of Supervisors. Dated November 8th, 1883"—large, n.d.

"Map Showing the Lands of the Tide Land Reclamation Company. Compiled & drawn by J. T. Gibbes, 1869"—large, n.d.

"Map Showing the Location of the San Francisco & Sacramento Rail Road & Its Connection. Theodore D. Judah, Chief Engineer, February 1st, 1856"—large, n.d.

"The Marine Mammals of the North. Western Coast of North America. Described and Illustrated . . . The American Whale Fishery 4° San Francisco, John H. Carmany & Co. 1874. Litho. plates by Britton & Rey"

"Masonic Cemetery. San Francisco, Cal. Masonic Cemetery situated between Masonic and Parker Avenues, Turk and Fulton Streets. Entrance on Turk Street and Golden Gate Avenue"—medium, n.d.

"National Eight Hour Law. Proclamation, 'I, U. S. Grant, President of the United States Do Hereby Direct That From This Date No Reduction Shall Be Made In Wages Paid By The Government By The Day To Such Laborers, Workmen & Mechanics On Account Such Reduction Of The Hours of Labor. In Testimony Whereof, [&c.,] Done At The City of Washington, This 19th Day of May, The Year Of Our Lord, 1869, & Of The Independence Of The United States, The 93rd.' Signed 'U. S. Grant, Hamilton Fish.' Entered . . . 1870"—medium. Three lines of reference on scroll held in eagle's bill.

"New Express Galop. Dedicated to the Late Patrons of the Pacific Union Express Company. 'Cape Horn' Placer County, Cal., and View of the Sierra Nevada, on the line of the Pacific Railroad. Copyrighted. Composed by Geo. T. Evans, Musical Director of the New California Theatre. San Francisco, Cal. Published by M. Gray, 609 & 613 Clay St., San Francisco"—music sheet, n.d. An interesting transportation item.

"Oceanic Steamship Company's Steamers Mariposa and Alameda. San Francisco & Honolulu. A. E. Mathews"—large, n.d.

"Official map of the city and county of San Francisco, prepared by William P. Humphreys, city & county surveyor, as per order 966 of the board of supervisors approved october 26, 1870. Scale 1000 feet to one inch. Entered . . . 1870"—large.

'Official Map of the County of Tehama, California. Carefully compiled from actual surveys by H. B. Shackleford. 1887"—large, n.d.

"The Original Design for the New City Hall and Law Courts. Entered . . . 1872"—medium.

"Plan of South Park. Property of George Gordon. Comprising an Area of 12 Acres between Second & Third, Bryant & Brannon Streets. George H. Cuddard, Architect. View of South Park from Third Street. Entered . . . 1862"—large. An early real estate development in the fashionable south end of San Francisco, after the titles were cleared in 1860. "Cuddard" may have been a misprint of George H. Goddard, the artist and civil engineer, who moved to San Francisco in 1862.

"The Presidential Elections of the United States. Designed & drawn by Henry Clay Donnell, San Francisco. Entered . . . 1877"—very large. Twenty-three colored maps showing division of electoral votes all over the country in the presidential elections from 1789 to 1876.

"Presidial Pueblo of San Francisco. With the Fort and the Golden Gate. A.D. 1830"—medium, n.d.

"Presidio Park, Fort Point, Golden Gate"—small, n.d.

"Public Buildings—San Francisco"—medium, n.d.

"The Resources of California. San Rafael"—small, n.d.

"St. Louis, Sears Diggings, Sierra Co. Cal. Drawn by W. H. Hackett. Published by Everts, Snell & Co., St. Louis, Cal."—small, n.d.

"San Francisco Clearing House Certificates"—small, n.d. (in $1, $5, $10, and $20 denominations).

"Santa Barbara. California. E. F. Cook, del."—large, n.d.

"Southern Approach to Jamestown, Tuolumne County, California. G. H. Goddard, del. Entered . . . 1853 by L. Jones"—small.

Stock certificates, all small, n.d., of the following companies:

"Antelope Silver Mining Company"
"Arizona Mining & Trading Company"
"Bear River & Auburn Water & Mining Company"
"Laurel Hill Mining Company"
"Meadow Valley Mining Company"
"Yule Gravel Mining Company"

"Treadwell's Birds Eye View of the Comstock Mines and Vicinity. Storey & Lyons Counties, State of Nevada. Entered . . . 1875"—large.

"U. S. Steam Frigate Mississippi . . . in a typhoon. W. Heine pinxt. Designed by Eliphalet Brown, Jr. Lith. Entered . . . 1854"—large.

"Ulysses S. Grant, President of the United States. H. Steinegger." Issued with the San Francisco *News Letter,* April 18, 1885.

"Under the Snow. Song and chorus sung by W. Hudson and T. W. Bree. Music composed by Geo. T. Evans. Published by M. Gray, 621 & 623, Clay St. San Francisco, 1869"—a music sheet, n.d. The lithograph is a copy of the picture called "God's Acre," by Emily Osborn.

"View of Calistoga Hot Sulphur Springs, Napa County"—large, n.d. Shows the terminus of the C. P. Railroad, the sulphur springs, the race track, etc.

"View of Goodyears Bar & Goodyears Creek. Sierra Co. Cala. With Monte-Cristo In The Distance. Published & drawn by Wm. B. Monmonier, Goodyears Bar, Sierra County"—small, n.d. This differs from the letterhead view, which is reproduced as Plate 42.

"View of Ham's Mammoth Aqueduct. California. Dedicated by Permission to the President and Members of the Bear-River and Auburn Water and Mining Company by their Obliged and Humble Servant the Artist, July 22th, 1852. From Nature by R. E. Ogilby. Entered . . . 1852"—medium.

"View of Minnesota with Orleans Flat in the Distance, taken from the hill in the rear of The Spring House. Drawn & published by Wm. B. Monmonier, Downieville, Cal. June 1st, 1858"—small, n.d.

"View of Santa Cruz. Published by A. J. Hatch & Co. San Francisco"—large, n.d.

"Yerba Buena (Now San Francisco) In The Spring of 1837. From a drawing by J. Vioget. Entered . . . 1867"—medium. This view was also issued in 1893 by George H. Baker. The reproduction in this volume is by Baker.

"Yreka, Siskayou Cy. A view from the Humbug Trail with Shasta Bute in the distance. Entered . . . 1853"—small.

PLATE 72 Britton & Rey had a close connection with Kuchel & Dresel, especially
PLATE 73 in the printing of the latter's series of California views (*q.v.*). It is also to be
PLATE 74 noted that many lithographs issued by them appear with the imprint of Justh,
PLATE 75 Quirot *et al.*, and that on these identical prints the address given is "California & Montgomery Streets"—the 1851–1852 address for the Justh and Quirot alignments, and Britton & Rey's from 1852 to 1853. Quirot & Company, and C. Quirot, carried on until 1853 at another address, "136 California Street," but it is possible that Britton & Rey moved into their old quarters and took over their stock, reissuing some lithographs with the new imprint.

Britton & Rey printed for G. H. Burgess "Mokelumne Hill," and "Port of Honolulu," one of the very few Hawaiian items in our story; and for J. B. Dunlap "U. S. Navy Yard." See also Cooke & Le Count's "Birds Eye View of San Francisco."

Britton & Company:

By far the most interesting lithograph done by Britton & Company is "California Stage Company. Incorporated December 1853"—large, n.d. It is almost identical with the "Overland Mail Company" of Woodward, Tiernan & Hale (*q.v.*), and although differences in detail convince me they were done on separate stones, the similarity leads me to believe they were done by the same artist. PLATE 108

A like similarity exists between Britton & Rey's "California & Oregon Stage Company" and Britton, Rey & Company's "Overland Mail Company." It will be noticed that the names of Barlow and Sanderson appear as owners on all but the "California Stage Company," so that apparently they all represent stage coaches of the same company, although the name changed from time to time. PLATE 21 PLATE 44

"The California Stage Company" was included as an illustration in *America on Stone*, as Plate 20. I am reproducing the other three in this volume because I consider them important as being among the few known lithographs of this American form of six-horse stage-coach travel. They are particularly interesting when we think of the very large gallery of stage-coach prints produced in Great Britain to commemorate that mode of travel there.

Britton & Company's other work seems to have consisted almost exclusively of maps:

"City and County of San Francisco. Compiled from official surveys and sectionized in accordance with U. S. surveys. Drawn by V. Wackenreuder, C. E. 1861. Published by Henry C. Langley for the 'San Francisco Directory.' Entered . . . 1861"—medium.

"Index Map of San Joaquin County. Showing all tracts of land, purchased or located upon, in the county to April 1st, 1862"—large, n.d.

"Map of Central California showing the different Railroad Lines Completed and Projected. Compiled by S. G. Elliott. Nevada: G. W. Welch, 1860"—large. Inset views of Nevada City, Auburn, Sacramento, Grass Valley, Folsom, and of a wood-burning engine and cars. The map has the early imprint of Nevada City, though it was lithographed by Britton & Co. of San Francisco. It shows the railroad in operation as far as Folsom, and the projected line to join the proposed Central Pacific at Nevada City. The inset tables give the census of Nevada City and Grass Valley, distances, votes of the counties, and other statistics.

"Map of the City & County of San Francisco. Drawn for the San Francisco News Letter and the Pacific Mining Journal by James Butler, 1864"—large, n.d.

"Map of the San Francisco & San Jose Rail Road. Entered . . . 1862"—large.

"Official Map of the City of San Francisco. Published by Josiah J. Le Count, 1859"—large, n.d.

"Railroad Map of the City of San Francisco, California. Published by A. Gensoul, Bookseller & Stationer"—medium, n.d. (c.1864).

"Sutters Fort, Sacramento, California. 1847"—medium.

"Woodbridge and Sacramento River Rail Road Company. Incorporated August 30th, 1862. Compiled from actual survey by R. H. Leonard, C. E."—small, n.d.

PLATE 18 PLATE 70 PLATE 71 Britton & Company printed many of C. C. Kuchel's lithographs (*q.v.*).

Britton, Rey & Company:

The following have turned up from Britton, Rey & Company:

PLATE 43 Certificate of membership in the "Territorial Pioneers of California. [Signed on stone:] H. Steinegger"—large, n.d. (certificate filled in "1878").

"Graphic Chart of the City and County of San Francisco. Respectfully dedicated to the leading interests of California and the Pacific Coast by Frederick Marriott, 1875"—large, n.d. Showing portraits of Tivis, Haggin, Colman, Mills, Wm. Babcock, Alvord, Mrs. Leland Stanford, Leland Stanford, Lucky Baldwin, Mrs. Coit (who when a girl was one of the fire company and ran with the machine and to whose memory a tower has recently been erected in San Francisco), and Dr. Gwin.

"Graphic Chart Of The Comstock Mines. State of Nevada. 1876. Scale 1000 Feet, Ave Inch. Compiled & Drawn by J. B. Treadwell, C. E. Issued Gratis With 'S. F. *News Letter*' June 3rd. With historical account of Mineral discoveries endorsed by the Superintendents of the leading mines of this wonderful lode. Entered . . . 1876 by J. B. Treadwell, Washington, D. C."—large.

"New map of the territory of Arizona, southern California and parts of Nevada, Utah and Sonora. Compiled by lieut. J. C. Mallery and J. M. Ward. 1876, 1877. Entered . . . 1877"—large.

"Overland Mail Company. B. S. & Co. [Barlow, Sanderson & Co.]"—large, n.d. (c.1860). The copy reproduced is proof before letters. It is very similar to Britton & Rey's "California and Oregon Stage Company" (*q.v.*), but a careful comparison shows that they were printed from two entirely different stones. Both are being reproduced. See also the note under Britton & Company's "California Stage Company." PLATE 44

BROOKS, VINCENT, DAY & SON — LONDON

Among the very fine series of Western views lithographed by this firm is "The Far West (Smoky Hill River)" showing the Halliday Express stage that played so important a part in the dime novel of a decade ago.

For a listing of this scarce series of views, see *America on Stone*.

BROWN (ELIPHALET, JR.), *ET AL.* — NEW YORK

1843–1844	4 John Street
1847–1848	73 Nassau Street
1848–1849	140 Fulton Street
1849–1858	142 Fulton Street

Brown, E. & J.

1848	140 Fulton Street

Brown & Severin

1851	142 Fulton Street
1853	unknown

Brown & Severin lithographed four of the plates in Letts's "Pictorial View of California," 1853, all drawn by G. V. Cooper (*q.v.*).

Brown was the designer of "United States Steam Frigate Mississippi," published by Britton & Rey.

I have seen nothing else of theirs pertaining to California, but their other work, covered in *America on Stone,* was of high rank. Severin was a Dane, of great merit as a lithographer; see *Currier & Ives: Printmakers to the American People,* Vol. I.

BROWN (GRAFTON T.) & COMPANY — SAN FRANCISCO

c. 1872	520 Clay Street
1877	540 Clay Street

According to the biography of Max Schmidt (*q.v.*), Brown was a colored man, who started in business as a lithographer sometime around 1872. Earlier than this, in the fifties and sixties, he is noted as the artist of Kuchel & Dresel's

"View of Santa Rosa," and C. C. Kuchel's "View of Fort Churchill" and

PLATE 71 "Virginia City."

"G. T. Brown & Company, 540 Clay Street" issued the 1849 view of San Francisco by Firks (*q.v.*).

They printed and published "San Francisco. Looking South from North Point. Drawn by C. B. Gifford. Entered . . . 1877"—large.

There are also from him three stock certificates, all small, n.d., of the "Goodshaw Mining Company," "Niagara Gold & Silver Mining Company," and "Wells Fargo Mining Company." The last has a vignette of a four-horse stage coach. As I have stated before, it is hard to find any examples of this early American (Deadwood Coach) type of travel vehicles, in any media. There are only about ten known, all lithographs. This is also an excellent example of the lithographed stock certificate of from 1850 to 1885. They were numerous.

BUFFORD, JOHN H. BOSTON AND NEW YORK

New York:

1835–1836	152 Broadway
1836–1837	114 Nassau Street
1837–1838	134 Nassau Street
1838–1840	136 Nassau Street

Boston:

1841–1842	204 Washington Street, with B. W. Thayer and J. E. Moody
1843–1844	204 Washington Street, with B. W. Thayer
1845–1851	204 Washington Street, with B. W. Thayer in 1851 and A. G. Dawes in 1845
1851–1855	265 Washington Street
1855	260 Washington Street
1856–1864	313 Washington Street
1867	34 Chauncy Street
1871	190 Washington Street
Finally	141 Franklin Street, and 93 Washington Street

Bufford was one of the noteworthy lithographers in the East, producing a large volume of fine work. This is quite fully described in *America on Stone*.

His California items are few:

"Map of the Valley of the Sacremento including the Gold Region. This map is a correct tracing of the map of Bidwell (land surveyor) by Thos. O. Larkin,

Esq: late Consul of the U. S. for California; and by him stated to be the best for reference in California. Boston. Published by T. Wiley Jr. 20 State St. J. H. Bufford & Co. Entered . . . 1848"—large. At about the middle of the left side of the map is "Table of Distances," including distances from Sandy Hook to Havana, Havana to Chagres, Chagres to Panama, Panama to San Diego, to San Francisco, etc. The map indicates by colored squares "Yerba Buena or San Francisco," San Raphael, Sonoma, and New Helvetia and gives the boundaries of the various ranches on the Sacramento River and its tributaries and the lower part of the San Joaquin River and its tributaries. The map shows the valley of the Sacramento to a point as about two Spanish leagues north of Barranca, Colorado, and the San Joaquin Valley to about two and a half Spanish leagues south of the Arroyo del Campa Frances. The entrance to the Bay of San Francisco is the boundary on the west. To the right of the Bay of San Francisco is printed, "To enter the Bay of San Francisco, keep White Island open with the south shore and run for it until within the harbor, then haul up and anchor abreast of the Town." The anchorage is indicated on the map by two anchors, placed between the Town and Yerba Buena island. This description was taken from the only known impression of the map, owned by the Cadmus Book Shop of New York City, which was also helpful in giving other information.

Three most interesting and extremely scarce music sheet covers, all with words by Bret Harte, music by F. B., and published by Oliver Ditson, 1871: PLATE 45
"Jim"; "Twenty Years"; and "Upon the Stanislow" PLATE 46

Two shipwreck scenes, both medium, n.d., drawn on the spot by Edwin Moody:
"View at San Quentin Bay, Lower California. July 20th, 1851. Embarkation of wrecked passengers from S.S. Union"
"Wreck of the Steamship Union on the Coast of Lower California. July 5th, 1851"—The original drawing turned up in New York City a few years ago. PLATE 47

BUFFORD, JOHN L. BOSTON

Bufford, listed as a lithographer from Boston, was a member of "The Bunker Hill Trading and Mining Association" which sailed on the clipper ship *Shooting Star* from Providence for California, February 22, 1849. So far, no work by him has been found. He may have been connected with the Boston firm of the same name.

BURGESS, GEORGE H. SAN FRANCISCO

1858 engraver on wood, res., 121 Pine Street

Burgess was born in 1831 in London, England. He studied art at the Somerset House School of Design in London and came to America as a young man, settling in San Francisco. His most noteworthy work was the 1849 view of San Francisco, which is listed under H. S. Crocker & Company. According to a biographical note on Burgess, he spent years in the painting of this picture, which when finished was twelve feet long and five feet high.

Burgess also sketched and lithographed "Mokelumne Hill, Calaveras Cy. Printed by Britton & Rey"—letterhead, n.d.; drew on stone "Port of Honolulu. Printed by Britton & Rey. Entered . . . 1857"—small; and drew on stone and lithographed "View of the City & Harbor of San Francisco. From the corner of Fremont & Harrison Sts. Drawn from a Daguerreotype by G. H. Johnson. Entered . . . 1854"—medium.

BURTON, G. W. UNKNOWN

The artist of Michelin's "View of Proposed Trinity Church."

This is most likely the "C. W. Burton," mentioned in *America on Stone*, who worked in New York for Michelin and several other lithographers.

BUTLER, BENJAMIN F. NEW YORK AND SAN FRANCISCO

New York:

1838	146 William Street
1846	17 Ann Street
1848	146 William Street
1849–1851	90 Fulton Street

San Francisco:

1851	Post Office Bldg., Clay Street
1852	Broadway between Kearny & Dupont Streets
1852–1853	86 Broadway
1854	bookseller & stationer, 110 Montgomery Street
1856–1857	lithographer, 88 & 90 Broadway
1858–1859	88–90 Broadway
1861–1864	Montgomery & California Streets
1865	338 Montgomery Street
1866	"Butler, B.F., widow"

LITH? & PUBL? BY BRITTON & REY. SAN FRANCISCO.

ST MARY'S CHURCH.

SAN FRANCISCO CAL.

Lith of Britton & Rey cor [illegible] San Francisco   Pub by S W Langton & Bro. Downieville, Sierra Co California.   Drawn by W. B. M.

VIEW OF GOODYEARS BAR, SIERRA CO. CAL.

42

THIS CERTIFIES
THAT
James Louis Martel
A VETERAN OF THE MEXICAN WAR
IS AN HONORARY MEMBER OF THE ASSOCIATION
OF "TERRITORIAL PIONEERS
OF CALIFORNIA".

44

Jim.

WORDS BY **BRET HARTE.** MUSIC BY **F. B.**

BOSTON.

Published by OLIVER DITSON & CO. 277 Washington St

PHILADA. LEE & WALKER. CINN. JOHN CHURCH JR. NEW YORK C.H. DITSON & CO BOSTON J.C. HAYNES & CO CHICAGO LYON & HEAD

45

Upon the Stanislow.

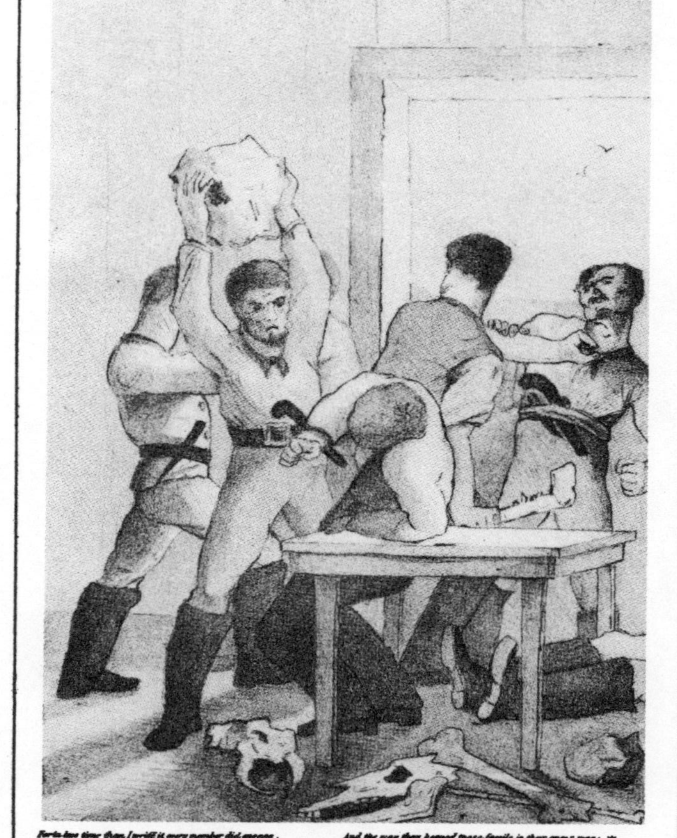

WORDS BY **BRET HARTE.** MUSIC BY **F—, B—.**

BOSTON.

Published by OLIVER DITSON & CO. 277 Washington

PHILADA. LEE & WALKER CINN JOHN CHURCH JR. NEW YORK. C.H. DITSON & CO BOSTON J.C. HAYNES & CO CHICAGO LYON & HEAD

46

WRECK OF STEAMSHIP UNION ON THE COAST OF LOWER CALIFORNIA. JULY 5TH 1851.

San Francisco May 26th 185[illegible]

This is to Certify that Jacob Lermen was ~~elected~~ an Original Member of the SAN FRANCISCO BLUES, on the 4th day of August 1852

Sect.y Wm R. Gorham, Capt.n

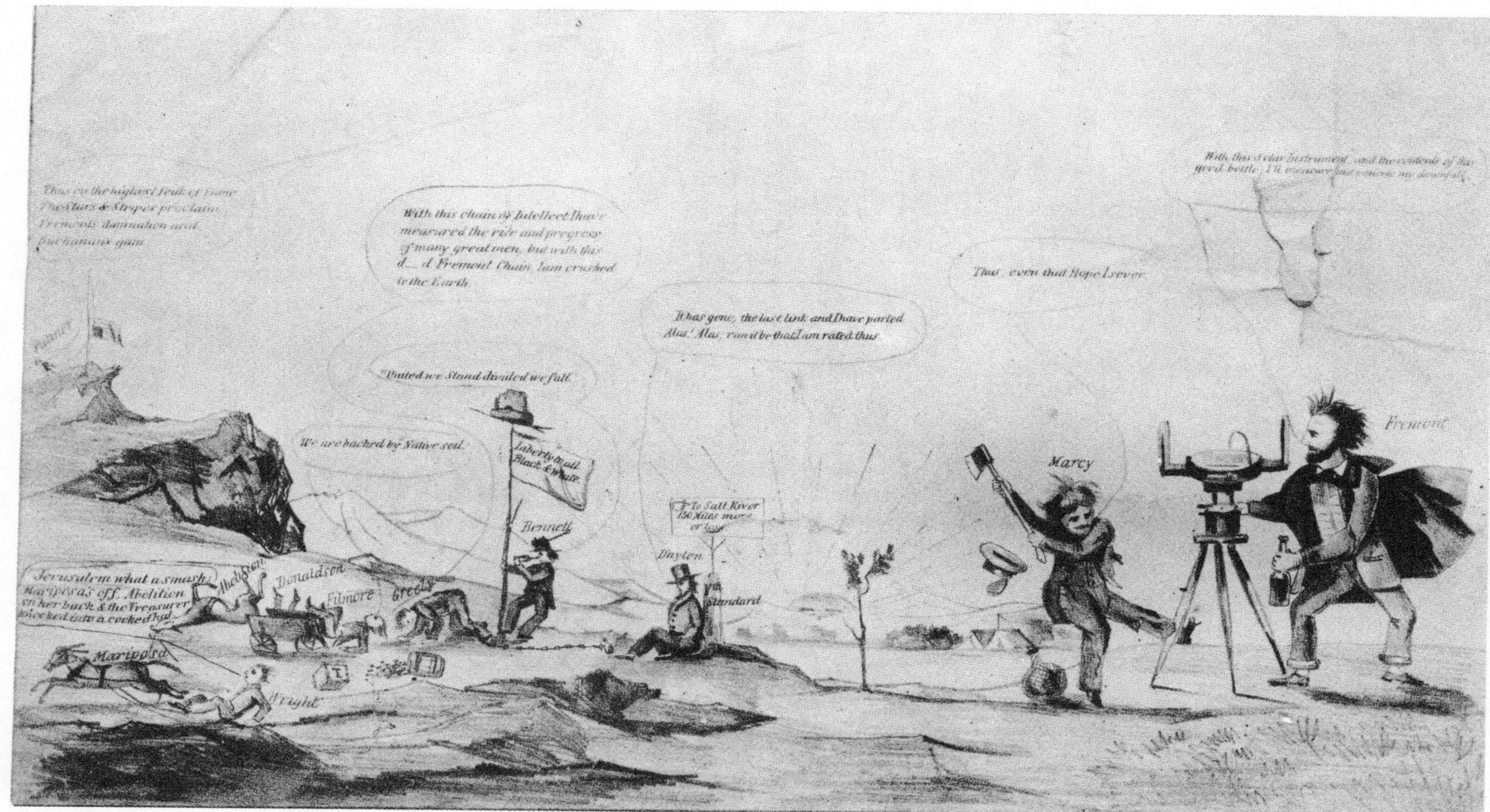

Defunct Ambition on the Road to Salt River, appearance and condition of the parties.

Butler's work in New York was varied, and is mentioned in *America on Stone*.

An article by Walter J. Thompson clipped without date from the San Francisco *Chronicle* states that most and the best of the early California caricatures were produced by Butler, "a pioneer of 1849 and the first man to establish a lithographing plant in the new city"; that he also made city and mine views; that he himself drew many of the caricatures; that he employed E. Jump, Nahl, and others; and that after his death in the mid-sixties many of his prints were pirated.

Butler was the lithographer of two of the very few portraits which I came across in looking for the California lithograph. A list of his work follows:

"Burning of the Steamers Santa Clara and Hartford, at San Francisco, on the morning of March 3rd, 1851. Published and sold by B. F. Butler, Clay St. S. F."—small, n.d.

Certificate of membership in the "San Francisco Blues"—small, n.d. The certificate is dated "1856." A colored view of a squad of "Blues" in full regalia. Signed on stone: "C. C. Kuchel." PLATE 48

"Cor. of Sacramento & Montgomery Sts."—large, n.d.

"Defunct Ambition on the Road to Salt River, appearance and condition of the parties. Sunset. San Francisco, December 1856. Entered . . . 1856 by Nhoj Mailliw Ettocetsew"—small. A note at the de Young Museum says this is a cartoon of Fremont's candidacy for President, done by Butler. PLATE 49

"Elephant & Prospector. Designed by McMurtrie"—letterhead, n.d. (c.1851). Below the picture appears the following:

"*Miner:* Well, How derdu? Put down your trunk
Your Journey makes you puff
You've travelled hard, I like your spunk
Say! Have you been up t'the 'Bluff'?
Elephant: I reckon, yes, have you?
Miner: 'Yes siree' I've been there tu.
Elephant: What saw you there? No Gold I swear!
To get it from the Sand, you can't.
Miner: I saw one chap when you was there.
Elephant: Who?
Miner: I saw the 'elephant.'"

See the note under Britton & Rey letterhead, "Miners' Ten Commandments."

"Funeral Procession of Henry Clay. Born April 12, 1777: Died June 29, 1852. Aged 75 years. Lith. Published and for sale by B. F. Butler, S. Francisco"—medium, n.d. A curious view showing the procession, winding in a serpentine form, across the full page of the sheet.

"Grace Church, San Francisco. (Interior view) On stone by J. H. Peirce from a drawing by G. H. Goddard"—small, n.d. This church was opened for service, October 20, 1851, with Rev. J. L. Mehr as pastor; consecrated October 8, 1855, by Rt. Rev. Wm. Ingraham Kip, missionary bishop to California. Kip was rector of Grace Church, New York, during the years 1835 to 1838 and was chosen missionary bishop to California in 1853.

"The Grand Plaza, San Francisco. Sold by Atwill & Co."—small, n.d.

"Hall & Crandal's Daily Line of U. S. Mail Coaches"—large, n.d.; also issued in small size. (Reproduced in *America on Stone.*)

"Infancy. J. H. Peirce, del. Published at the Noisy Carrier's Hall, Long Wharf, San Francisco"—small, n.d. A Butler version of the Frenchman Boilly's caricature.

"International Hotel"—medium, n.d.

"James Evrard Comedian. From life and on stone by J. H. Peirce"—small, n.d. Evrard was the proprietor of the San Francisco Dramatic Museum, which he established in 1850.

"Jenny Lind Theatre & Parker House. Drawn on stone by J. H. Peirce"—medium, n.d. In the margin: "The Parker House contains two spacious Billiard and one Bowling Saloon. The Billiard Saloons contain 12 tables, the Bowling Saloon 6 alleys. Portsmouth Square, San Francisco Cal. T. Maguire Proprietor."

Letterhead, across the top, advertisements and views of J. L. Riddle & Co., Auctioneers; Revere House; and Pioneer Club House—n.d.

Letterhead, same as above, with views of the Union Hotel; Jenny Lind Theatre; and various business concerns—n.d.

"The Lumber Merchant Reading His Account of Sales from California. Sold by Atwill & Co. S. F. Cal."—small, n.d.

"The Map of the Burnt District. Night of May 3d 1851. Lith. & Published by B. F. Butler, Clay St."—letterhead, n.d.

"Map of the Northern Portion of San Francisco County. Compiled from Surveys June 1st, 1852 by Clement Humphreys, County Surveyor. January 1853"—medium, n.d.

"Map of the State of California. Compiled from the most recent surveys and explorations, and comprising an accurate description of the county boundaries. Also a complete delineation of the Gold Region, Post Office Routes, &c. 1851. Lith. & Published by B. F. Butler, Post Office Bldg., San Francisco. Entered . . . 1851"—large.

"Map of Waterlot Property To be Sold on Monday, Dec. 26th, 1853, at the Musical Hall, Bush St., by the City of San Francisco. Surveyed for the City of San Francisco by J. J. Gardner. Shows four blocks (122 lots) bounded by Clay, East, Sacramento and Davis Streets"—large. This is the first map showing lots sold under the city ordinance, approved December 5, 1853.

"Miners Cabin, Result of The Day. Published by C. A. Shelton, San Francisco. Painted and Drawn on Stone by C. Nahl and A. Wenderoth. Entered . . . 1852"—small. Interior of a cabin with a man cooking at open fire, three others examining gold, another asleep in bunk; the moon is seen through doorway.

"A Miner Prospecting. Published by C. A. Shelton. Painted and Drawn on Stone by C. Nahl and A. Wenderoth. Entered . . . 1852"—small.

These last two prints are among the most artistic lithographs produced in California during the Gold Rush period. They are painter-lithographs of the finest quality, and will stand comparison with any lithographs of any period or place.

"Miss Cathrine Hayes in the 'Bridal Scene' of Lucia de Lamermoor. [Signed on stone:] Peirce; [also the signature of:] Cathrine Hayes"—medium, n.d.

"Montgomery St. between Sacramento & Commercial"—letterhead, n.d.

"Montgomery Street, between Washington & Clay Sts."—letterhead, n.d.

"Official Map of the City of San Francisco full and complete to the present date. Compiled by Wm. M. Eddy, City Surveyor. January 15, 1851. John B. Brady, Delr. B. F. Butler's Lith. Clay St., S. F."—medium, n.d. This print also appears "Lith. by Britton & Rey."

PLATE 50 "Re-Opening of Duncan's Chinese Salesroom, and display of Goods for the Second Art-Union, January 1855"—medium, n.d.

"The San Francisco Quadrilles. Arranged from the Most Famous Negro Melodies for the Pianoforte. Respectfully Dedicated to the Ladies of California by Their Sincere Admirer George Peck. Published by Atwill & Co. [Signed on stone:] Rey. Entered . . . 1852"—a music sheet, with three vignette views.

Stock certificate of the "Cedar Hill Tunnel & Mining Company"—small, n.d.

"A Testimonial of the High Regard Entertained for Col. James Collier Collector of Upper California by the Officers of Customs of the Port of San Francisco. January 15th, 1851. Sold by J. F. Atwill & Co. Post Office Bldg., Clay St."—medium, n.d. This is lithographed on silk; a loving cup on which the title is inscribed, underneath the cup: "Manufactured by Jacks & Brothers, San Francisco, from California gold. Weight 30 oz. Cost $1,500."

PLATE 51 "Tompson in a Quandary. San Francisco 'Local Hits' Cross Reading to be Read Downwards. [On stone:] San Francisco 1862. Appleton, Genl. Agent, 508 Montgomery St., San Francisco. Entered . . . 1862"—medium. A billboard with humorously jumbled advertisements, similar to the "Bill Poster's Dream," reproduced as Plate 58 in *America on Stone*.

"View of the Conflagration of Nevada City on the Morning of March 11th 1851. Estimated Loss, $1,500,000, From a sketch by E. G. Withington"—small, n.d.

BUTLER, JAMES — SAN FRANCISCO

1854 Messenger, U. S. Surveyor General's Office
1864 unknown

James Butler drew Britton & Company's "Map of the City & County of San Francisco." I have seen nothing else by him. Any reference to "Butler" in this book is meant to indicate Benjamin F. Butler.

CAMERER, E. — SAN FRANCISCO

Drew from nature these Kuchel & Dresel views: "The Great Yo-Semite Fall in Mariposa County Cal."; "Shasta Butte & Shasta Valley"; "Stockton, Cal. 1858"; and "View of That Portion of the City of San Francisco Seen From the Residence of N. Larco, Esqre."

CAMERON, JOHN NEW YORK

1852–1855	208 Broadway
1856–1858	33 Spruce Street
1859	12 Dutch Street, with Henry Lawrence
1860–1861	32 John Street
1862	208 Broadway

Cameron did on stone the frontispiece and thirty-nine of the plates, drawn by G. V. Cooper (*q.v.*), in Letts's "Pictorial View of California," 1853.

This was the brilliant hunchback lithographer who deserves much of the credit for the Currier & Ives horses, comics and caricatures. He also did some work on his own, and in partnership as Lawrence & Cameron and Cameron & Walsh. Whether or not he himself ever went to California is not known; it does not seem probable. For further information on Cameron, see *Currier & Ives: Printmakers to the American People,* p. 130.

CAMPBELL, A. H. UNKNOWN

Drew many of the originals for the lithographs by Sarony, Major & Knapp appearing in "The Pacific Railroad Explorations and Surveys."

CASILEAR, GEORGE W. NEW YORK

Drew from nature, with Henry Bainbridge, Sarony & Major's "View of San Francisco . . . 1851," and Napoleon Sarony's "View of Sacramento City."

The frontispiece in Letts's "Pictorial View of California" was drawn by G. V. Cooper (*q.v.*) "from a sketch by G. W. Casilear."

CHAM.

See "Noé, Amédée de." PARIS

CHITTENDEN, J. SAN FRANCISCO

The only work by this man I have come across is "San Francisco College . . . Drawn, designed, and lithographed at the College by J. Chittenden"—large, n.d.; reproduced because it is a most unique item. PLATE 56

CHORIS, LOUIS PARIS

Choris, a Russian of German stock, was born March 22, 1795. In 1816 he visited San Francisco as an artist with the Kotzebue expedition. On his return to France he issued the monumental "Voyage Pittoresque autour du

Monde," Paris, P. Didot, 1822. The work contains upwards of a hundred finely drawn and executed lithographs, of which twelve are part of the California story. Choris himself drew some of the prints upon the stone, others were done by Victor Adam, Franquelin, Marlet, Vorblin, and Noblin. Choris left France in 1827 for South America, and while en route to Vera Cruz was killed by robbers on March 22, 1828.

The following twelve plates, all numbered and sometimes found beautifully colored, comprise the California section of the book:

"Cap de los Reyes. L'entree du port de Sn. Francisco. Rochers Farelones"

"Vue du Presidio Sn. Francisco. Lith. par V. Adam d'après Choris. Lith. de Langlumé, r. de l'Abbaye N.4"

"Danse des habitans de Californie à la mission de St. Francisco. Par Franquelin d'après Choris. Lith. de Langlumé, r. de l'Abbaye N.4"

"Jeu des habitans de Californie. Par Noblin d'après Choris. Lith. de Langlumé, r. de l'Abbaye N.4"

"L'Ours gris de l'Amérique Septentrionale. dessé. et Lithé. par Choris. Lith. de Langlumé, r. de l'Abbaye, N.4"

"Habitants de Californie. desé. et Lithé. par L. Choris"

"Habitants de Californie. Lith. par Marlet. desé. par L. Choris"

"Armes et ustensiles de Californie. dessiné et Lith. par L. Choris"

"Bateau du port de Sn. Francisco. lithé. par Vorblin d'après Corris. Lith. de Langlumé, rue de l'Abbaye N.4"

"Jeune lion marin de la Californie. dess. et Lith. par Choris. Lith. de Langlumé"

"Coiffures de danse des habitans de la Californie. dess. et Lith. par Choris. Lith. de Langlumé"

"Tcholovonis à la chasse dans la baie de St. Francisco. lithé. par Franquee in d'après Choris. Lith. de Langlumé, r. de l'Abbaye N.4"

CLARKE, GEORGE P. UNKNOWN

See Stringer & Townsend's "View of the Chagres."

COLLINSON, CAPTAIN LONDON

Artist of Hanhart's "View of The Town and Harbour of San Francisco, 1851."

COLTON, J. H. NEW YORK

"California. 1854. Published by J. H. Colton, No. 86 Cedar Street, New York. Entered . . . 1853"—small, map in "History of California. By E. S. Capron. Boston, John P. Jewett & Co. 1854." No lithographer mentioned.

COOK, S. F. or E. F. UNKNOWN

These names appear on two Britton & Rey views: "Los Angeles Cal. S. F. Cook del." and "Santa Barbara. California. E. F. Cook, del." As they are both obviously the work of the same man, it is assumed that the initials are erroneously given on one print or the other.

COOKE (WILLIAM B.) & COMPANY SAN FRANCISCO

1850	Portsmouth Square
1850–1852	Cooke & Le Count (*q.v.*)
1852 on	Bookseller & Stationer, 153 Montgomery Street

The only lithographs done by Cooke, before he joined with Le Count, are:

"Great Fire in San Francisco. May 4th, 1850. 400 Buildings Burned! Loss $5,000,000! Pub. by W. B. Cooke & Co, Portsmouth Square"—letterhead, n.d. This was one of the earliest lithographs made in San Francisco. Below the view is a small map of the area burned. On the copy seen at the Huntington Library there is a most interesting letter written in 1850 by a man living in Sacramento. It follows: PLATE 52

Sacramento City
May 26th, 1850

Dear Friend—

Yours of April 1st is received, my thanks for the same. You say you have written four or five times. I have not received so many. I will immediately send to Frisco for those you sent by private conveyance. I am still here in the City in good health and doing very well—feel satisfied to remain—and not try mining—so long as it is healthy here. It is one of the places you better believe I enjoy myself first rate. Obliged to you for calling on Mr. Small—glad to learn of his prosperity—tell him it is no excuse for not writing. [illegible] . . . it is no consideration at all when one can have news from their friends. You ask what I am going to do with a Piano-forte. In answer I will say—the same as I would do were I in Boston—pass my leisure hours in the enjoyment. In regard to the fair sex they are not very numerous at present—but from the accounts we have there is a probability of a large increase in their numbers this season. You speak of sending out a venture—were I certain that prices would remain as they now are I would say send, but no calculation can be made, so fluctuating is the market—and so long it takes to get an order answered. I paid for a pair of thin calf pegd Boots 12 dollars I could buy the same in Boston for 3 . . . [illegible] You will see at present prices it would pay. Should you choose to make any such arrangement I will most willingly assist you all in my power. I have been engaged in building since I have been here excepting at times when the rise of water has prevented—Am now putting up a large Bathing Establishment on I st. at the foot of 4th bordering upon the Lake that runs up into the City about half or three fourths of a mile—It is to be a very showy building four stories high with a Piazza and Balustrade at each story 80 ft. fronting I st. and two wings extended over the Lake for bathing rooms, one for ladies the other for gents. The Upper story is designed for a dancing hall—There is soon to be put up a magnificent theatre building—I have seen the plans and judge it will be *some pumpkins*—Tell Bill I have not yet seen Amasa believe he still remains in Francisco—Sullivan has been to the Sandwich Islands returned and gone into the Southern Diggins—on the Cavalaris I think—Previous to his going into the mines he had not been very successful but is very persevering, and will undoubtedly do well if he has health—You ask if I lost by the flood? All my clothing, Books & papers were spoiled the long Black Chest being under water several days. I was so fortunate as to have my tools in a Dry place & kept them above water—In compliance with your request I will endeavor to answer as many of your questions as my sheet admit. 1st Is Sacramento a plain? It is a perfect level for 4 or five miles from the bank of the river & some distance beyond the fort, by the way, I wish you could see the fort, tis *some pumpkins* again—Is the land fit for Cultivation? Some of the best garden sauce I have ever seen has been raised here this spring—We have had green Peas now for two weeks past also string beans—turnips—radishes—beets—summer squash—tomatoes—onions—lettuce—new potatoes—&c—all of which were equal to any in Boston markets—and the cabbage surpasses any I ever saw.

It is now nearly headed. What kind of trees, plants & fruits? The trees are principally large spreading Oaks & Sycamores & very thick along the banks of the river—farther back on the plain is thick shrubbery & herbs—Here upon the plain there were not many flowers owing to so many mules and cattle grazing—but a little back in the country it is truly beautiful—such a profusion of flowers—I couldn't begin to give you a description. Fruits there are none to my knowledge—plenty of berries. I was out and picked some last Sunday—thimble berries were fine. Our City is laid out in squares, a Levee extending the whole length. The Sts. named alphabetically commence at the Levee and run back to the fort east and west. Those by numerals run at right angles N. & S. the same as the river. The distance between the Sts. is 340 ft each way, and all sts. 80 ft wide. There are not 5 vacant lots that front the Levee, from I st where the Lake comes in, until you get as far down as the letters extend and most of the improvements are very fine & substantial frame buildings. I think you can form some idea of the view it presents as you come up the river. I St. is built back as far as 9th about $\frac{1}{3}$ of the lots improved. Next comes J St. houses have been built as far out as 14th not a vacant lot on this st. until you get to 9th. K St. is improved as far as 12th about $\frac{1}{2}$ the lots built upon. L about the same as K. All the Sts. beyond this are not improved farther out than 4th. The cross Sts. are not so much improved. The Pacific Theatre is on M between Front & 2nd. The Tehama Theatre is on 2nd between I & J Sts. The new theatre will be built on 2nd adjoining the Tehama. For want of room I close—love to all—write every opportunity. I will answer the rest of the questions in my next. Yours

[signed] G W W

[On back of picture fold]:

You ask how Francisco looked after the fire—you can see how it looked in two weeks time after the first fire—the same ground having been burnt over again. I see by the Alta of yesterday that nearly all are again built & occupied. The large building on the left of the sketch was the Miners Bank. The large building on Kearny St. fronting the square was the U. States formerly the Parker house—the low building next to it on corner of Jackson St. is the El Dorado—before the first conflagration it was the largest building in town, 3 stories high. They rebuilt it but 1-½ stories—The white spots on the ground plan were brick buildings —The building next but one to the Miners Bank was where Amasa tended bar in an eating saloon on Kearny St.

"Leland's Map of Marysville Officially Surveyed and Drawn by Cushing & Co. 1850. Published by W. B. Cooke & Co., Portsmouth Square. Beuch Del." —small, n.d.

COOKE & LE COUNT — SAN FRANCISCO

The firm of Cooke & Le Count was established in March, 1850, and continued until November, 1852, when Cooke dropped out, and it became Le Count & Strong, Booksellers & Stationers—a firm which apparently produced no lithographs. Josiah J. Le Count is found listed individually during these years as a bookseller and stationer, and we have also run across two lithographs by him, both dated 1852. When and where Le Count Brothers worked, I do not know.

From Cooke & Le Count are the following:

"Birds Eye View of San Francisco. Drawn from Meream's model & nature. July 1852. J. Britton, del. Entered . . . 1852"—letterhead, with view extended across two folds. One of the earliest birds'-eye views. I have also seen a copy "Lith. & Pub. by Britton & Rey."

PLATE 53 "Celebration of the Fourth of July in San Francisco Cal. the 5th July 1852" small, n.d. Part of the title has been torn on the copy reproduced.

"Downieville, Sierra County, Cal. Sketched by Mrs. M. N. Horton. Entered . . . 1852"—small.

"San Francisco in 1851. From Nature and On Stone by J. H. Peirce. Printed by Charles E. Peregoy"—letterhead, n.d.

PLATE 54 "Stockton. June 1, 1852. J. Britton, del. Entered . . . 1852"—small. [Stamped in margin:] "Noisy Carrier's."

"View of Sacramento City. June 1, 1852. J. Britton, del. Entered . . . 1852"—small.

PLATE 55 "A View of the [Elephant]"—letterhead, n.d., lithographed in gold. Center view of an elephant, surrounded by eight views:

"The Eliza Ship for California"; "Arrival at St. F. A Monte Bank"; "Travelling about the Mines"; "Camping Out"; "Miners preparing their

Fodder"; "Washing Gold in a Cradle"; "One of the few that return"; and "The End of the Many."

See also Peirce & Pollard, Pollard & Britton, and Fishbourne & Gow. PLATE 87 PLATE 88

From Josiah J. Le Count we have:

"Map of San Francisco . . . Lith. of Josiah J. Le Count"—medium, n.d. (c1853).

"View of Grass Valley, Nevada County, California. By R. E. Ogilby, Aug. 6, 1852. Lith. of J. J. Le Count, San Francisco"—medium, n.d. (c.1852). One of the finest of the California lithographs.

Le Count also published Britton & Company's "Official Map of the City of San Francisco."

From Le Count Brothers:

Stock certificate, small, n.d., for the "Maybelle Consolidated Mining Company." (See Galloway.)

COOPER, GEORGE V. NEW YORK

1844	103 Spring Street
1847	613 Houston Street
1848	77 Varick Street
1849	2 Sullivan Street
1849–1852	In California
1852	221 Wooster Street
1860–61	627 Broadway
1862	77 Bleecker Street
1863	31 Washington Place
1864	76 West 19th Street
1865–66	25 Greenwich Avenue
1869	421 West 33rd Street
1870	116 Christopher Street
1872	226 West 20th Street
1874	307 West 15th Street
1876	506 West 50th Street
1877	523 West 50th Street
1878	300 East 57th Street

George V. Cooper was born in Hanover, New Jersey, January 12, 1810, and died in New York City, November 12, 1878. He was known as a lithographer, painter, cameo cutter and sculptor, two of his outstanding works being a portrait of Lincoln, in 1865, and a marble bust of Senator Truman Smith. To us, the most interesting fact is that from 1849 to 1852 he was in California, traveling about the heart of the mining country, apparently as the working partner of J. M. Letts. In the latter's book, Cooper has left us a pungent, graphic record of the long trip to and from the gold fields, of the young cities he found mushrooming there, of booming San Francisco and Sacramento, of the lovely vestiges of the mission-founding padres in early California, and of the actual life of the Forty-niners, with its flavor of roughing it, humor, hope, and all the luring magic of the yellow streak.

Cooper drew all of the plates in Letts's "Pictorial View of California: including a Description of the Panama and Nicaragua Routes, with Information and Advice Interesting to All, Particularly Those Who Intend to Visit the Golden Region. By a Returned Californian. New York: Published by Henry Bill. 1853."

Of these plates, Brown & Severin lithographed the following:

"Between Sacramento and the Mines"

"Mormon Bar, on the North Fork, American River"

"South Fork, American River"

"Chagres, from the Castle, Looking Down. 1851"

No lithographer is mentioned on the following, "G. V. Cooper Del." only being given:

"Chagres from the Anchorage, Feb. 14th 1849"

"Interior of the Castle at Chagres"

"Entrance to the River Chagres"

"Castle at Acapulco"

The frontispiece and thirty-nine plates were "on stone by J. Cameron":

"Part of San Francisco, from a sketch by G. W. Casilear"—(frontispiece)

"Preparing Breakfast on the Chagres River"

"Passing a Rapid"

"New Granadean Mother"

"Battery, Panama"

"Grand Cathedral, Panama"

"The Islands, from Panama"

"Sutter, 3 miles below Sac City"

"Encampment at Sac City, Nov. 1849. My own tent."
"Sutters Fort"
"Rear of Sutters Fort, during the Spring months"
"Author and Artist"
"Teamsters Breakfasting, on the Road to the Mines"
"J. C. Tracy and Myself 'Prospecting' "
"Sutters Mill, Coloma, the spot where Gold was first found"
"Coloma"
"The Yankees House at Hangtown. So much lower than their heads, they had to crawl in and double up like jack knives"
"Placer Ville (Hang Town)"
"White Oak Spring"
"Looking Down the Big Canon"
"The Plains near Sac City in the Flowry Season"
"Sacramento City, From the Foot of J Street. 1849"* PLATE 60
"St. Lucas, Lower California (Looking Northwest)"
"Coast of Lower California. Showing the Peculiarity of the Sky"
"Santa Barbara, Upper California"
"Mission House at Santa Barbara"
"St. Lucas, Lower California (Looking East)"
"Acapulco"
"Market Place, Acapulco"
"Baraco Realejo"
"Church in Shinandagua"
"Batheing and Washing Corn at Chinandaga"
"Harbour of Realajo"
"Our Arrival at Masaya"
"Breakfasting on Shore, Nicaragua Lake"
"San Carlos, Nicaragua Lake, at the entrance of the San Juan River"
"San Juan de Nicaragua"
"The Barbour at San Juan, Nicaragua"
"Panama, from the Battery, Gerro Lancon in the background"
"Coaling Up, Kingston, Jamaica"

*This view of Sacramento by Cooper was lithographed in a more finished form by William Endicott & Company (*q.v.*).

COQUARDON, A. UNKNOWN

I have seen two things done by Coquardon. He drew on stone for Britton
PLATE 23 & Rey "A Correct View of Weaverville," and for Zakreski & Hartman, "View
PLATE 110 of the Procession in Celebration of the Admission of California."

COX, H. F. UNKNOWN

Cox was the artist of "Post Office, San Francisco" for William Endicott & Company.

He was mentioned in *America on Stone* as "H. S." Cox.

CROCKER (H. S.) & COMPANY SAN FRANCISCO

"San Francisco In 1849. George H. Burgess, pinxit. Lithographed by H. S. Crocker & Co. Copyrighted, 1894 by Elisha Cook"—large. A highly colored lithograph showing Mexicans and miners in the foreground, shipping in the harbor. The view is from the present site of the San Francisco Stock Exchange. The Crocker firm, which is still operating in San Francisco, started late in the period of our story, but Burgess was on the scene in the fifties.

CROFUTT, GEORGE W. UNKNOWN

Publisher of the anonymous "Allegorical View of The Conquest of The Continent"—large, n.d. (c.1873). Lithograph portraying in pictorial allegory the conquest of the Continent by the various methods of Western overland travel. The successive waves of the conquest are indicated by the elements of the picture. At the extreme left (the western horizon) are a herd of receding bison; a fight between soldiers and Indians; a group of peaceable Indians on their way towards the sunset; and a grizzly bear. Following them are an ox-drawn prairie schooner and a group of hunters and miners on foot and on horseback. Rapidly approaching these slow-moving groups are seen a six-horse stage coach labeled "Overland Mail" and a galloping pony-expressman. Somewhat to the east of these westbound movements are a log cabin and a patch of cleared ground within a rail fence, where settlers are plowing by the aid of oxen. Last of all, and at the right, come the pioneer overland railroad trains, with their huge smokestacks and red-painted engines. In the center of the picture, and above the various groups and vehicles shown crawling westward on the earth, is seen the flying spirit of Progress. On her brow is the Star of Empire. In one hand she bears a volume, and with the other she is uncoiling and dropping behind her a telegraph line that stretches backward to the eastern shore of the continent. At the extreme right, in the far eastern distance, ships are seen, and New York City and the outlines of the Brooklyn Bridge are dimly discernible.

Crofutt, its publisher, was likewise the editor of the series of Overland guidebooks which began to appear as soon as the continent was spanned by iron rails.

CULLBERG, EDWIN — UNKNOWN

Drew some of the plates listed under W. H. Dougal.

CURRIER & IVES, *ET AL.* — NEW YORK

Stodart & Currier:

1834–1835 137 Broadway

N. Currier:

1835–1836 1 Wall Street
1836–1837 148 Nassau Street
1838–1856 152 Nassau Street, and 2 Spruce Street

Currier & Ives:

1857–1865 152 Nassau Street, and 2 Spruce Street
1866–1872 152 Nassau Street, and 33 Spruce Street
1872–1874 125 Nassau Street, and 33 Spruce Street
1874–1877 123 Nassau Street, and 33 Spruce Street
1877–1894 115 Nassau Street, and 33 Spruce Street
1894–1896 108 Fulton Street, and 33 Spruce Street
1896–1907 33 Spruce Street

Charles Currier:

Over a period of years } 33 Spruce Street

It is to be noted that there is a record of Stodart & Currier at 137 Broadway in 1834, but few prints were produced by this combination. The story really starts at 1 Wall Street in 1835. Charles Currier, the brother of Nathaniel Currier, used mostly the 33 Spruce Street address, and was loosely affiliated with the firm at all times. James Merritt Ives came into the firm as bookkeeper in 1852. In 1857 he became a partner, and the firm name was changed to Currier & Ives.

This firm did over seven thousand listed lithographs of the American scene, including a few of California to fill their line. The more important of these latter are listed below, with their checklist numbers in parentheses. It would seem that the large folio colored "View of San Francisco, California. On stone by F. Palmer. McMurtrie" (3881), issued by N. Currier, is the most important. It shows the house flags on the clipper ships in the harbor so vividly they can readily be identified. This scarce print has been most useful to those interested in that phase of our history. Also, the very important series of cartoons, six in number, show the trials and tribulations, as well as the hoaxes of the Gold Rush.

For full and further information, see *Currier & Ives: Printmakers to the American People,* Volumes I and II, by the author.

Nathaniel Currier:

(The numbers given in parentheses are H.T.P. Check-list numbers.)

"California Gold"—small, n.d. (1537).

"Californian Seeking the Elephant"—small, n.d. (1535).

"The Gold Seekers"—small, 1851 (1527A).

"The Grand Patent India-rubber Airline Railway to California"—small, 1849 (1528).

"Independent Gold Hunter on His Way to California"—small, n.d. (1536). This greatly resembles the H. R. Robinson "A Gold Hunter on his Way to California" (*q.v.*), differing only in the background, and is identical with the Kelloggs & Comstock print of the same title.

PLATE 58 "View Of San Francisco, California. Taken from Telegraph Hill, April 1850. By Wm. B. McMurtrie, Draughtsman Of The U. S. Surveying Expedition. Published by N. Currier, N. Y.—Wm. B. McMurtrie, San Francisco. Clarkes Point—Rincon Point—Happy Valley—Long Wharf (building)—Pacific St. Wharf (building)—Apollo Warehouse—Niantic Warehouse—Sansome St.—Portsmouth Square. On Stone By F. Palmer. Lith. & Pub. By N. Currier, 152 Nassau St. Cor. Of Spruce, N. Y. Entered . . . 1851"—large (3881). This is a fine early view of San Francisco, and probably the most important California item of the Curriers.

A series medium, 1849:

"The Way They Cross the Isthmus" (1530).

"The Way They Raise a California Outfit" (1531).

B.F. Butler's Lith San Francisco

The opening of DUNCAN'S CHINESE SALESROOM, and display of Goods for the SECOND ART-UNION, January 1855

50

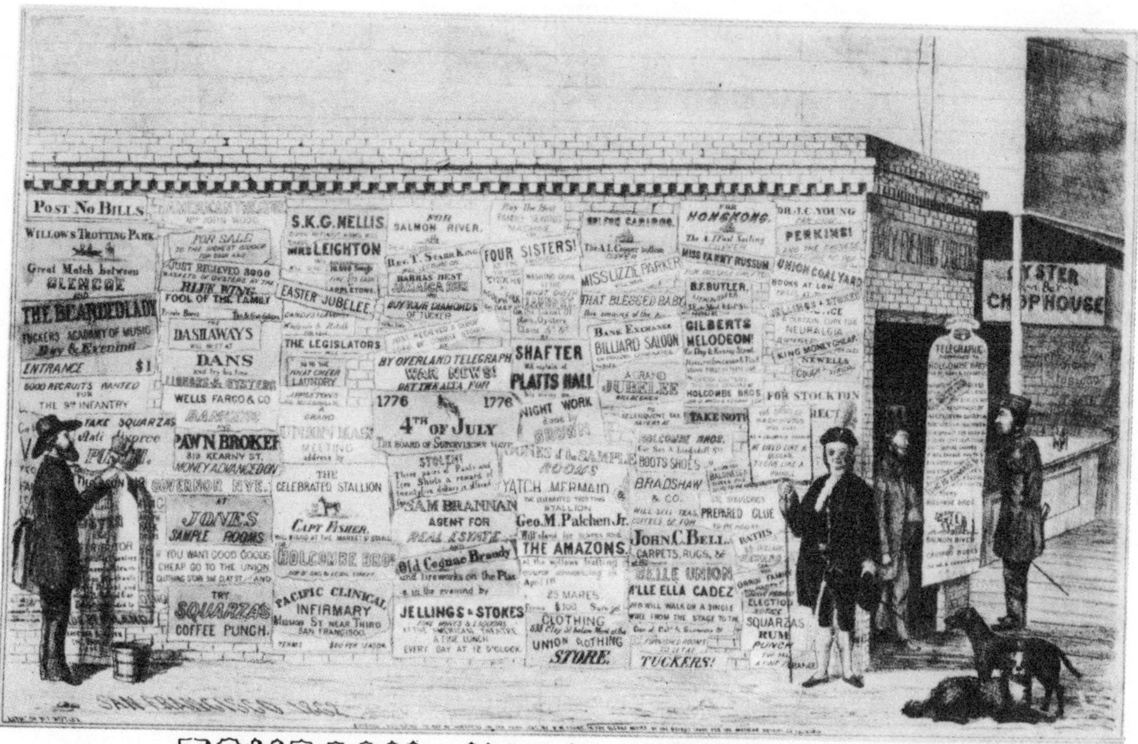

TOMPSON IN A QUANDARY.

SAN FRANCISCO "LOCAL HITS" CROSS READINGS TO BE READ DOWNWARDS.

APPLETON GENL. AGENT 508 MONTGOMERY ST SAN FRANCISCO.

51

CREAT FIRE IN SAN FRANSISCO.

May 4th, 1850.

400 BUILDINGS BURNED!

Loss $5,000,000!

Pub. by W.B. Cooke & Co, Portsmouth Square.

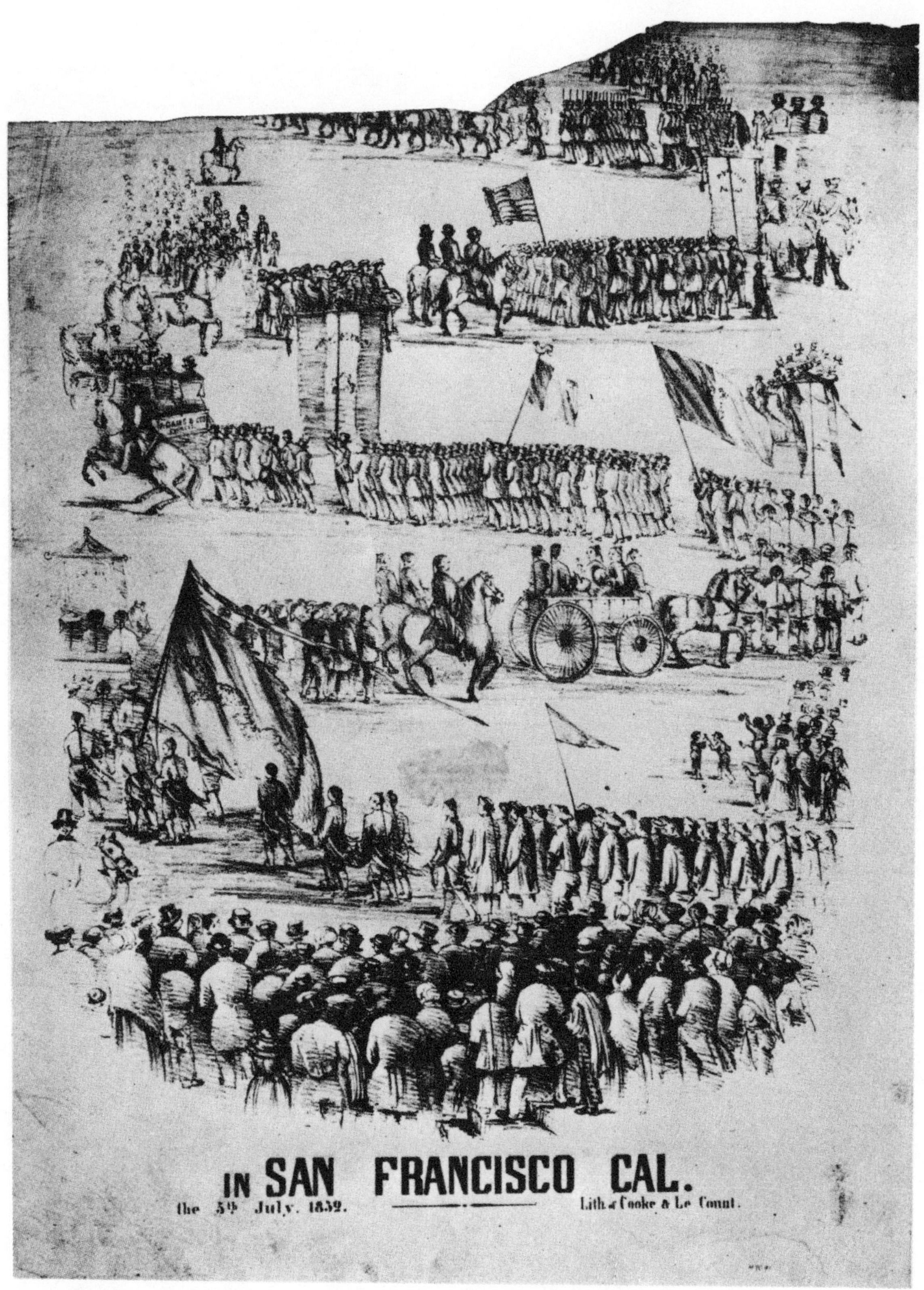
IN SAN FRANCISCO CAL.
the 5th July. 1852.
Lith. of Cooke & Le Count.

J. Britton del

STOCKTON.

June 1st 1852.

Lith & Published by Cooke & Le Count San Francisco.

Published and Sold by [illegible] San Francisco.

SAN FRANCISCO COLLEGE
BUSH STREET.
THIS COLLEGE.
A HEALTHY AND DELIGHTFUL RESIDENCE,
A THOROUGH CLASSICAL AND COMMERCIAL EDUCATION.
MODERN LANGUAGES
Mathematics &c.
The Study of NATURAL PHILOSOPHY is illustrated by the BEST APPARATUS in the State.
DRAWING, PAINTING, & VOCAL MUSIC are taught WITHOUT EXTRA CHARGE.
N B The Institution has been particularly celebrated for teaching the art of Writing
TEACHERS.
John Chittenden, Principal.
REFERENCES.
TERMS MODERATE. see PROSPECTUS.

SIXTH GREAT CONFLAGRATION IN SAN FRANCISCO. JUNE 22d 1851

J. De Vere, del.

NOISY CARRIER'S PUBLISHING HALL
77 LONG WHARF SAN FRANCISCO
CHARLES P. KIMBALL PROPRIETOR

VIEW OF SAN FRANCISCO, CALIFORNIA.

TAKEN FROM TELEGRAPH HILL. APRIL 1850, BY Wm B. McMURTRIE, DRAUGHTSMAN OF THE U. S. SURVEYING EXPEDITION.

58

A full color reproduction of this plate appears in the color section in this book.

LITH. OF G. & W. ENDICOTT

VIEW OF THE MISSION OF S[T] GABRIEL

"The Way They Go to California" (1532).

"The Way They Come From California" (1533). PLATE 2

"The Way They Get Married in California" (1534).

"The Way They Wait for the Steamer at Panama" (1529).

This set of six cartoons, of the balloon type, is the only series depicting the entire story. They are extremely scarce, very well done, and deserve a very high ranking. "The Way They Come From California" was copyrighted in 1849 by N. Currier. It is here reproduced in color as one of the outstanding California cartoons.

Currier & Ives:

"Bridal Veil Fall, Yo-Semite Valley, California"—small, n.d. (3886).

"The California Beauty"—small, n.d. (2754A).

"California Scenery. Seal Rocks—Point Lobos"—small, n.d. (3879).

"California Yo-Semite Falls"—small, n.d. (3884).

"The City of San Francisco"—small, 1877 (3882A).

"The City of San Francisco. Birds Eye View from the Bay, looking Southwest. Sketched & drawn by C. R. Parsons"—large, 1878 (3882).

"Col. Fremont's Last Grand Exploring Expedition in 1856. For Sale at No. 2 Spruce St. N. Y."—small, n.d. (1635A).

"El Capitan—From Mariposa Trail"—small, n.d. (3878).

"Gold Mining in California"—small, 1871 (1527).

"Golden Fruits of California"—medium, 1869 (773).

"The Home of the Seal (California Coast)"—small, n.d. (2587).

"Looking Down the Yo-Semite"—small, n.d. (3888).

"On the Coast of California"—small, n.d. (3880).

"The Pioneer Cabin of the Yo-Semite Valley"—small, n.d. (1563).

"The Route to California. Truckee River Sierra-Nevada"—small, 1871 (2111).

"Silver Creek—California"—small, n.d.

"The Washington Columns, Yo-Semite Valley"—small, n.d. (3889).

"Yo-Semite Falls, California"—small, n.d. (3887).

"Yo-Semite Valley—California. 'The Bridal Veil' Fall"—medium, 1866 (3885).

DAHLGREN — UNKNOWN

"Carmelo Mission. Lithographed by Dahlgren"—small, n.d. This was the mission founded at Monterey and known as the San Carlos Mission. It was later removed to Carmel.

DANIELS, J. H. — BOSTON

See Britton & Rey's "Mammoth Arbor Vitæ."

DAUMIER, HONORÉ — PARIS

French painter, lithographer and caricaturist. Born in Marseilles, 1808, died in Valmondois, 1879.

"Actualités. Actionnaires Californiens. 'J'ai versé hier cinq mille francs pour prix de mille actions de la Societé des Jaunets Californiens. Nous avons l'exploitation de toute la rive gauche du Sacremento. Je crois que j'ai fait une bonne affaire et le geraut en est convaincu comme moi. Je prefere la Societé de la Carotte d'or, j'y ai placé tout ce que j'avais d'argent.' Chez Aubert & Cie. Pl. de la Bourse, 29, Paris. Imp. de Me. Ve. Aubert, r. de l'Abbaye 5, Paris"—small, n.d.

D'AVIGNON (FRANCIS), *ET AL.* — NEW YORK AND BOSTON

Entered as lithographer except as noted:

Francis D'Avignon, New York:

1844	unknown
1847	artist, 33 Spruce Street and 132 Nassau Street
1848	artist, 289 Broadway
1849–1853	323 Broadway; 1849, D'Avignon & Hoffman; 1850, Brady, D'Avignon & Co., 111 Nassau Street
1853–1854	323 and 341 Broadway
1854–1855	house, 306 Ninth Avenue
1855–1856	80 Leonard Street
1857	painter, no address
1858	327 Broadway
1859	346 Broadway

D'Avignon & Brainerd, Boston:

1859–1860	134 Washington Street; associated with Elliott & White

This lithographer of the very first rank is best known for his portrait work. He was born in St. Petersburg of French parents and educated at a military school. His family took him to Paris in 1830, where he studied drawing and lithography. His work is fully listed in *America on Stone*.

But two prints of his pertaining to our present story have turned up. They are:

"The City of Monterey, California. 1842. para Sr. Larkin. On stone by Gildemeister. Lith. of D'Avignon, 323 Broadway, N. Y."—large, n.d. This is one of the earliest California views, and extremely rare. There are sixty-two references in the margin, most of the names being of Spanish residents, a few of English. Monterey was founded in 1770, when Portola built a Presidio there, and Padre Junipero Serra established the Mission of San Carlos de Borromeo de Monterey. It was for many years the Spanish and Mexican capital of California. On October 19, 1842, the surrender of Monterey was demanded by Commodore Thomas C. Jones, commander of the Pacific Fleet, who through some error thought the United States was at war with Mexico. The American flag flew over the plaza for several days before Jones realized his mistake, lowered the flag, and withdrew. One of Jones's officers made a sketch of Monterey at this time, which was later lithographed and sent to Thomas Larkin, an American of some importance then living in Monterey. This was undoubtedly the D'Avignon lithograph.

"Map of the City of Benecia. Surveyed & Drawn by Benj. W. Barlow. Pub. by B. W. Barlow. Lith. of F. D'Avignon, 323 Broadway, New York. Entered . . . 1851"—large. In one corner are two vignette views: "South-east View of Benecia" and "South-west View of Benecia." Benecia was the capital of California from 1853 to 1854. Perhaps it was more widely known as the home town of John C. Heenan, "The Benicia Boy," once champion of the world.

DAY & HAGHE — LONDON

Day & Haghe, "Lithrs. to the Queen," lithographed all but two of the plates in "California: A History of Upper and Lower California. By Alexander Forbes, Esq. London: Smith, Elder & Company. Cornhill. 1839." The other two plates were lithographed by L. M. Lefevre (*q.v.*). Of those done by Day & Haghe, all but the frontispiece were drawn by Captain William Smyth, R.N.

"Father Antonio Peyri (Aet.67) Missionary at San Luis Rey. Upper California from 1799 to 1832. S. Drummond Pinxt. Mexico 1832"—(Frontispiece)

"Portrait of a Native Indian"
"The Presidio and Pueblo of Monterey, Upper California"
"The Bay of Monterey, Upper California"
"San Francisco Harbour, Upper California"
"The Temescal or Hot Air Bath of Upper California"
"Mission of San Carlos and Bay of Carmel, Upper California"
"The Mission of San Francisco, Upper California"

DEROY PARIS

"Vue De San-Francisco Vista De San Francisco Paris, L. Turgis Fne. Impr. Editeur, r. des Ecoles, 60-Maison a New-York Dessiné et Lithog. par Deroy"—large, n.d. From "Ports de Mer D'Amérique."

DE VERE, J. UNKNOWN

De Vere was the lithographer of two letterheads, both n.d., showing views of the fire of June 22, 1851:

PLATE 57 "Sixth Great Conflagration in San Francisco, June 22nd, 1851. J. De Vere, del. [Stamped in margin:] Noisy Carrier's Publishing Hall, 77 Long Wharf, San Francisco. Charles P. Kimball, Propr[i]etor"

"View of the Conflagration from Telegraph Hill, San Francisco, June 22nd, 1851. J. De Vere, del." San Francisco was burned over a number of times in its early days, especially in the fifties. The fires were often set by the hoodlums and "Sydney men," and it was the fires, together with the constant robberies and murders committed by these men, that brought about the organization of the first Committee of Vigilance by the long-suffering citizens of the city.

DONNELL, HENRY CLAY SAN FRANCISCO

Designed and drew Britton & Rey's "Presidential Elections of the United States . . . 1877."

DOUGAL, W. H. WASHINGTON

Dougal (originally named McDougal) was born in New Haven, Conn., about 1808. He was an engraver of landscapes and portraits. He was working for the United States Treasury Department in 1853. The following California views are the only lithographs that I have seen by him. The views are attractive and well drawn, and are the plates in:

"A Series Of Charts, with Sailing Directions, State Of California. By Cadwalader Ringgold, Commander, U. S. Navy. Washington. 1852":

"View of San Francisco from Yerba Buena Island. Rincon Pt. Signal Hill. Ft. Finley. Fort. Pta. Boneta"

"Entrance to San Francisco. Monte Diablo. Yerba Buena. Punta Boneta. Fort Miley. Pto.Lobos. C. Ringgold, U.S.N."

"View of Sacramento City from the west bank. Edwin Cullberg"

"View of Benicia from the Anchorage East of Seal Island. West Entrance Straits of Carquines. Navy Point. S. F. Blunt, U.S.N."

"View of Monte Diablo from Garnet Island. Monte Diablo. New York. E. Cullberg"

"View from the Forks of the Sacramento. Monte Diablo. Gillespie Id. Suisun City. E. Cullberg"

"Mark for Invincible Buoy Point Smith, east end of Angel I. on with Signal Hill. Signal Hill. Motate I. Pt. Smith. Angel I. S. F. Blunt, U.S.N."

"Mark for Invincible Buoy North extreme of Marin Is. on with Clump of trees north of San Rafael. Clump. Marin I. S. F. Blunt"

"Mark for Tongue Shoal. Pt. San Joaquin. Monte Diablo. Single Tree. N.York Plain Tree. Pt. Hansen. E. Cullberg"

"Entrance to the Sacramento River. Pt. Cullberg. Montezuma House. Burnett I. Chain islets. Montezuma Hills. Pt. Sacramento. Edwin Cullberg"

"Marks for entering the Sacramento and its Forks at their confluence. West Fork. Middle Fork. Sacramento River. Edwin Cullberg"

"Marks for entering the second section of the Middle Fork of the Sacramento River. West Fork. Middle Fork. Edwin Cullberg"

DRESEL, EMIL SAN FRANCISCO

See Kuchel & Dresel.

DROUAILLET SAN FRANCISCO

"Official Map of the City of Oakland, compiled from Records and Surveys by J. E. Whitcher. San Francisco. Drouaillet Lithographer, 1860"—medium, with twenty-one marginal views. Especially valuable for these views of early buildings, which include the College of California, which later became the University of California, in the year of its organization; Alameda County Agricultural Society Pavillion; Washington Brewery; Young Ladies Seminary; Capt. Michelsen's Wharf; Behren's Lumber Yard; residences of Mr. Blake, G. W. Fountain, William Dove, Dr. Cole, Hon. J. A. Hobart, Gen. R. W. Heath, and others.

DUNLAP, J. B. UNKNOWN

The only lithograph of Dunlap's I have seen is "U. S. Navy Yard. At Mare Island, California. Taken from the City of Vallejo. Printed by Britton & Rey, S. F. Drawn & lithd. by J. B. Dunlap"—small, n.d.

DUVAL (PETER S.), *ET AL.* PHILADELPHIA

c.1831–1835	working for Childs & Inman
1835–1836	Lehman & Duval, 7 Bank Alley (Childs & Lehman, 45 Walnut Street, at the same time)
1839–1840	Huddy & Duval, 7 Bank Alley
1840–1848	7 Bank Alley
1849–1855	5 Ranstead Place
1856	Rosenthal, Duval & Prang, 8 South Fifth Street
1857	P. S. Duval & Son (Stephen C.), and P. S. Duval, Son & Co., 8 South Fifth Street
1858	22 South Fifth Street
1859–1860	22 & 24 South Fifth Street
1863	22 & 24 South Fifth Street; also Duval & Ludlow
1864	22 & 24 South Fifth Street
1879	P. S. Duval retired, followed by Duval & Hunter, until:
1893	the business was sold by the sheriff.

Duval was one of the most important and early American lithographers, whose story is connected with many others. No attempt to describe the great volume of his work can be made here, but it is fully dealt with in *America on Stone.*

I have come across but few California prints of his:

"Plan of the Alameda Gardens, within and adjoining the City of San Jose, originally known as El Potrero de Santa Clara. 1850. P. S. Duval's Steam Lith. Press, Philada."—large, n.d.

"View of San Francisco. 1850. Taken from a high point on the south side. Published by the Author of 'Sights in the Gold Region &c.' Kuchel, delt. Lith. of P. S. Duval. Entered . . . 1850"—small.

Duval lithographed the plates in "Central Route To The Pacific, From The Valley Of The Mississippi To California: Journal Of The Expedition of E. F. Beale, Superintendent of Indian Affairs In California, And Gwinn Harris Heap, From Missouri To California, In 1853. By Gwinn Harris Heap. Philadelphia: Lippincott, Grambo, and Co. 1854." They were all "G. H. Heap, del.":

"Rafting Across Grand River"
"Spanish Peaks. Huerfano Butte"
"Lower Mouth of Huerfano Canon"
"Huerfano Butte"
"First Camp. In the Sangre de Cristo Mts."
"Entrance of Sah Watch Valley. San Luis Valley and the Sierra Blanca in the distance"
"Scenery In Sahwatch Valley"
"Coochatope Pass. 'The Gate of Buffaloes,' in Sahwatch Mts."
"Coochatope Pass"
"Rio De La Laguna. Sierra de la Plata"
"Crossing Laguna Creek"
"Grand River, Below the junction of the Uncompagre"
"View On Green River"

EASTMAN, HARRISON — SAN FRANCISCO

1854 designer & engraver, Taylor Street
1856–1858 designer & engraver, Taylor Street near Clay

Eastman sketched the Pollard & Britton "San Francisco, January 1852" and, with A. Nahl, Nagel's "Lombard, North Point." PLATE 80

ELLIOTT (WALLACE W.), *ET AL.* — OAKLAND AND SAN FRANCISCO

1878 Smith & Elliott, Oakland
1879 Wallace W. Elliott & Company, San Francisco
1881 Elliott & Moore, 106 Leidesdorff Street, San Francisco
1885 W. W. Elliott, 921 Broadway, Oakland

See also C. L. Smith & Company.

Elliott, in various alignments, published and lithographed the plates in the following county histories:

"Illustrations of Contra Costa County, California. With Historical Sketch. Smith & Elliott, Oakland, 1878"

"Colusa County, California. Wallace W. Elliott & Co. San Francisco. 1879"

"Santa Cruz County, California. Wallace W. Elliott & Co. San Francisco. 1879"

"History of Merced County, California. Elliott & Moore, 106 Leidesdorff Street, San Francisco. 1881"

"History of San Benito County, California. Elliott & Moore, 106 Leidesdorff Street, San Francisco. 1881"

"Oakland and Surroundings. W. W. Elliott, 921 Broadway, Oakland, 1885"

ELTON, ROBERT H. — NEW YORK

Elton evidently had a lithographic establishment, 1848–1850, at 90 Nassau Street, but few of his prints are recorded anywhere. A very well colored
PLATE 68 print is "A California Gold Hunter Meeting a Settler. Published by Serrell & Perkins—75 Nassau St. N. Y. R. H. Elton 90 Nassau St, N. Y."—small, n.d. The "settler" is a puma.

ENDICOTTS, THE, *ET AL.* — NEW YORK

Entered also, besides as lithographers, at various times, as music dealers, depository of the fine arts, pianofortes, general engravers and printers:

1828	date of founding, on trade lists
Endicott & Swett:	
1830–1834	111 Nassau Street
George Endicott:	
1834–1840	359 Broadway
1840	152 Fulton Street
1841	16 or 22 John Street; also William Endicott
1842–1844	22 John Street; also William Endicott
G. & W. Endicott:	
1845	22 John Street
1846–1859	59 Beekman Street
1849	Sarah L. Endicott, widow of George, 59 Beekman Street

William Endicott & Company:

1849–1852 59 Beekman Street

Endicott & Company (William and Francis):

1852–1856 59 Beekman Street

1857–1858 59 Beekman Street and 89 Ann Street

1859–1870 59 Beekman Street

1871–1886 57 Beekman Street

George Endicott (II):

1887 75 Murray Street

1888–1891 10 Barclay Street

1892–1896 insurance, 51 Cedar Street

The Endicotts did a huge volume of work, but they are difficult to summarize. They did everything and did it well, had Parsons with them for years, worked with and for Currier & Ives, yet in spite of all that much of their work lacks real individuality. Their prints seem to be, and actually were, the first machine-made lithographs in mass production. The true spirit of lithography lies only in their early work. This may be an unjust summary, but go through a large pile of their assorted work and then see how you feel about this summary if you know and like lithographs.

Their work is fully covered in *America on Stone,* and we list here only their California prints.

G. & W. Endicott:

The 1849 view of San Francisco. See Firks.

Frontispiece and eight illustrations in "Life in California: During a Residence of Several Years in That Territory, Comprising a Description of the Country and the Missionary Establishments, with Incidents, Observations, Etc., Etc. By an American To Which is Annexed a Historical Account of the Origin, Customs, and Traditions of the Indians of Alta-California. Translated from the Original Spanish Manuscript. New York: Published by Wiley & Putnam, No. 161 Broadway. 1846":

"View of the 'Presidio' or Town of Santa Barbara, Taken from a Hill Near the Fort. A. Robinson Del. [Signed on stone:] F. Swinton"—(frontispiece)

"View of the Mission of St. Luis Rey. A. Robinson Del. [Signed on stone:] F. Swinton"

PLATE 59 "View of the Mission of St. Gabriel. A. Robinson Del. [Signed on stone:] F. Swinton"

"View of the Presidio or Town of Santa Barbara. A. Robinson Del. [Signed on stone:] F. Swinton"—(differs from frontispiece)

"A View of the Mission of Santa Barbara. A. Robinson Del. [Signed on stone:] F. Swinton"

"View of the Mission of St. Buenaventura. A. Robinson Del. [Signed on stone:] F. Swinton"

"View of the Place of Anchorage at 'Yerba Buena' in St. Francisco. F. Teschmaker Del."

"Father Geronimo Boscana, Missionary at St. Juan Capistrano"

"An Indian Dressed in the 'Tobet.' A. Robinson Del. [Signed on stone:] F. Swinton"

William Endicott & Company:

"Monterey Capital of California"—small, n.d. The California capital until 1847.

"Post Office, San Francisco, California. A faithful representation of the crowds daily applying at that office for letters & newspapers. H. F. Cox, del."—small, n.d. (c.1850).

"Sacramento, Cal. Plan of Sacramento city, state of California. Original survey by capt. W. H. Warner, U. S. A. in dec. 1848; extended by the city charter, adopted by the people octr. 13th, 1849 and surveyed by Clement W. Coote cty. engr. decr. 1849. Copied by H. Ehrenberg, surveyor. Entered . . . 1850"—large.

PLATE 60 "Sacramento City Ca. From the foot of J. Street, showing I. J. & K. Sts. with the Sierra Nevada in the Distance. Drawn Dec. 20th 1849 by G. V. Cooper. New York, Published by Stringer & Townsend, 222 Broadway. Entered . . . 1850"—large. (Le Breton's "Ville de Sacramento" is identical with this.) This view shows the full pageant of California life, and travel by sea and land, of the Gold Rush period. In the margin is a key to the principal buildings. It is one of the most typical of larger Gold Rush prints, and is found reduced in size, with many details left out, in Letts's "Pictorial View of California." (See G. V. Cooper.) Sacramento, now the capital of California, was built up by the Forty-niners as a trading center and "jumping-off place" for the mines. For a description of the city in its early days, see the letter written on the Wm. B. Cooke & Company's letterhead.

Endicott & Company:

"City of San Francisco. From Rincon Point. Lithographed by C. Parsons, New York. Del't. by F. N. Otis, M.D. Surgeon in U.S.M. Steamship Co's Service. Entered . . . 1855"—large. The artist served with the steamship company from 1853 to 1859. He drew the originals for Endicott's "View of Panama" and "The Steamship Illinois." For an account of his work see, *Medical Record,* New York, Vol. 57, pp. 1073–5.

The plates, all small, in "A Tour of Duty in California Including a Description of the Gold Region" by Joseph Warren Revere, published New York, 1849:

"Monterey, Capitol of California"; "Quicksilver Mine—near Santa Clara"; "Monte Diablo—from the Sacramento River"; "A Ranchero Feat"; "Sutter's Fort—New Helvetia"; and "A 'Pui' Day"

ENSIGNS, THE, *ET AL.* NEW YORK

Timothy and Edward Ensign:

1841–1843	7½ Bowery; also Phelps, Humphrey
1843–1845	160 Nassau Street; also Phelps, Humphrey, 1844–1845
1845–1846	36 Ann Street
1847–1849	36 Ann Street; also Ensigns & Thayer; also Phelps, Humphrey
1849–1851	50 Ann Street; also Ensigns & Thayer; also Phelps, Humphrey
1861	156 William Street; also Ensign, Bridgman & Fanning

The Ensigns produced a considerable amount of work in various associations and alignments. However, only two California prints have been discovered:

"Gold Regions of California, showing the routes via Chagres and Panama, Cape Horn, &c."—large, n.d. (c.1849). This map shows none of the overland trails; it has a descriptive text.

"Map of the United States," listed under McLellan.

See also The Kelloggs, *et al.*

PLATE 69

FELGNER, A. BERLIN

"Sacramento in Californien. Des Auswanderers Hoffnung. Druck Verlag A. Felgner in Berlin"—medium, n.d.

FERRAN, AUGUSTO HAVANA, CUBA

See Marquier.

FIRKS, HENRY SAN FRANCISCO

Firks was the artist of one of the best-known early San Francisco views:

"San Francisco 1849. Drawn on the spot by Henry Firks for W. H. Jones, Esq. of San Francisco, U.C."

The history of the various issues of this view is somewhat difficult to trace, but it seems to have been about as follows:

PLATE 102 It was first lithographed by "T. Sinclair, 101 Chestnut St. Phila. On Stone by Ibbotson. Entered . . . 1849 by G. T. Deveraux for W. H. Jones"—rectangle 13.12 x 33, in colors, with forty-five marginal references.

Next seems to have been the issue, "Lith. of G. & W. Endicott N. Y. Entered . . . 1849 by G. T. Deveraux for W. H. Jones"—arched rectangle 13.4 x 32.4, in colors, with forty-six marginal references. This is considered the first authentic and correct view, but is the second issue.

It was printed by G. T. Brown & Company—arched rectangle 14.6 x 32.6, in colors, with fifty-one marginal references. Just below the old 1849 copyright date are the words: "Reentered in San Francisco 1868." This issue has also appeared with neither the lithographer's name nor the new copyright date given.

There was a printing by "Snow & Company, 20 Post Street, San Francisco"—rectangle 13.2 x 32.4, in tints, with fifty-two marginal references. As Snow & Company did not exist, so far as we know, until 1880, this would make it a late issue.

The latest issue that has turned up was from "Schmidt Label & Litho. Co. S.F. Cal.—Copyright 1886 by Max Burkardt, San Francisco, Cal. For Sale By All Principal Art & Book Stores. Latest Edition Corrected By A Committee of Pioneers Consisting Of Richard M. Sherman—William Heath Davis—Ferdinand Vassault"—rectangle 13.5 x 32.4, in tints, with sixty-two references.

I have heard of an issue of this print by Fishbourne, but I have not seen it and so cannot give any accurate record of it.

FISHBOURNE (R. W.), *ET AL.* SAN FRANCISCO

1851	Ohio Street; also Fishbourne & Gow, unknown
1852–1853	16 Ohio Street
1854	18 Ohio Street
1855	Ohio Street
1856–1857	Ohio Street, near Broadway
1858	draftsman, U. S. Surveyor General, Ohio Street
Unknown	"& Company," Clay Street

See Nagel, Fishbourne & Kuchel; and Henry Firks.

Fishbourne was one of the earliest lithographers on the scene. Prints of his I have seen are:

"A Correct View of the Mammoth Tree Grove, by D. A. Plecker. Entered . . . 1855"—letterhead.

"Execution of Rafael Escobar"—letterhead, n.d. Below the view is printed the story of the crime for which Escobar hung. A note at the Huntington Library says the execution took place August 10, 1855.

"Map of the Burnt District of San Francisco, Showing the Extent of the Fire. S. J. Gower, del."—letterhead, n.d. On the second fold of the letter paper is a key to buildings. This was the fire of May 4th, 1851.

"Map of the Mining Region of California. 1854. Drawn & compiled by Geo. H. Baker. Published by Barber & Baker, Sacramento, Cal. [Stamped in margin:] "Noisy Carriers, San Francisco. Entered . . . 1854"—small.

Stock certificate of the "Silver Peak Silver Mining Company"—small, n.d.

"Chinese Life!!! Dupont Street. San-Francisco, Cal. Beutler, delt. Fishbourne & Co. Lithogrs. S.F."—letterhead, n.d. Dupont Street, now Grant Avenue, was from the first the Chinatown of San Francisco. The street was laid out in 1839 by Jean Jacques Vioget (*q.v.*) as Calle de la Fundacion, under the order of the Spanish alcalde. It was renamed Dupont Street in honor of Captain Dupont, who commanded the sloop of war *Cyane* during the Mexican War. Dupont Circle in Washington, D. C., was also named for him when he later became an admiral. In the seventies the street was again renamed, this time for General Grant on the return from his trip around the PLATE 61 world. A newspaper item of 1932 says this last rechristening was "due to the unsavory record of that thoroughfare" as Dupont Street.

"San Francisco. View & Plan of the Burnt District, San Francisco, The Day After The Fire, 22nd June 1851. As Seen from the Corner of Washington & Montgomery Streets. Published by Cook & Le Count San Francisco 1851. From a Photograph by Gow. Fishbourne & Gows Lithog."—letterhead. Plan and references in two columns on lower half of the sheet. In the field of the print is the monogram G^s. This is the only print with their imprint that I have seen. The view was drawn on stone by Gow from a photograph that he made.

FRIEND & AUB — PHILADELPHIA

1854 80 Walnut Street

See "Map of the City of San Francisco," listed under Wagner & McGuigan.

GALLOWAY, W. T. — SAN FRANCISCO

Unknown 540 Clay Street

Galloway lithographed stock certificates, all small, n.d. (but near the 80's) for the following companies:

"Kentucky Mining Company"

"Maybelle Consolidated Mining Company"—this also appeared with the imprint of "Le Count Bros. S.F."

"Phil. Sheridan Gold & Silver Mining Company"—with a portrait of Sheridan.

The only other work of his I have seen is:

"Nevada county, Cal. Map of Nevada county, Cal. Compiled from the latest authentic sources, showing towns, villages, roads, streams, mining ditches etc. By J. G. Hartwell, county surveyor. 1880. San Francisco, lith. W. T. Galloway"—large, n.d. (c. 1880).

GARIBOLDI, G. G. — UNKNOWN

See Britton & Rey's "At the Play."

GIBBES, C. D. — UNKNOWN

See Quirot & Company's "Map of the Southern Mines. 1852."

GIBBES, J. T. UNKNOWN

See Britton & Rey's "Map Showing the Lands of the Tide Land Reclamation Company."

GIFFORD, CHARLES B. SAN FRANCISCO

See Gray & Gifford.

Gifford was the artist of G. T. Brown & Company's "San Francisco Looking South from North Point" and Nahl Brothers' "Mission Dolores."

Also see Nagel's "Camano Island," "First Annual Encampment," PLATE 79
"Hayes' Valley," "L.&.A.B. Burr's North Beach," "Lombard, North Point," PLATE 80
"San Francisco. Panoramic View," "Private Signals," "San Francisco Birds PLATE 81
Eye View," "Bay-View-Park Galop," and "U.S. Navy-Yard." PLATE 112

"North Beach, San Francisco From Russian Hill. C. B. Gifford, del. & Lith. Published by Thomas Hackett. 1864"—medium, n.d.

GIHON & BUTLER SAN FRANCISCO

In the San Francisco directory for 1852 and later there is a Thomas Gihon listed as an engraver. I do not know whether the Butler in the combination was Benjamin F. Butler.

One lithograph by them has turned up:

"The Plaza, Portsmouth Square, San Francisco; as it should and as it may be, according to the plan proposed by J. J. Chauviteau, Esqre. View taken from Kearney & Merchant streets. Gihon & Butler, Lith."—small, n.d. PLATE 62

GILDEMEISTER, CHARLES NEW YORK

Gildemeister was entered in the New York directories from 1850 to 1858 as an artist and architect. He did a number of views in and around New York, but the thing that interests us here is that he drew on stone the rare view of Monterey mentioned under D'Avignon (*q.v.*).

Also see Nagel & Weingaertner.

GILDERSLEAVE, CHARLES F. NEW YORK

Unknown 17 William Street

The only thing of his I have seen is "The Great Pictorial Romance of the Age or Steam Ship Commodores & United States Mail Contractors. Published by Chas. F. Gildersleave, 17 William St. N.Y."—small, n.d. This is a cartoon, showing a huge balloon labeled "California Mail Balloon via Nicaragua."

GLOVER, EDWIN UNKNOWN

Drew and published Justh, Quirot & Company's "Big Bar." Possibly the same as E. S. Glover, although the technique differs from that in the Bancroft prints.

GLOVER, E. S. PORTLAND, OREGON

Drew A. L. Bancroft & Company's "Birds Eye View of Santa Monica" and "View of Los Angeles from the East," and drew and published the same firm's "View of New Tacoma and Mount Rainer."

GODDARD, GEORGE HENRY

SACRAMENTO AND SAN FRANCISCO

Goddard was born in Bristol, England, in 1817 and went to California in 1850, settling in Sacramento. He was appointed a government surveyor, and in the course of his work produced many sketches and paintings of the country. Most of these were destroyed in the 1906 fire in San Francisco, where he moved in 1862 and lived until his death in 1906. One of the highest peaks in the Sierras was named after him, "In honor of a Civil Engineer who has done much to advance our knowledge of the geography of California."

PLATE 90 See Butler's "Grace Church"; Pollard & Britton's "Sonora January,
PLATE 89 1852," "Columbia, Stanislaus County, in 1852," "Columbia January, 1852";
Britton & Rey's "Birds Eye View of San Francisco, 1868," "Birds Eye View of the City of San Francisco, 1868," "Map of the State of California," "Southern Approach to Jamestown," and their letterheads "Sonora from the North, 1853," "Sonora, Jany. 1853," and "Springfield, Tuolumne County."

GOODRICH, LEVI SAN JOSÉ

The artist of Bancroft's "State House. 1849. San Jose" and Kuchel & Dresel's "San Jose, from City Hall. 1858."

GOUPIL, VIBERT & COMPANY, *ET AL.* NEW YORK

1849 289 Broadway

Goupil & Company:

1852 289 Broadway

1854 366 Broadway

1854–1857 M. Knoedler, 366 Broadway

The New York branch of this famous house, published, in conjunction with various lithographers, several views of American cities. Their most im-

DRAWN DEC. 20TH 1849 BY G.V. COOPER.

LITH. OF WM. ENDICOTT & CO. N. YORK.

A Hensley, Redding & Co
B Peoples Market
C T. McDowell & Co
D S. Taylor
E Round tent (S. Weeks)
F Montgomery & Warbour (Zinc Store)
G Myrick Nelson & Co
H The Gem
I Depacker Brothers
J Machonikins
K Oregon Bowling Saloon
L Colton Hoxie & Co

SACRAMENTO CITY CA.

FROM THE FOOT OF J. STREET,

SHOWING I. J. & K. STS WITH THE SIERRA NEVADA IN THE DISTANCE.

NEW YORK PUBLISHED BY STRINGER & TOWNSEND 222 BROADWAY.

Entered according to Act of Congress in the year 1850, by A. Brainerd in the Clerks Office of the District Court of the Southern Dist. N.Y.

M R. M. Jessup & Co
N Robert M. Folger & Amos Clift
O Barnes Hotel
P Van Dornes Hotel
Q Gondola
R H. R. Robinson & Co (Post Office)
S Empire
T Mansion House (formerly S. Brannan's Store)
U United States Hotel
V J. B. Starr & Co
W Jackson's Hotel
X Lenard & Co Express Office

60

A full color reproduction of this plate appears in the color section in this book.

Bentler del. Fishbourne & Co. Lithogr. S.F.

CHINESE LIFE!!!
Dupont Street. SAN-FRANCISCO, CAL.

61

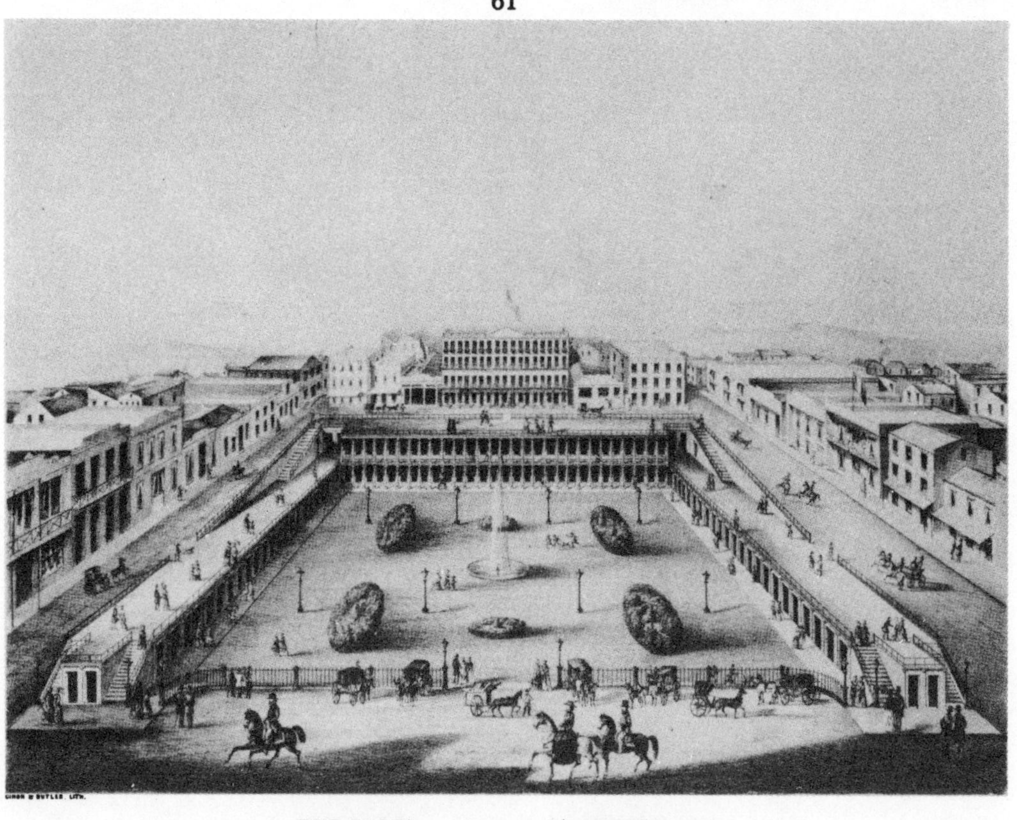

Simon & Butler, Lith.

THE PLAZA, Portsmouth Square, SAN FRANCISCO,
as it should and as it may be, according to the plan proposed by J. J. Chauviteau, Esqr.
View taken from Kearny and Merchant streets.

62

EARTH QUAKEY TIMES,
SAN FRANCISCO, OCT. 8, 1865.
SALOON
SHAVING
E. Jump
Entered according to an Act of Congress in the year 1865 by E. Jump in the Clerks Office of the District Court of the United States.

John Whitford

San Fco Lith Justh & Co Montgomery St. 253.

PLACERVILLE (HANGTOWN) EL DORADO Co. CAL

Published by Albert W. Bee, Placerville, 1851.

64

Lith. Justh & Co Broadway between Dupont & Stockton St. S.F.

VIEW OF MONTGOMERY ST. FROM SACRAMENTO WHARF THE MORNING AFTER THE GREAT FIRE.

Both of the pictures I send convey a poor idea of the fire or the ruins, as they are far more extensive than represented.

65

del after the nature by W. C. K.

THE FIRST TRIAL & EXECUTION IN S. FRANCISCO ON THE NIGHT OF 10th OF JUNE AT 2 O'CLOCK

John Jenkins, *a Sidney man, entered the store of M.r [illegible] Wharf in the evening of 10th of June & carried off a safe after he was captured he was brought to the corner of Sansome & Bush Str. where he was tried by a jury of the highest respectability, and condemned to be hung. The execution took place on the Plaza on the same night at 2 o'clock. Immediatly after sentence of death was passed upon him, he was asked if he had anything to say, he replied: No, I have nothing to say, only I should wish to have a cigar & brandy & water, which was given him.*

66

VIEW OF THE PLAZA OF SAN-FRANCISCO
On the 4th of July 1851.

Publ. & Lith. by Justh Quirot & C.o Calif. Corn. Montg. Sts.

67

Pub. by Serrell & Perkins 75 Nassau St. N.Y. — H. H. Kilton 90 Nassau St. N.Y.

A CALIFORNIA GOLD HUNTER MEETING A SETTLER.

KELLOGG & COMSTOCK, 150 FULTON ST NEW YORK & 136 MAIN ST. HARTFORD CONN.

ENSIGN & THAYER 33 EXCHANGE ST BUFFALO.

THE INDEPENDENT GOLD HUNTER ON HIS WAY TO CALIFORNIA.

I NEITHER BORROW NOR LEND

370

Printed by Britton & Rey.

On Stone by C. C. Kuchel, 118 Montgomery St. S.F.

DRAWN FROM NATURE, BY GRAFTON T. BROWN.

BRITTON & Co PRINT.

C.C. KUCHEL LITH. 176 CLAY ST S. FRANCISCO, CAL.

VIRGINIA CITY,

NEVADA TERRITORY

1861.

PUBLISHED BY GRAFTON T. BROWN

71

COLOR PLATES

LITH. & PUB. BY N. CURRIER,

Entered according to Act of Congress in the year 1849 by N. Currier, in the Clerk's office of the District Court of the Southern District of N.Y.

152 NASSAU ST. COR. OF SPRUCE N.Y.

THE WAY THEY COME FROM CALIFORNIA.

WORKS, POTRERO. OFFICE, 28 CALIFORNIA ST.

ARCTIC OIL WORKS.

SAN FRANCISCO, CAL.

Fort Yuma, Colorado River. California.

FROM NATURE & ON STONE BY T. GROB

NAGEL, FISHBOURNE & KUCHEL, 529 CLAY ST., SAN FRANCISCO, CAL

PUGET MILL Co's MILLS.

TEEKALET W.T.

W. C. Talbot & Co.

SAN FRANCISCO, CALIFORNIA.

15

LITH. BRITTON & REY S.F.

BRADLEY BARLOW.
J. L. SANDERSON.
JAMES W. PARKER.
CHAS C. HUNTLEY.
} PROPRIETORS.

CALIFORNIA & OREGON STAGE COMPANY.

E. F. HOOKER
SUPERINTENDENT.

CARRIES WELLS, FARGO & CO'S EXPRESS AND THE U.S. MAIL.

VIEW OF MOUNT SHASTA 14.442 FT ABOVE THE SEA - ON C.& O. STAGE ROUTE.

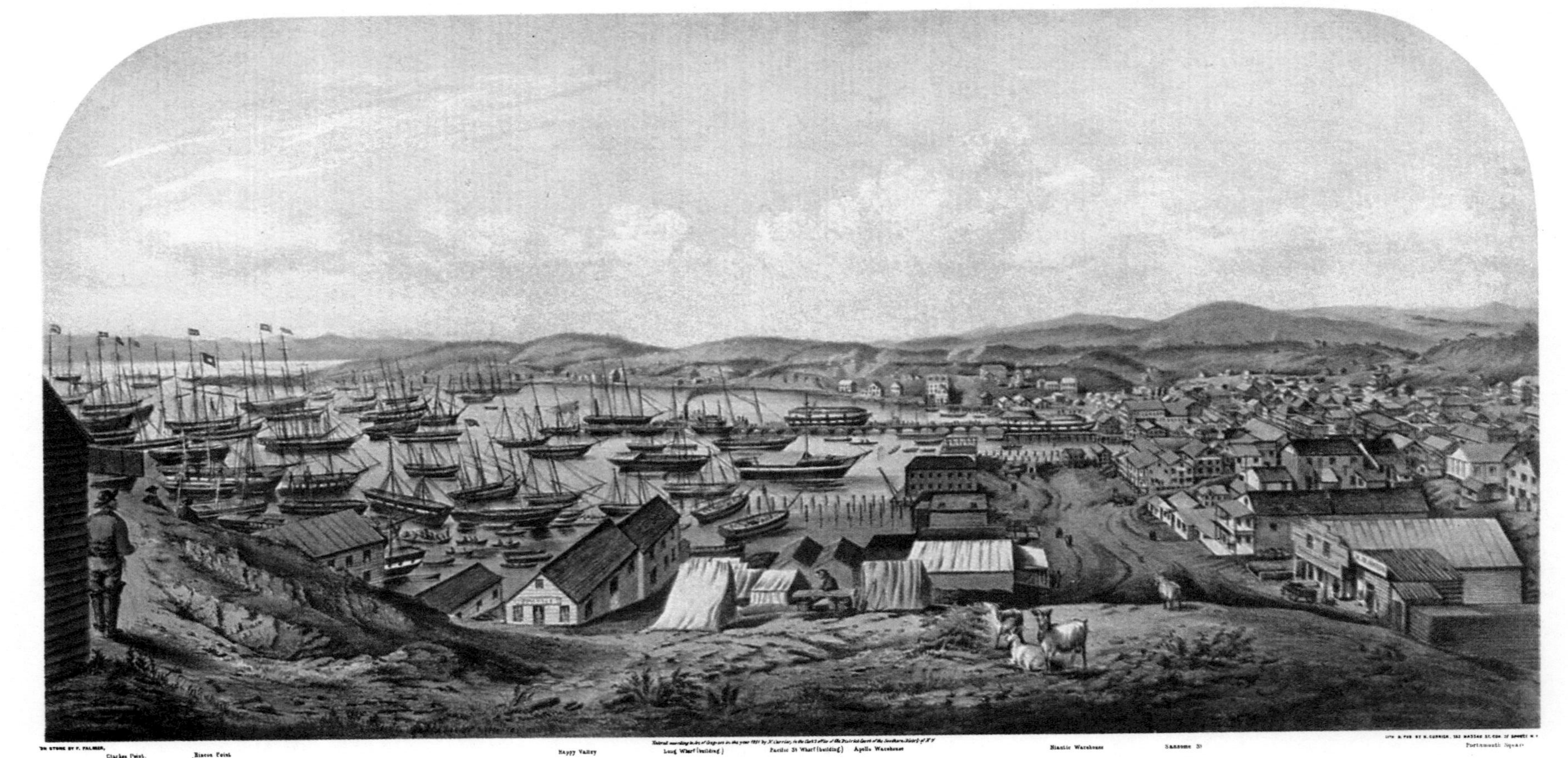

ON STONE BY F. PALMER,

Clarkes Point. Rincon Point. Happy Valley Long Wharf (building) Pacific St Wharf (building) Apollo Warehouse Niantic Warehouse Sansome St Portsmouth Square

VIEW OF SAN FRANCISCO, CALIFORNIA.

TAKEN FROM TELEGRAPH HILL, APRIL 1850, BY Wm B. M^c MURTRIE, DRAUGHTSMAN OF THE U. S. SURVEYING EXPEDITION.

Published by N. Currier. N.Y. Wm B. Mc Murtrie, San Francisco.

DRAWN DEC 20TH 1849 BY G.V COOPER.

LITH. OF WM. ENDICOTT & Co N. YORK.

SACRAMENTO CITY Ca.

FROM THE FOOT OF J. STREET,

SHOWING I. J. & K. STs WITH THE SIERRA NEVADA IN THE DISTANCE.

A Hensley, Redding & Co
B Peoples Market
C T. Mc Dowell & Co
D S. Taylor
E Round tent (S. Weeks)
F Montgomery & Warbour (Zinc Store)
G Myrick, Nelson & Co
H The Gem
I Desperker Brothers
J Machonikins
K Oregon Bowling Saloon
L Colton Hoxie & Co

M R. M. Jessup & Co
N Robert M. Folger & Amos Clift
O Barnes Hotel
P Van Dornes' Hotel
Q Gondola
R H. R. Robinson & Co (Post Office)
S Empire
T Mansion House (formerly S. Brannan's Store)
U United States Hotel
V J. B. Starr & Co
W Jackson's Hotel
X Lasselle & Co Express Office

NEW YORK PUBLISHED BY STRINGER & TOWNSEND 222 BROADWAY.

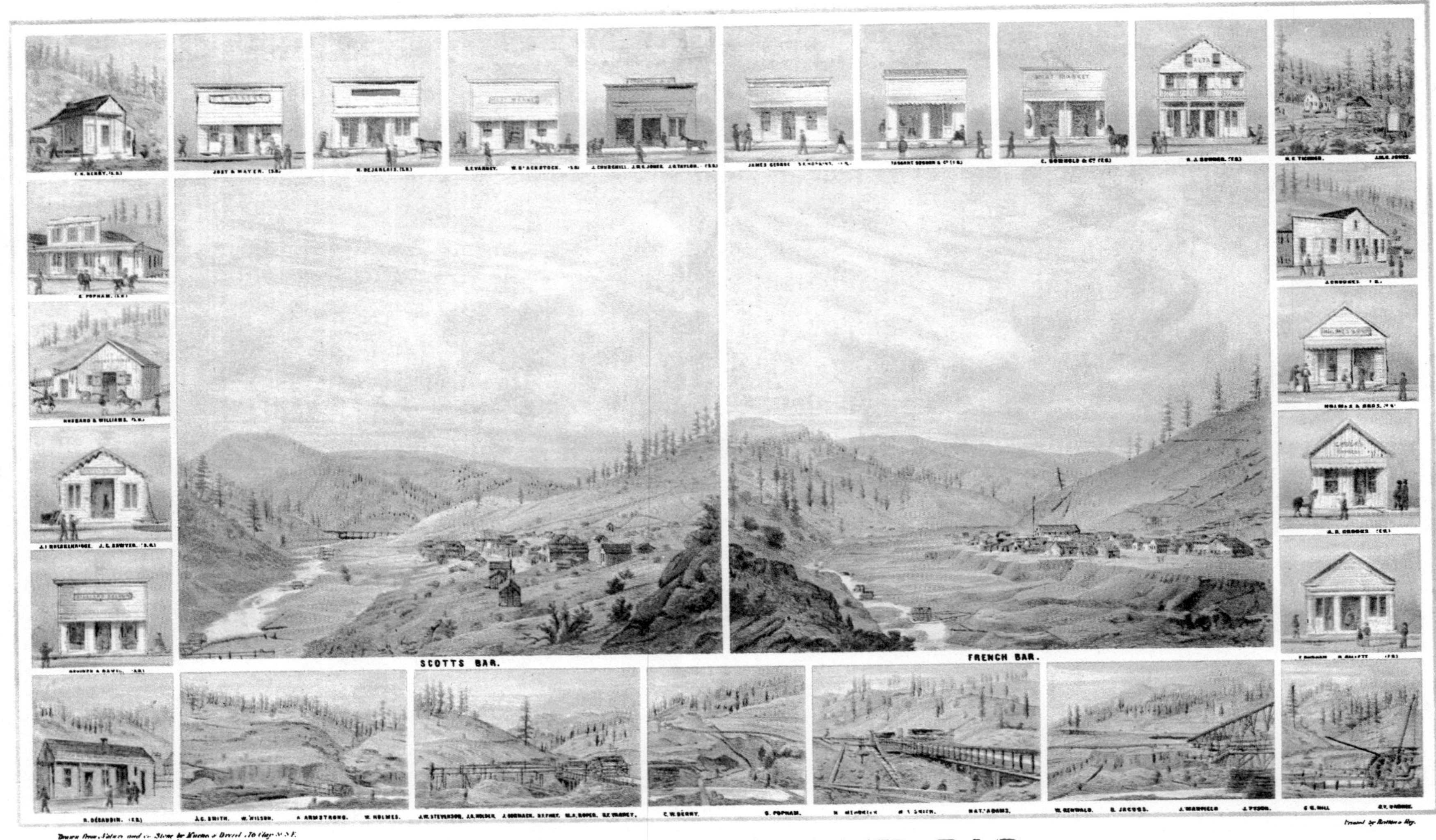

SCOTTS BAR AND FRENCH BAR,

ON SCOTTS RIVER, SISKIYOU COUNTY, CALIFORNIA.

1856

Published by J. M C. Jones.

PRIVATE SIGNALS
OF THE MERCHANTS OF NEW YORK AND SAN FRANCISCO.
RESPECTFULLY DEDICATED TO THE MERCHANTS OF SAN FRANCISCO BY CHARLES B. GIFFORD.

1. Am. Sh. Huntress 2 Br. B Amnah 3. Dan. B. Neptunus 4 Fr B Stanaul 5 Fr Sh. Chateaubriand 6 Mr Sh Victoria 7 Am. Sh. Forrester 8 Am. B Oberon 9 Am. B Superior
10 Am. Sh. Philadelphia burnt June 24th 11 Ch. B Carmen 12 Haw B Mary Frances 13 Am. Sh. Edwin 14 Fr Sh. Ronald 15 Dan Sh. Addie 16 Am. Sh. Grey Eagle
17 Br B John Paton 18 Am B Col. Fremont 19 Ch Sh Virginia 20 Am. Sh. Sea Queen 21 Ch B Maria Louisa 22 Ch B Romano.

SAN-FRANCISCO

1849.

DRAWN ON THE SPOT BY HENRY FIRKS, FOR

W. H. JONES, ESQ.

OF SAN-FRANCISCO U.C.

23 Am. Sh. Thomas 24 Am B Quito 25 Am B Louisiana 26 Am Sh Greyhound 27 Ch. Sh. California Dorado 28 Am. Steamer Panama 29 Am Br Col. Benton.
30 Am. Sh. Mass. Anecta 31 Am B Lucy Penniman 32 Fr B Limousine 33 Ch. Sh. Gen. Ferrias 34 Am Schoon. Honolulu 35 Fr B Olympe 36 Am. Sh. Huber
37 Am. Steamer Oregon 38 U.S.S Warren 39 U.S.S Southampton 40 Quarter P Inveneble 41 H B M Inconstant 42 Launch for Stockton (Emily & Jane) 43 Customhouse 44 Golden Gate 45 Parker Hotel. Isl.d Yerba Buena.

LITH OF SARONY & MAJOR NEW YORK

A VIEW OF SUTTER'S MILL & CULLOMA VALLEY.

ON THE SOUTH FORK OF THE AMERICAN LINE, ALTA CALIFORNIA

Respectfully dedicated to Capt. John A. Sutter,

by his obedient Servant John T. Little

SUTTER'S FORT, SACRAMENTO, CALIFORNIA 1847.

portant work was, of course, the series of beautiful early American sporting scenes. For fuller mention of them, see *America on Stone*.

The only prints of theirs which concern our story in this book are Sarony & Major's "San Francisco Upper California in January 1849," which Goupil, Vibert & Company published, and Lemercier's large view of San Francisco published by M. Knoedler & Company.

GOW — SAN FRANCISCO

See Fishbourne & Gow.

GOWER, S. J. — SAN FRANCISCO

Drew Fishbourne's "Map of the Burnt District."

In *America on Stone* as J. S. Gower.

GRAHAM, CURTIS B. — NEW YORK AND WASHINGTON

1836–1838	7 John Street & 119 Fulton Street
1838–1839	119 Fulton Street
1839–1841	90 Nassau Street
Unknown	Washington, D. C.

California lithographs from Graham are:

"Official map of San Francisco, compiled from the field notes of the official re-survey made by William M. Eddy. 1849. S. W. Higgins draftn. Copied by P. M. McGill. Washington, C. B. Graham, lith. (1849)"—large.

"San Diego from the Old Fort. C. B. Graham Lith."—small, n.d.

The following four maps are from "A Series Of Charts, with Sailing Directions, State of California. By Cadwalader Ringgold, Commander U. S. Navy. Washington, 1852":

"Chart of Suisun & Vallejo bays with the confluence of the rivers Sacramento and San Joaquin, California, by Cadwalader Ringgold, 1850. Constructed, projected and drawn by Fred. D. Stuart. Washington, C. B. Graham, (1851)"—large.

"Chart of the bay of San Pablo straits of Carquines and part of the bay of San Francisco, California, by Cadwalader Ringgold, 1850. Projected, constructed & drawn by Fred. D. Stuart. Washington, C. B. Graham, (1851)"—large.

"Chart of the Farallones and entrance to the bay of San Francisco, California, by Cadwalader Ringgold, assisted by Simon F. Blunt, 1850. Constructed, projected and drawn by Fred. D. Stuart. Washington, C. B. Graham, (1851)"—large.

"Sacramento river, Cal. Chart of the Sacramento river from Suisun city to the American river, California, by Cadwalader Ringgold, 1850. Projected, constructed & drawn by Fred D. Stuart. Washington, C. B. Graham, (1851)"—large.

GRAY, MATTHIAS — SAN FRANCISCO

Unknown	609 & 613 Clay Street
c.1862	613 Clay Street
1869	621 & 623 Clay Street

Published Britton & Rey's "New Express Galop" and "Under the Snow"; and Nahl's "Abraham's Daughter" and "An Hour at the Cliff," all music sheets.

GRAY & GIFFORD — SAN FRANCISCO

I have seen but three lithographs by this firm:

"Birds Eye View of the Bay of San Francisco and Adjacent Country. Designed, lithographed and published by W. Vallance Gray & C. B. Gifford, 645 Market Street, S.F. Entered . . . 1869"—medium, with two columns of references.

"Birds Eye View of the City & County of San Francisco, 1868. Published by A. L. Bancroft & Company, 721 Market Street, San Francisco. W. V. Gray & C. B. Gifford, delt. & lith. Entered . . . 1868"—medium, with a separately printed key. This view was also issued as of 1869 and of 1872, both with the copyright date of 1868.

"Birds Eye View of the City of San Jose, California. Designed and Lithographed by W. Vallance Gray and C. B. Gifford. L. Nagel, Print. Published by George H. Hare, San Jose, 1869"—large, n.d.

GROB, TRAUTMAN — SAN FRANCISCO

1856–1857	artist, Montgomery & Clay streets
1858	teacher of drawing, Montgomery & California Streets
Later	unknown

Grob was the artist of F. Kuhl's "Execution of James P. Casey & Charles Cora"; Nagel's "First Annual Encampment"; and Nagel, Fishbourne & Kuchel's "Puget Mill Co's Mills." PLATE 77 PLATE 15

HACKETT, THOMAS UNKNOWN

Publisher of Gifford's "North Beach."

HACKETT, W. H. UNKNOWN

See Britton & Rey's "St. Louis, Sears Diggings, Sierra Co."

HAEHNLENS, J. PHILADELPHIA

This is probably the "Jacob Haehlen" listed in *America on Stone*.

The only California print of his I have seen is "Big Oak Flat, Tuolumne County, California. J. Haehnlen's Lith. Philada. Entered . . . 1858"—small.

HAMERTON, R. J. LONDON

See Metchim & Company.

HANHART, M. & N. LONDON

"San Francisco, 1851. View of the Town and Harbour of San Francisco, California. From the Signal Hill. Drawn on stone by W. Boosey from a sketch by Capt. Collinson, R.E. M. & N. Hanhart, lith. printers, London. Published Nov. 12, 1851, by Ackermann & Co., 96 Strand"—large.

There is also a Hanhart 1851 view of San Francisco, "Marryat delt. July 1st 1851"—large. They are among the most important and interesting of the early views.

They also lithographed the plates in "Three Years in California," by J. D. Borthwick (*q.v.*).

HARRISON, WILLIAM P. SAN FRANCISCO

"Masonic Temple March. Respectfully dedicated to the Masons of California. Published by Wm. P. Harrison, San Francisco. Entered . . . 1863 by Wm. P. Harrison . . . California"—music sheet. Title taken from an imperfect copy which lacked the lithographer's name.

HARTMAN, J. W. SAN FRANCISCO

This is very possibly the Hartman of Zakreski & Hartman (*q.v.*). I have seen but one lithograph by Hartman alone:

"Map of Northern California. Exhibiting a reliable view of the Rich Gold Region. By N. Schofield, C. E. Lith. by J. W. Hartman, San Francisco. Entered . . . 1851"—medium.

HASKELL & ALLEN BOSTON

1871–1875 61 Hanover Street
Unknown 14 Hanover Street

Haskell & Allen produced a considerable volume of lithographs, and while the general level was not high, some were very important. Their work is listed, and some of their prints reproduced, in *America on Stone*.

Two California views are: "California Scenery"—small, n.d., and "Union Pacific Rail Road. Entered . . . 1872"—large. The first is a view of the old Cliff House, San Francisco. General William B. Parsons, who lent me the copy reproduced in *America on Stone*, considered the second one of the best of all the Western lithographs, and I agree with him.

HATCH (A. J.) & COMPANY SAN FRANCISCO

See Britton & Rey's "Los Angeles, Cal." and "View of Santa Cruz."

HEALY, L. B. UNKNOWN

PLATE 95 Drew Quirot & Company's "View of Shasta City."

HEAP, GWINN HARRIS UNKNOWN

Author and artist of the plates in "Central Route To The Pacific," listed under Duval.

HILDEBRANDT, E. UNKNOWN

"San Francisco. View Looking up California Street from Montgomery, showing the First Congregational Church, Knob Hill, St. Mary's Cathedral and the Parrott Building. In the field of the print, San Francisco,—E. Hildebrandt"—small, n.d. (c.1862). This attractive and rare view, printed in colors, was probably made abroad. Whether Hildebrandt was the artist or lithographer is unknown. The print bears a striking resemblance to the *vue d'optique* print of the same location by Winckelmann & Söhne of Berlin.

HOEN (A.) & COMPANY BALTIMORE

An historical outline of this firm is given in *America on Stone*. The only lithographs of theirs I have seen pertaining to California are the plates in "Report Of A Geological Reconnaissance In California: Made in Connection with the Expedition to Survey Routes in California, to Connect with the Surveys of Routes for a Railroad from the Mississippi River to the Pacific Ocean, under the Command of Lieut. R. S. Williamson, Corps Top. Eng'rs, in 1853. By William P. Blake, Geologist and Mineralogist of the Expedition. New York: H. Bailliere, 290 Broadway":

"Sierra Nevada From The Four Creeks. Drawn by W. P. Blake. (1853)"—small.

"Ravines In The Bed Of The Ancient Lake. From a sketch by Chs. Koppel. (1853)"—small.

"Rounded Hills, Tertiary, (Between Ocoya Creek and Ponsuncula River) From a sketch by Chs. Koppel. (1853)"—small.

"Valley In The Slope Of The Great Basin, Leading from the Tejon Pass. From a sketch by Chs. Koppel. (1853)"—small.

HOLDERTINE ST. LOUIS

Signed on the stone the "Overland Mail Company" of Woodward, Tiernan & Hale. PLATE 108

HOLTZMANN, F. COLUMBIA, CALIFORNIA

The artist and publisher of Kuchel & Dresel's "Views of the New Ditch of the Columbia & Stanislaus River Water Co." PLATE 76

HORTON, MRS. M. N. UNKNOWN

Mrs. Horton is the only woman we have run across in our search for the California lithograph. She sketched Cooke & Le Count's "Downieville, Sierra County, Cal."

HOWELL SAN FRANCISCO

" 'Magnolia.' Savannah and Florida Packet," by Bard, lithographed by Howell, San Francisco—large, n.d., is the only thing of his I have seen.

HUTCHINGS, C. LIVERPOOL

"San Francisco, California, from the Bay, C. Hutchings, Liverpool"—medium, n.d.

This is not the Hutchings of Hutchings & Rosenfield.

HUTCHINGS & ROSENFIELD SAN FRANCISCO

See A. Rosenfield.

Publishers of Kuchel & Dresel's "Yo-Semite Falls . . . 1855" and "Nahl Brothers' "General View of the Great Yo-Semite Valley . . . 1859."

The Kuchel & Dresel view was reproduced in *America on Stone*.

IBBOTSON, A. PHILADELPHIA

PLATE 102 Drew on stone for T. Sinclair the important view, "San Francisco, 1849." See Firks.

Ibbotson did other work for Sinclair, which is mentioned in *America on Stone*.

JANNIN PARIS

"View of San Francisco. Original by Lopez. Litho. of Jannin. Gallè, Paris"—large, n.d. This is one of the rare and early views of San Francisco. In the foreground a group of Mexicans. In the middle distance, the city, with barely two hundred houses and tents. In the bay, many sailing vessels and two side-wheel steamers. The print was copied, in smaller form, by Le Breton.

JONES, WILLIAM H. SAN FRANCISCO

William H. Jones was listed in the San Francisco directories from 1850 to 1853 as an auctioneer, and he merits inclusion in this volume for one achieve-
PLATE 102 ment. It was for him that the well-known 1849 view of San Francisco was drawn by Henry Firks (*q.v.*). This fine, early view is without doubt one of the most lithographed of all the California views. To date it has turned up as issued by six different firms: Thomas Sinclair, G. & W. Endicott, Fishbourne, Schmidt, Snow & Company, and G. T. Brown & Company. It would not be surprising to find that it was also done by others.

JUDELS, A. AMSTERDAM

"Sacremento Rivier Vraar Het Grootste Bekende Stuk Goud Gevondenis, Californie, [etc.]"—(1850), small.

"Stad en baaij S.Francisco, men ziet het binnen kommen van een transport stofgoud"—(1850), small.

"De Goudzoekers Colonie aan de St. Joachim Rivier, Californie"—(1850), small.

"Het nitbaggeren van het goudzand, het wasschen, en drogen van hetzelve, aan de St. Joachim Rivier Colonie"—(1850), small.

JUMP, EDWARD — SAN FRANCISCO

Jump was an excellent caricaturist. His specialty was to do a whole crowd in one lithograph. His mass grouping was poor, but his individual figures were humorously conceived and well drawn. He came to San Francisco in the early sixties and got his start in graphic work making labels for whisky bottles. In 1868 he was in Washington where he was very successful, often making as much as five hundred dollars a week doing portrait work. In the early seventies he was in St. Louis. Between the Washington and St. Louis periods he worked for *Leslie's* in New York and made cartoons for "The Budget of Fun" and "Wild Oats." Jump was of French extraction. While in St. Louis he married a member of a visiting French opera company. Jump worked at one time for B. F. Butler (*q.v.*).

The following lithographs were all signed on the stone "E. Jump," with no information as to lithographer or publisher:

"Earth Quakey Times, San Francisco, Oct. 8, 1865. Entered . . . 1865"— medium. A cartoon. PLATE 63

"Grand Municipal Turn 'em-out. 1866"—medium. A political caricature, with men astride mules, tilting in an arena.

"The Last Jump"—small, n.d. A self-portrait of Jump descending in a balloon. (Jump committed suicide, by what means I do not know.)

"The Law and the Profits"—small, n.d. A courtroom scene, with caricatures.

"San Francisco at the Fair"—medium, n.d. Caricatures of prominent San Franciscans.

"Spring Races"—small, n.d. Cartoon of a mayoralty race in San Francisco.

See also Nagel's "Steamer Day in San Francisco." PLATE 82

1851	Justh & Company, Broadway Street and 253 Montgomery Street
1851	Justh, Quirot & Company, corner California & Montgomery Streets
1851–1852	Quirot & Company, California & Montgomery Streets
1852–1853	Quirot & Company, 136 California Street; also C. Quirot, same address

Justh, Quirot, *et al.*, were early on the scene, and their realization of the "news value" of lithography is obvious. The mines, the growing city of San Francisco, the Vigilance Committee, the fires—all are vividly portrayed by their work.

Little enough of it has survived. They existed in those rather wild early San Francisco days when the very events they pictured were at destructive height, and there is little doubt that most of their stock was destroyed, as was Britton & Rey's in the later 1906 catastrophe. In the 1850's, fire after fire razed parts of the flimsily built young city; in one of them, it has been said, a river of molten type ran down to the Bay from a burning printer's establishment. The wonder is that we have even this little by which to know any of the pioneer California lithographers.

A number of lithographs appear, sometimes with a Quirot imprint, sometimes with Britton & Rey's. Many of these identical prints have been so noted in the listing, and the collector will no doubt run across many more. In production of letterheads, Justh, Quirot, *et al.*, were exceeded only by Britton & Rey.

Justh & Company:

"A Complete Map of the Feather & Yuba Rivers, with towns, ranches, diggings, roads, distances. . . . Compiled from the recent Surveys of Mr. Milleson and R. Adams. Insert views of The Marysville Bookstore, News Emporium, City Drug Store and Express Building. Published by R. A. Eddy, Marysville, 1851. Entered . . . 1851"—medium. One of the earliest detailed maps of the mining district of Central California.

"The Morning After the Great Fire of May 4th. Taken from the corner of Broadway & Sansome Sts. Lith. & Pub. by Justh & Co., Broadway St. Sn Francisco"—small, n.d.

"Placerville (Hangtown) El Dorado Coy. Cal. Published by Albert W. Bee, Placerville, 1851. John Whitford. San Fco. Lith. Justh & Co. Montgomery St. 253"—small, n.d. An explanation of its name appears on a woodcut view of Placerville: "It was first settled in 1849. . . . For a long time it was known far and wide by the euphonious name of Hangtown, an appellation bestowed upon it because of the very many executions there under the code of Judge Lynch. In 1850, it received its present name, and under a respectable cognomen has attained a respectable position." PLATE 64

"View of Montgomery Street from Sacramento Wharf the Morning After the Great Fire"—letterhead, n.d. Written in ink on margin: "Both of the pictures I send convey a poor idea of the fire or the ruins, as they are *far more* extensive than represented." PLATE 65

Justh, Quirot & Company:

"Adventures of The Firm of Brown & Jingo. San Francisco, Lithographed by Justh & Quirot, Jackson St. Published and sold by Cooke & LeCount. (1851)."—small. Illustrated with thirty humorous caricatures.

"Big Bar—Middle Fork. Drawn & Published by Edwin Glover"—medium, n.d.

"Execution of Jose Forner, Dec. 10, 1852, On Russian Hill, San Francisco, for the Murder of Jose Rodrigues"—letterhead, n.d. The Huntington Library catalog notes this as "the first capital execution under sentence of a lawful tribunal in the County of San Francisco."

"Fire in San Francisco. In the night from the 3d–4th May, 1851"—letterhead, n.d.

"The First Trial & Execution in S. Francisco on the Night of 10th of June at 2 o'clock. del. after the nature by W. C. K."—letterhead, n.d. Under the view appears the following text: "John Jenkins, a Sidney man, entered the store of Mr. Van long Wharf, in the evening of 10th June & carried off a sale after he was captured, he was brought to the corner of Sansome & Bush Sts., where he was tried by a jury of the highest respectability, and condemned to be hung. The execution took place on the Plaza on the same night at two o'clock. Immediately after the sentence of death was passed upon him, he was asked if he had anything to say, he replied: No, I have nothing to say, only I should wish to have a cigar & brandy & water, which was given him." PLATE 66

"James Stuart Hung by the Vigilance Committee on Market Street Wharf, on the 11th of July, 1851. View taken from the Storeship Byron, Foot of Market Street Wharf, San-Francisco"—letterhead, n.d.

Business letterhead of Justh, Quirot & Company

"Tremendous Excitement! Samuel Whittaker and Robert McKenzie rescued from the authorities and hung by the Vigilance Committee on Sunday, August 24th, at 3 o'clock P.M. in the presence of Fifteen Thousand People" —letterhead, n.d. The copy of this letterhead in the Templeton Crocker Collection at the California Historical Society has the following letter:

San Francisco
Aug 30 / 51

Dear Wife

This day closes the year since I arrived at San Francisco and before a second year shall have expired I hope to be with you at our old residence in Lower 4th Street at what time I shall be able to leave here / if my life is spared / depends on my success in business during the twelve months that I have been here I have cleared about one hundred dollars per month the hundred dollars I send with this will make but eleven hundred but if I had all that is due me I could add the other hundred

The job I now have on hand I think will pay me two or three hundred for the next month When you get the money for the enclosed bill of One hundred and fifty dollars you must Pay Mrs James Newbanks fifty dollars and take a receipt for it Jim has been at work for me during the last four weeks at seven dollars per day I have paid him but 10 or 12 dollars a week in order to keep back enough to send some to his wife as I expect to employ him some weeks longer perhaps I may send her some more the same way Some folks have thought that I did not pay them well when I was at home but I think Newbanks's money is safer in my hands than in his own anyplace

I owe Old Mr Dayton two or three dollars when he calls on you for it I wish you to pay it Sammy Haslett did hold a note against me if he still has it I would like for you to pay him 10 or 15 dollars I owe James Reed I think about a dollar & a half send for him and if he says that is the amount pay him the residue or balance of the money you had better keep for your own use during winter Once more I will caution you not to pay any thing to any person / except Jimmy Reed / unless they present a note and sign a receipt for the same on the back of the note or the whole note is paid and you take it I think there is some folks about New Albany that say I owe them that I do not owe one cent to Should it be necessary for you to pay any more money for street improvements taxes or the like than you can well spare you need not be afraid to borrow some for the purpose as I will probably be able to send you some more in six or eight weeks from this time Mr Rogers and the Daytons are in town on their way home I have bought another cane for Father which Mr Rogers undertakes to deliver to him It was made in China and required ten days labour of a Chinaman to cut the figures on it he was paid ten cents a day for his labour and I bought the cane here for two dollars

Your letter of the 2d July came to hand last mail the 19th Aug that of the 23 June which you supposed would not come by the mail you intended it should did come as designed I am glad you begin to think of taking my advice to return to the house on Lower 4th St and dont put it off till wet fall weather as I believe you would enjoy better health there than on Spring Street Once more I want to caution you to take better care of yourself and not confine yourself so much to work as you have been doing go out often stir around among your friends and take Eleanor with you and your health will be improved by it It would be poor satisfaction for me to return home after an absence of two years or more and find you broken down by hard work I take work in such a way as not to hurt me and want you to do the same Again I will remind Susan that she should do something to cure herself of the scrofula I believe the pokeberry medicine if persevered in six or eight months will effect a cure I omitted to mention in its proper place that I want you to keep a regular account of all you pay on old debts so that I can have it when I return

Runkle is still at Stockton Mr Cowan Newbanks and Charles Tuley are at work here Dunsan & Sabin have just arrived with their schooner on their first trip from Sacramento and have done tolerable well I have not heard from William since my last It is yet uncertain what vessel Rogers and the Daytons will go in whether a ship or steamer I do not know whether I will put up Bragdons boat or not but I think it is likely I will not she has not yet arrived

I have sent you some account of the Vigilance Committee and now I send you a view of some of their doings From information obtained from the many different prisoners they have had it was evident that Whittaker and McKenzie were part of the gang of desparadoes who had committed the many murders and robberies in the city during the past year They were arrested at Sacramento by the Committee tried and condemned to be hung on Wednesday the 20th About 3 o'clock in the morning the Governor Sheriff Mayor and Marshall and a posse of Police officers came suddenly on the guard at the Committee room and took the two men from them and hurried them off to the county jail On Sunday last 36 of the committee came as suddenly upon the jail guard retook the Prisoners and had them hanging by the neck in front of their room ¾ of a mile from the prison in 21 minutes from the time of leaving there I saw it and think six or seven thousand people were present collected in that short space of time probably 15 thousand persons may have seen them while hanging as crowds were continually coming and going This is a very correct view of the scene although but a small portion of the crowd is represented large numbers myself among them being on the opposite side of the street on piles of lumber buildings wharves and in boats on the water

Directly where the horses are seen is the place that John W Tuley met with the accident that caused his death The railroad is not shown in the view The Street is a plank one over the water The view in the distance is telegraph hill with the telegraph house and flagstaff and windmill

The Committee room is on Battery Street between Pine & California by consulting the map you can perceive it is close to where I live Stuart was hung by the Committee on Market Street wharf I have lately received a letter from McElroy he was just recovered from a spell of sickness He wished to be remembered to you and I with my sincere hopes for the happiness of you all

remain yours for ever

(Signature illegible)

P.S. I want the children to write to me and dont forget to send your likeness It is reported that the committee have three prisoners to hang Send for Mrs Newbanks to come to the house

"View of Downieville, Forks of the North Yuba River. Del. W. H. O'Grady. Published and Sold by Samuel W. Langton of Langton's Express Downieville, California."—letterhead, n.d. Reproduced in *America on Stone* as Plate 80.

"View of the Conflagration of Marysville, on the night of August 30th, 1851. Three entire squares consumed. Loss estimated $500,000. Published by R. A. Eddy, Stationers Warehouse, Marysville, Cala."—small, n.d.

"View of the Fire in San Francisco, May 3d, 1851"—small, n.d.

"View of The Golden Gate and North Beach, from the Telegraph"—(1852), small.

"View of the Last Great Conflagration in San Francisco on the 22nd of June, 1851"—letterhead, n.d.

"View of the Plaza of San-Francisco On the 4th of July 1851"—small, n.d. PLATE 67
This is identical with the Quirot & Company letterhead of the same title, except that on this one "F.C.Buttler Lithographer" appears over Atwill & Company's store, where on the Quirot view "Post Office" replaces the Butler sign. Who F. C. Buttler was, I do not know, none of his work having been found.

Quirot & Company:

"The California Pioneers a Song respectfully inscribed to Mrs. J. Emerson PLATE 93
Sweetser. Words & Music by Dr. M. A. Richter. Lith & del. by Quirot & Co., cornr. Califa. & Montgomery Sts. S-F. Published & Sold by Atwill & Co. in San-Francisco. N.B. The First Piece of Music Pubd. in Cala. Entered . . . 1852"—music sheet. Cover contains a large and spirited lithograph of pioneers crossing the Sierra.

"City Hall, San-Francisco, Cal."—letterhead, n.d. Also issued by Quirot & Company as "Jenny Lind Theatre."

"A Company of prospecting miners"—letterhead, n.d. PLATE 92

"Interior View of Merchants Exchange, San Francisco, Cal. As Draperied on PLATE 94
the occasion of the Obsequies of the Hon. Henry Clay. Sweeny & Baugh, Proprietors. Entered . . . 1852"—medium. This was also issued showing the Exchange without the funereal draperies. On the right-hand wall of the room can be seen a picture of a bridge, the setting of which would indicate that as early as 1852 San Francisco dreamed of bridging the Golden Gate.

The "Annals of San Francisco," published in 1854, describes the Merchants' Exchange as being established by Sweeny & Baugh, supported by subscription, and "in the spacious rooms of which are always to be found the latest papers from all parts of the world." Sweeny & Baugh, in 1849, had built both the inner and outer telegraph stations, and in 1853 opened the first electric telegraph between Point Lobos and San Francisco.

"Jenny Lind Theatre, San-Francisco"—letterhead, n.d. See "City Hall" above.

"Map of San Francisco. Entered . . . 1852"—small.

"Map of San-Francisco, California"—letterhead, n.d.

"Map of the Southern Mines. By C. D. Gibbes. 1852"—small, n.d.

"Mariposa City"—letterhead, n.d.

"Miners at Work with Long Toms"—letterhead, n.d.

"Mission Dolores"—letterhead, n.d.

"Placerville"—letterhead, n.d.

"San Francisco Upper California, in November 1851. Engraved by C. Quirot" —letterhead, n.d., with view running across two folds. This is identical with Britton & Rey's letterhead, "San Francisco Upper California."

"The Times!!!"—letterhead, n.d. Shows several members of the Vigilance Committee arresting a man who was about to start a fire. Two city officials look on, one saying, "I say Judge, these Vigilant Bhoys take all the business out of our hands." The other replies, "Yes, Othello's occupation's gone—I am off to the diggings." A scarce letterhead.

"View of Agua Fria Town"—letterhead, n.d.

"View of Agua Fria Valley. C. Riehn, del."—letterhead, n.d.

"View of Mokelumne Hill. Borthwick, del."—small, n.d.

PLATE 95 "View of Shasta City. L. B. Healy, del. Published by Geo. W. King, Shasta"—small, n.d.

"View of the Fire in Sacramento City on the night of 2d & 3d of November 1852, taken from the levee. Loss Ten Millions of Dollars!!!"—letterhead, n.d.

"View of the Plaza of San-Francisco, on the Fourth of July 1851"—letterhead, n.d. See Justh, Quirot & Company's view of the same title.

KELLER, F. UNKNOWN

See F. Korbel & Brothers' certificate of the "Society of California Pioneers," and Britton & Rey's "Haverley's Theatre."

The only other things of his that have turned up are:

"Hospital of the German Benevolent Society, San Francisco. F. Keller, del."—medium, n.d.

"Wreck of The Ship 'Frank Jones' Off Fort Point, S. F. F. Keller. Litho."—small, n.d.

Keller also drew caricatures for the *Wasp.*

KELLOGGS, THE, *ET AL.* HARTFORD, NEW YORK, AND BUFFALO

Any tabulation of the addresses of this group would be more confusing than helpful, but the following rough outline may be of some use: D. W. Kellogg & Co. seems to have been the pioneer, from about 1833 to 1842, at 110 Main Street, Hartford. About 1843 he is joined by E. B. and E. C. Kellogg at 136 Main Street, which remains the headquarters until 1852. Meanwhile they have had an office with Horace Thayer, 1846–1847, at 144 Fulton Street, New York, and with J. G. Comstock, 1849–1852, at 150 and 136 Fulton Street, New York. About 1852 the Comstock connection is terminated, the New York office moved to 87 Fulton Street, and the Hartford office to 73 Main Street. The New York office at 87 Fulton Street is kept up until about 1860, and the Hartford office, after a year, 1856–1857, at 128 Main Street, runs on into the sixties at 245 Main Street. Meanwhile, J. G. Kellogg has had a separate office, 1844–1855 (with an interval, 1848, at 9 Central Row, Hartford, and a partnership, 1845, with Samuel Hanmer, Jr.) at 1 Central Row, Hartford, and 1856 on into the sixties at 258 Main Street. During the Thayer and Comstock connections, D. Needham was the Buffalo agent, at 232 Main Street and 12 Exchange Street, and Horace Thayer or Ensign, Thayer & Co. also appear in the alliance, at 127 Main Street, Buffalo. Another combination, with Frank Bulkeley, who married into the family, is located at Hartford, and seems to have occurred in the sixties. I have seen a print published by Willis Thrall of Hartford. Also, Charles E. Kellogg, the son of E. B. Kellogg, appears in the business about 1860. This should enable collectors to date roughly their undated but addressed Kellogg prints.

The Kelloggs were the only group of whom it is at all possible to say that they were for a time near-rivals of Currier & Ives, but they completely lacked the news sense of the Curriers. There are a few large folios; there is no outstanding print of great merit—just a long record of places and events done in craftsmanship above the average. Their work is fully described in *America on Stone.*

It would seem that the Kelloggs took small interest in the Gold Rush in California, for but few of their lithographs having anything to do with it have turned up. Three are from "Kelloggs & Comstock," and as this particular combination existed only from 1849 to 1852, it would make all three prints early in our story.

"California Gold Diggers. Mining Operations on the Western shore of the Sacramento River"—small, n.d. This particular lithograph, for some reason, has been reproduced more often in books than almost any other California print I know.

"The Gold Seeker. 195"—small, n.d. A cartoon of the "Independent Gold Hunter" type.

PLATE 69 "Independent Gold Hunter on His Way to California. I neither borrow nor lend"—small, n.d. This is probably a steal from N. Currier's of the same title (*q.v.*), with which it is identical. See also H. R. Robinson's "A Gold Hunter on His Way to California."

From Kellogg & Bulkeley, sometime in the sixties, came:

"Yosemite Falls. Lith. by Kellogg & Bulkeley"—small, n.d.

KIPP, A. K. UNKNOWN

See Britton & Rey's "Mammoth Arbor Vitæ."

KNOEDLER (M.) & COMPANY NEW YORK

See Goupil, Vibert & Co.

KOCH, AUGUSTUS SAN FRANCISCO

Koch was the artist of a series of bird's-eye views, all 1871, for Britton & Rey. We have seen the following, and there may be many others: "Los
PLATE 20 Angeles," "City of Oakland," "City of Nevada," "City of Petaluma," and "Woodland."

KUCHEL & DRESELS CALIFORNIA VIEWS

DRAWN FROM NATURE AND LITH. BY KUCHEL & DRESEL, ... SAN FRANCISCO.

PRINTED BY BRITTON & REY.

COLOMA, 1857.

EL DORADO COUNTY, CALIFORNIA.

First discoveries of Gold in Cal was made at this place early in February 1848 by Jas. Marshall & P. L. Wimmer in the Tailrace of Sutters Saw mill situated at the extreme lower end of the Town. The Mill was torn down in 1856.

⊕ Place where Sutters mill stood

Published by George Searle Coloma.

KUCHEL & DRESELS CALIFORNIA VIEWS.

Drawn from Nature & on Stone by Kuchel & Dresel, 176 Clay St. S. Francisco.

LOS ANGELES,

LOS ANGELES COUNTY, CAL 1857.

Published by Hellman & Bro.

THE MAMMOTH TREE GROVE,
CALAVERAS COUNTY CALIFORNIA.
LAPHAM & HAYNES Prop^rs
SKETCHED FROM NATURE BY T. A. AYRES, 1855.
PRINTED BY BRITTON & REY.
DRAWN ON STONE BY KUCHEL & DRESEL 146 CLAY St. S.F.

SCOTTS BAR AND FRENCH BAR,

ON SCOTTS RIVER, SISKIYOU COUNTY, CALIFORNIA.

1856

Published by J. M C. Jones.

A full color reproduction of this plate appears in the color section in this book.

PART OF THE FLUME NEAR DONNELL'S FLAT.

ENTRANCE OF THE TUNNEL, 3,162 FEET LONG.

DONNELL & PARSONS SAWMILL.

DOME ROCK.

THE HIGH FLUME. 200 FEET HIGH FROM LOW WATER MARK TO THE TOP.

THE FALL. 50 FEET HIGH.

DRAWN FROM NATURE BY F. HOLTZMANN.

L. NAGEL, PRINT.

KUCHEL & DRESEL'S LITH. 176 CLAY ST. S.F.

VIEWS OF THE NEW DITCH,

OF THE COLUMBIA & STANISLAUS RIVER WATER Cº

Published by F. Holtzmann, Columbia, Tuolumne Cº CALIFORNIA

Drawn by T. Grob. Printed by F. Kuhl.

EXECUTION OF
JAMES P. CASEY & CHARLES CORA
by the Vigilance Committee of San Francisco Thursday May 22d 1856.

77

78

HAYES' VALLEY,
SAN FRANCISCO.

LOMBARD, NORTH POINT and GREENWICH DOCKS,
SAN FRANCISCO.
SHIPS GREAT REPUBLIC, HURRICANE AND ZENOBIA DISCHARGING.

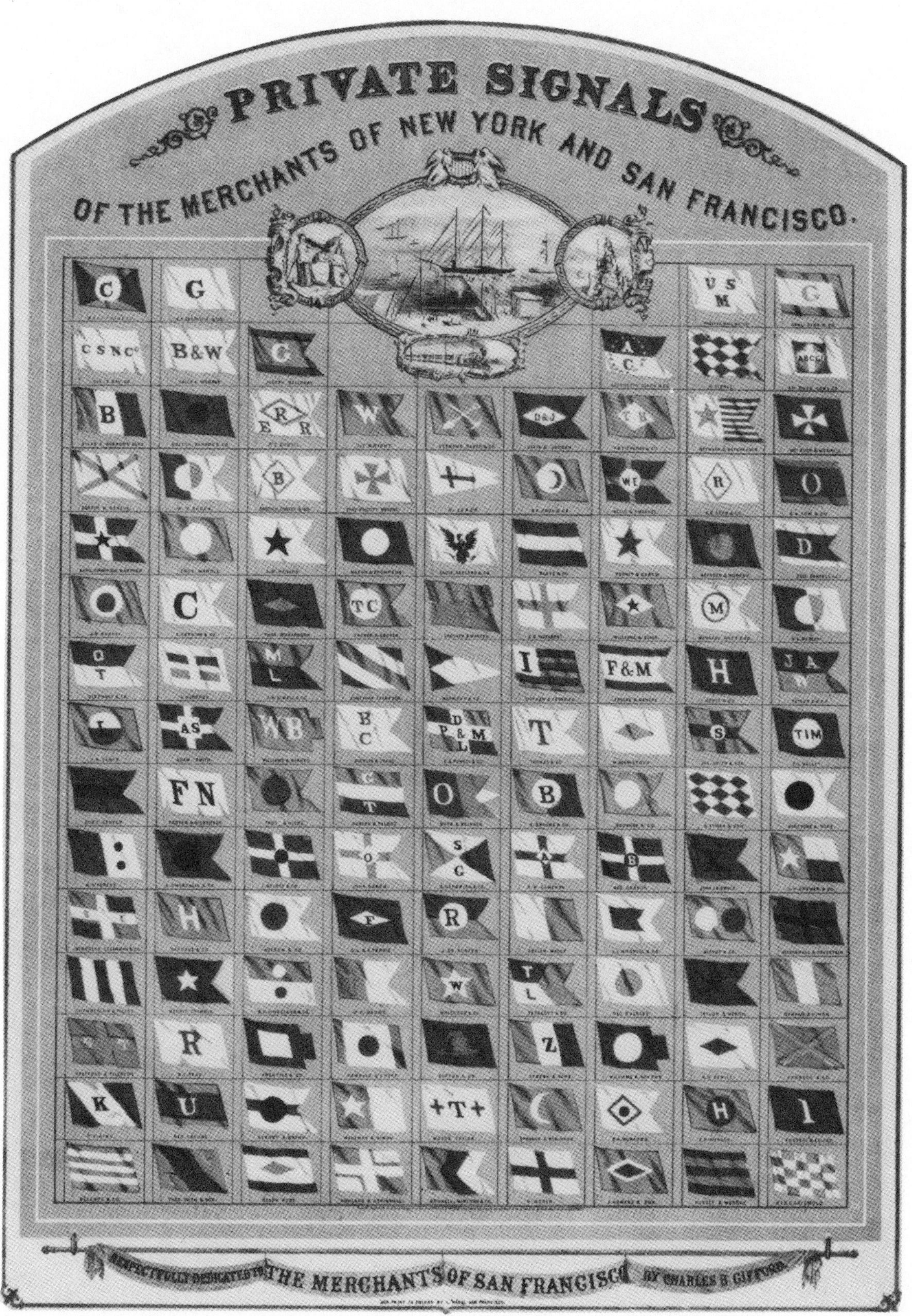

81

A full color reproduction of this plate appears in the color section in this book.

STEAMER DAY IN SAN FRANCISCO.

Published by Snow & Roos, San Francisco

82

SAN JUAN DEL NORTE or GREYTOWN.

83

KOHLER, ANDREW SAN FRANCISCO

1852–1853 grocer, 276 Stockton Street

1856–1857 music and fancy goods, 276 Stockton Street

Unknown 178 Washington Street and 276 Stockton Street

The publisher of Nagel's "The Exhibition Fair," a music sheet.

A note on a woodcut view of his shop says that Andrew Kohler founded Kohler & Chase in 1850, and that this shop was the musical headquarters in San Francisco at that time.

See Baker's "Independent City Guards Quick Step." PLATE 11

KOPPEL, CHARLES UNKNOWN

"Los Angeles. Charles Koppel, del."—small, n.d. (c1856). The earliest known lithographed view of Los Angeles.

See also Sinclair's "View of Benecia from the West"; three of the plates listed under A. Hoen & Company; and some of those in "Report of a Geological Reconnaissance" under Sarony, Major & Knapp and T. Sinclair.

KORBEL (F.) & BROTHERS SAN FRANCISCO

Unknown 437 Brannan Street

I have seen but two lithographs by this firm.

"In Memory of Wm. C. Ralston. Late Pres. of the Bank of Calif. Respectfully Presented to the Subscribers of the S. F. News Letter. Entered . . . 1875"—large. Portrait of Ralston, view of the bank, and on each side five other views.

Certificate of membership in "The Society of California Pioneers. [Signed on stone:] F. Keller"—large, n.d. (certificate filled in, "1876").

Korbel Brothers were the original owners of the *Wasp* (*q.v.*).

KUCHEL & DRESEL SAN FRANCISCO

Kuchel (Charles C.) & Dresel (Emil):

1853–1855 146 Clay Street

1855–1858 176 Clay Street

1856–1857 174½ Clay Street

1858 174 Clay Street

Charles C. Kuchel:

1856–1857	"of Kuchel & Dresel," 174½ Clay Street
1860	174 Clay Street
1861–1862	622 Clay Street
1863–1865	543 Clay Street
1866	"Kuchel, Louisa, widow"

Charles C. Kuchel was born in Zweibrucken in 1820, and after coming to this country worked for P. S. Duval in Philadelphia. Just when he went to California is not known, but he formed the association with Emil Dresel in 1853.

The outstanding work of this firm was a series entitled "Kuchel & Dresel's California Views," including all the important cities and mining towns, with a few of Oregon and Washington, issued during 1855, 1856, 1857, and 1858. They were sometimes published by a local merchant, often the bookseller. Many of them were framed by a border of views of the important buildings, ranches, and mines in and about the town portrayed, and on these titles we have noted in parentheses the number of these smaller views. Unless otherwise noted, all we have listed were drawn and lithographed by Kuchel & Dresel, printed by Britton & Rey, and were medium in size. Mr. John Howell, of San Francisco, who has so kindly lent us some of his lithographs for reproduction in this volume, has considered this series of enough importance to merit a book.* Kuchel & Dresel's other work is listed after the series, which follows:

"Angels, Calaveras County, Cal. 1857. Published by C. G. Lake, Angels. Entered . . . 1857"—(nineteen views).

"Auburn, Placer County, California. 1857. Published by W. K. Parkinson. Entered . . . 1857"—(24 views).

"Chinese, Tuolumne County. Southern Mines, California"—small, n.d. (twelve views). A most interesting view of a Chinese camp. The place was started by an importer of Mongolian labor, and it was for a long time the headquarters of that race.

PLATE 72 "Coloma, 1857. El Dorado County, California. First discovery of Gold in Cal. was made at this place early in February 1848 by Jas. Marshall & P. L. Wimmer, in the Tailrace of Sutter's Sawmill, situated at the extreme lower end of the town. The Mill was torn down in 1856. [Symbol, cross in small

*"California in the Fifties: Fifty Views of Cities and Towns in California and the West." Text by Douglas S. Watson. San Francisco: John Howell, 1935.

circle, with hook at top]: Place where Sutters mill stood. Published by George Searle, Coloma. Entered . . . 1857"—(twenty views).

"Columbia, Tuolumne County"—n.d.

"Crescent City, Klamath County, Cal. 1857. Entered . . . 1857"

"Downieville, Sierra County. Entered . . . 1856"

"Eugene City, Oregon,"—n.d.

"Forest Hill, Placer County. 1857"—n.d. (ten views).

"French Bar. 1857. Siskiyou County"—n.d.

"The Golden Gate. Entrance to the Bay of San Francisco. Sunrise. View off Point Lobos—Looking Towards the Bay—with the Steamship John L. Stephens and the Clipper Ship Flying Cloud Just Entering the Golden Gate. Sketched from nature by T. A. Ayres. Printed by Britton & Rey. Entered . . . 1855"—medium.

"Grass Valley, Nevada County, California. 1858. Published by W. K. Spencer, Bookseller & Stationer"—n.d. (thirty-five views).

"Jackson, Amador County, Cal. 1857. Published by Wesley Jackson. Entered . . . 1857"—(sixteen views).

"Lachryma Montis. Residence of General M. G. Vallejo, near Sonoma, California. Paint. by S. W. Shaw"—n.d.

"Lone Mountain Cemetery, San Francisco. View towards the Bay. Entered . . . 1857"

"Los Angeles, Los Angeles County, Cal. 1857. Published by Hellman & Bro. PLATE 73 Entered . . . 1857"—(twenty views).

"The Mammoth Tree Grove, Calaveras County California. Sketched from PLATE 74 nature by T. A. Ayres, 1855. Entered . . . 1855"—large. In the center of this print is: "General View of the Hotel & Surrounding Forest." At top: "The Father of the Forest, 112 Feet in circumference. Estimated Height when standing 450 Feet." At left: "The Mother of the Forest. 90 feet in Cir. 327 feet high. Bark taken off 120 feet." At right: "The Three Graces. Circum. of the Three 90 feet, 300 feet high." Lower left: "The Big Tree 96 Feet in Circumference. 300 Feet high. Was cut down in July 1852, employed 5 men 25 days in boring and sawing it off." Lower right: "The

Horseback Ride Distance through 75 Feet. 12 feet in the clear." Lower center view is of people standing in hollowed-out tree bases. In the margin is the following:

> "The Mammoth Tree Grove, Calaveras County California. Lapham & Haynes Proprs. These Gigantic Trees are found in a Valley at the source of one of the tributaries of the Calaveras, 15 miles above Murphys. According to Botanists they belong to the Family of Taxodimus and have been justly named Washingtonia Gigantea. Within an area of 50 acres 92 trees of this specie are found standing, & are beyond doubt the most stupendous vegetable products on earth. They were discovered early in 1850 by hunters, whose accounts were considered fabulous until confirmed by actual measurement. The Valley contains 160 acres of land & was located & settled by Wm. W. Lapham (one of the present proprs.) in July 1852. The House is at present conducted by A. S. Haynes (one of the proprietors) and offers any accomodation to parties, visitors or boarders. The charges are reasonable, it being the aim of the proprs. to make the Grove a fashionable & popular place of resort. A daily line of Stages from Stockton, Sacramento City & Sonora, arrive at Murphys, where Animals & Carriages can be procured, thence by a splendid road through a magnificent open forest the Grove is reached in 2½ hours. The scenery in the vicinity is beautiful & the Climate from the elevation of the valley (4000 ft. above the sea) is delicious. The vegetation fresh & green during the summer."

"Marysville. Published by G. & O. Amy, Music & Booksellers, Marysville. Entered . . . 1856"—(thirty-two views).

"Mokelumne Hill, Calaveras County"—n.d.

"Murphys, Calaveras County, Cal. 1857. Published by Wm. W. Latham. Entered . . . 1857—(seventeen views).

"Nevada. 1856"—n.d.

"North San Juan, Nevada County, California. 1858. Published by Theodore Green"—n.d. (sixteen views).

"Oregon City, Oregon"—n.d. (c.1857).

"Petaluma, Sonoma County, Cal. 1857. Published by S. C. Haydon, Petaluma. Entered . . . 1857"—(fourteen views).

"Placerville, El Dorado County. Entered . . . 1856"

"Portland, Multnomah County, Oregon. 1855. Published by J. J. McCormick, Franklin Book Store"—large, n.d. (forty views).

"Rabbit Creek, 1856. Sierra County, Cala. Published by Everts, Wilson & Co." —n.d. (fourteen views).

"Salem, Marion County, Oregon. 1858. Published by W. C. Griswold & Company, Salem"—large, n.d. (twenty-six views). At top: "Kuchel & Dresel's Pacific Views." The Oregon and Washington views were possibly a separate series.

"San Jose, 1856. County of Santa Clara, Cala. Entered . . . 1856"—large (twenty-three views).

"San Jose, from City Hall. 1858. Published by Levi Goodrich, San Jose. Sketched from nature by Levi Goodrich"—n.d.

"Santa Clara, 1856. Entered . . . 1856"—large (thirteen views).

"Scott's Bar, Trinity County"—n.d.

"Scotts Bar and French Bar, on Scotts River, Siskiyou County, California. 1856. Published by J. M. C. Jones. Entered . . . 1856"—large (twenty-five views). This is an unusual one of the series because of the two separate views in the center—the only one like this I have seen of the series. PLATE 75

"Shasta, Shasta County, Cal. Entered . . . 1856"—small.

"Sonora, Tuolumne County, Southern Mines, California"—n.d. (twenty-one views).

"St. Louis, Sierra Co. Cal."—n.d.

"Stockton, Cal. 1858. Published by Rosenbaum & Van Allen, Booksellers. Drawn from nature by E. Camerer"—n.d. (twelve views).

"Stockton. Entered . . . 1855"—small.

"Todd's Valley, Placer County, California. 1857. Published by Read & Hall. Entered . . . 1857"—(fifteen views).

"Union, on Humboldt Bay, Humboldt County, Cal. 1857. Published by B. Henry Wyman, Union. Entered . . . 1857"—(fourteen views).

"Vancouver, Washington Territory"—n.d. (c.1858).

"Weaverville, 1856. Trinity County, California. Published by Fagg & Feast. Entered . . . 1856"

"Yankee Jim's, Placer County, California. 1857. Entered . . . 1857"

"The Yo-Semite Falls. Sketched from nature by T. A. Ayres. Published by Hutchings & Rosenfield. Entered . . . 1855"—large. Reproduced in *America on Stone* as Plate 22. This sometimes appears as "The Yo-Hamite Falls."

"Yreka, Siskiyou County, California. Published by A. Roman & Brother. Entered . . . 1856"

Other lithographs by Kuchel & Dresel are:

"Bavaria Brewery, By Jacob Gundlach, Vallejo St. between Dupont & Stockton Streets, San Francisco, Cal. Drawn by Kuchel & Dresel, 176 Clay St. S. F. Print. by Britton & Rey"—letterhead, n.d.

"Church of St. Francis"—medium, n. d.

"Design for the Mechanics Institute, 1857"—medium, n.d.

"The Great Yo-Semite Fall in Mariposa County, Cal. Drawn from nature by E. Camerer. L. Nagel, print."—large, n.d.

"Jackson, Amador County. Published by Wesley Jackson, Jackson News Depot. From nature & on stone by Kuchel & Dresel, 146 Clay St. S.F. Printed by Britton & Rey"—letterhead, n.d. This is not the same as the view of Jackson listed in the series. This letterhead shows three small settlements: "Jackson; Butte City; The Gate."

"Haraszthy, Uznay & Company's Gold & Silver Refinery, Cor. Brannan & Harris Sts. San Francisco, Cal. Print. by Britton & Rey"—small, n.d.

"Henston, Hastings & Company"—medium, n.d.

"Map of the Overland Route"—small, n.d.

"Mechanics Hotel"—medium, n.d.

"Shasta Butte & Shasta Valley. Siskiyou County Cala. Drawn by E. Camerer. Kuchel & Dresel's Lith. 174, Clay St. San Francisco. L. Nagel Print."—small, n.d.

"View of Santa Rosa. From Sketches by Grafton T. Brown"—medium, n.d.

"View of that Portion of the City of San Francisco Seen from the Residence of N. Larco, Esqre. Green Street, Telegraph Hill, Looking South. 1859. Drawn from nature by E. Camerer. L. Nagel, print."—large, n.d.

"Views of the New Ditch, of the Columbia & Stanislaus River Water Co. Drawn from nature by F. Holtzmann. L. Nagel, print. Published by F. Holtzmann, Columbia, Tuolomne Co. California"—medium, n.d. [c.1856], with six views: PLATE 76

"Part of the flume near Donnell's Flat"; "Entrance to the Tunnel. 3162 Feet Long"; "Donnell & Parson's Sawmill"; "Dome Rock"; "The High Flume. 200 Feet High from Low Water Mark to the Top"; and "The Fall. 50 Feet High"

C. C. Kuchel drew on stone several of Edward Vischer's Mammoth Tree Grove series (*q.v.*). See also Butler's "San Francisco Blues" certificate; Duval's "View of San Francisco 1850"; and Nagel, Fishbourne & Kuchel. PLATE 48

Kuchel alone lithographed the following prints:

"1860. Fourth German May Festival. Return of the Procession at the Close of the Festival [title repeated in German]. Weaverville, Trinity County, Cal. Ambrotype taken by C. H. P. Norcross. Britton & Co. Print. C. C. Kuchel, Lith. 176 Clay St. S. Francisco. Published by Charles Schutz"—medium, n.d. PLATE 18

"Knickerbocker Engine Company N. 5. San Francisco. Printed by Britton & Co."—medium, n.d. PLATE 70

"Lick House. Kenitzer & Farquharson, Architects. Britton & Co. Print."—medium, n.d.

"San Francisco Masonic Temple. (1862)"—large.

"San Francisco Pacific Sugar Refinery. Britton & Co. Print."—medium, n.d.

"View of Fort Churchill, N. T. Grafton T. Brown, del."—large, n.d. (c.1856).

"Virginia City, Nevada Territory. 1861. Drawn from nature by Grafton T. Brown. Britton & Co. Print. Published by Grafton T. Brown"—medium, n.d. (twenty-one border views). PLATE 71

"Woodward's Whatcheer House. Printed by Britton & Co."—medium, n.d.

Although the following "Commandments to California Wives" is not a lithograph, it is included because it is interesting and amusing. The illustration at the top shows an angel appearing before a Forty-niner in his cabin, the angel being a ringleted damsel with a wasp waist. At the right is a view of home life, with four children being dandled on parental knees or teasing a mottled cat. In the margin is a sketch of a camp in the mining country, with a miner sitting on a rock under a tree while his offspring climb trees and pick daisies. The illustration is signed: "W. C. Butler, S. F." At the bottom of the print is, "C. C. Kuchel, del. W. C. Butler, S. F. Mercantile Job Print, 130 Sansome St. S. F. Entered . . . 1855, by James M. Hutchings."

COMMANDMENTS TO CALIFORNIA WIVES
COMMANDMENTS ARE GIVEN TO MAKE A HAPPY HOME

Now it came to pass that as thy servant sat alone and at night watching the dying embers of his cabin fire, behold the latch of his cabin door was softly lifted, and before him stood an angel! clothed in female apparel. As in duty bound, I immediately rose from my only stool, and invited her to be seated: this she gracefully declined; but, placing her white and beautiful fingers upon the bosom of my woolen shirt, in a voice of musical distinctness she thus addressed me, "Young man, hast thou courage?" I was almost speechless, for I felt what little I possessed fast oozing away, and I modestly answered that I had none to boast of, yet "dare do all that may become a man." "It is enough," she replied, "I therefore commission thee to give the following—

"COMMANDMENTS TO CALIFORNIA WIVES

"1. Thou shalt not 'put on airs' of self-importance, not indulge in day-dreams of extravagance, nor allow thy vanity and love of dress to turn thy head, and unfit thee for the sober duties of life, or make thee MERELY an expensive toy and walking advertisement of the latest fashions.

"2. Thou shalt not believe thyself to be an angel 'all but wings'—nor over-estimate thine own and under-estimate thy husband's value; because the scarcity of thy sex leads men to bow, almost in worship, to silk or calico made into woman's garments. Neither shalt thou be intoxicated by the personal attractions and flattering attentions of men with finger-rings, fine apparel and prancing horses; nor by the glittering equipage and wonderful promises of the unprincipled and gay gallant—lest thy weakness and folly tempt thee to prefer him to thy husband, and soon under the plea of 'incompatibility of temper,' or other phantom of the imagination—thou become dissatisfied, and in the end 'seek a separation,' or 'pray for a divorce,' to gratify thy vain desires, or cover thy sin.

"3. Thou shalt not consider it fashionable, cleanly, or economical, to sweep the streets with one-hundred-dollar dresses—when at home thou considered thyself fortunate to get calico;—nor to promenade muddy sidewalks in long satin robes and bedraggled underclothes; nor to wear jewels and flowers on thy head, while thy feet go 'flipety click' in buskin shoes run down at the heel, and discover to strangers the holes in thy stockings.

"4. Thou shalt not starve thyself and family twenty-nine days out of thirty, to feast thy circle and give a party, nor by the purchase of expensive gew-gaws and finery keep thy husband poor, nor run up bills for pills and furbeloes, while the dry goods merchant and thy husband are at their wits' end how to pay their way; nor spend hard eaanings foolishly; nor lose a half day shopping, to invest your bits. Neither shalt thou devour all thy savings at cotillion parties and balls; nor waste thy substance by improv'dence or neglect.

"5. Thou shalt not fret, nor sulk, nor faint, nor fly into hysterics because thine unfortunate husband cannot buy for thee 'that beautiful moon, made of such nice green cheese,' and a riding dress to match; nor quit his business at any moment, and take you out riding to—Paradise. Neither shalt thou ride or walk with other men, nor associate with profligates and spend-thrifts in the ball room, or by the way-side, in preference to thy husband; nor, under the excuse of saving his purse, treat him as a simpleton, or slave, to stay at home and nurse the children nor follow thee—at a proper distance—to await thy pleasure, or carry thy lap-dog.

"6. Thou shalt not accept presents of Cashmere shawls, specimen shawl pins, embroidered elastics, diamond rings, or other baubles, as the price of thy husband's and thine own dishonor—supposing they will bring thee happiness, for—after thou hast forsaken honor, husband, children and home—as ministers of retribution they will dog thy footsteps, and haunt thy sleep with withering memories of the happy PAST, and shut for ever out the angel images of innocence and love, that hovered around thy parents' dwelling and in thy husband's home;—while thy poor abandoned children, the objects of charity and pity, wander as outcasts, and he that was thy husband perish in sorrow and the gutter—a miserable drunkard, or a broken-hearted, premature, old man.

"7. Thou shalt not substitute sour looks for pickles; nor a fiery temper for stove-wood; nor cross words for kindlings; nor trifling talk for light bread; nor tart language for dessert; nor excuses for anything. Neither shalt thou serve up cold looks or cold meats for breakfast, nor scoldings and hard potatoes for dinner, nor what remains of the other two meals for supper—no, not even on washing days. Neither shalt thou allow hard feelings or unwashed dishes to accumulate; nor withhold either secrets or shirt buttons from the bosom of thy husband; and NEVER omit LITTLE KINDNESSES of any kind.

"8. Thou shalt not neglect to make thy person and thy home attractive—that when thy husband cometh from his daily toil, or business care, thy cheering looks of loving welcome may greet his footsteps at the cottage door, and charm him into forgetfulness of all but thee. And should he be unfortunate—as many are—thou shalt not increase his sorrows—as many do—by weeping and repining; but, with all thy noblest sympathy and womanly love, seek to lift the heavy burden from his manly heart, and thus renewed, again to dare the rugged and slippery steep that leads to fortune and success,—believing 'there's no such word as fail,' while thou art near to cheer him on, and share with him the victory.

"9. Thou shalt not seek to break up friendships and injure character by fabricating slander. Neither shalt thou indulge in insinuating inuendoes; nor use half-spoken and surmising sentences, nor suspicious and knowing or upturned looks, that seem to say, 'Oh, my; if you but knew what I know;' (yet what you DON'T KNOW would make a very large book, PRE-haps.) Neither shalt thou go about with thy gadding-needle, gossip-thread, and scandal-basket of evil speaking, with which to mend the character and manners of thy neighbors; for when thy handy-work is returned unto thee—as it will be—magnified, and twisted, and changed, thou wilt reply in anger, 'I never said it,' yet will not be believed, but hence-forth be considered a busy-body and mischief-maker—and thy FRIENDS shall say of thee, 'It's just what I expected.'

"10. Thou shalt not give these commandments a revengeful interpretation; nor curl thy lip in insulted contempt, nor flash fire from the corners of thine eyes. Neither shalt thou allow thy finger-nails to be drawn inwards, in imaginary and Amazonian heiroglyphics and scratches upon the frontispiece of thy servant; but, instead thereof, thou shalt speak a kind word for him to thine unmarried sister, and present him with 'a piece of a plate,' or 'a leather medal,' with which to commemorate to posterity his good intentions. Yet thou shalt not take pleasure in thinking—'Won't these suit Mrs. So-and-So?' but examine carefully where they speak unto thee, that peradventure by their admonition and by reading twice a week the last chapter of Proverbs and the fifth chapter of Ephesians, thou mayest profit thereby, and thy children by thy example, and thy children's children after thee, rise up to call thee blessed.

"LASTLY:

"To Unmarried Ladies—Thou shalt not become weary of waiting for thy lover's return; nor expect him at thy side before his purse is full; nor forsake him because he is poor; nor marry another because he is rich—(for here the rich become poor and the poor become rich.) Neither shalt thou hesitate—if thou lovest him—when he sendeth for thee; yet, LET HER REMAIN who, if a room is not carpeted, or a dinner needs cooking, or a shirt requires washing, expects to drown irrecoverably in briny tears, or die immediately in agonizing spasms, because she 'never soiled her fingers before, and now—it is so provoking!'—poor thing. Moreover, whisper ye to the wives at home, that they 'cut up no capers,' while, uncheered and alone—frequently against hope—their husbands toil unremittingly on from weary month to month, without one murmuring thought of what they suffer or forego for the dear ones, far, far away. AMEN—So mote it be."

FORTY-NINE.

KUHL, F. PHILADELPHIA AND SAN FRANCISCO

Philadelphia:

Unknown	$46\frac{1}{2}$ Walnut Street
Unknown	120 South 2nd Street

San Francisco:

1856–1857	lithographic printer, 109 Sutter Street

In the East, Kuhl did a series of Mexican War scenes and a view of Philadelphia.

California lithographs are:

PLATE 77 "Execution of James P. Casey & Charles Cora by the Vigilance Committee of San Francisco Thursday May 22d 1856. Drawn by T. Grob. Printed by F. Kuhl"—letterhead, n.d.

PLATE 78 "Monetary Panic in California!!! San Francisco, February 1855. [Signed on stone:] Sv,EG. Published by Leland F. Schlesinger. Printed by F. Kuhl"—medium, n.d.

KURZ & ALLISON — CHICAGO

One of the firms which had the real news sense and lithographic touch. Their work is described and illustrated in *America on Stone.*

"The Miners Pioneer Ten Commandments of 1849. Copyright . . . 1887 by W. P. Bennett, Gold Hill, Nevada. Kurz & Allison's Art Studio, Chicago, U.S.A."—very large. This is late, but the commandments are amusing, and it has been included for that reason. The text is framed by a border of eleven views of life in the mines, illustrating humorously the points made in the commandments. There are also three border views of emigrants crossing the plains. The commandments follow:

MINERS PIONEER TEN COMMANDMENTS OF 1849

A Man Spake These Words, And Said: I am a miner who wandered from "Away Down East," and came to sojourn in a strange land and "See the Elephant." And behold I saw him, and bear witness, that, from the key of his trunk to the end of his tail, his whole body passed before me; and I followed him until his huge feet stood still before a clap-board shanty; then with his trunk extended, he pointed to a candle-card tacked upon a shingle, as though he would say "READ!" and I read

PIONEERS' TEN COMMANDMENTS

I

Thou shalt have no other claim than one.

II

Thou shalt not make unto thyself any false claim, nor any likeness to a mean man by jumping one. Whatever thou findest, on the top above, or on the rock beneath, or in a crevice underneath the rock, or I will visit the miners around to invite them on my side; and when they decide against thee, thou shalt take thy pick, thy pan, thy shovel, and thy blankets, with all that thou hast, and go prospecting to seek good diggings; but thou shalt find none. Then, when thou hast returned in sorrow thou shalt find that thine old claim is worked out, and yet no pile made thee to hide in the ground or in an old boot beneath thy bunk, or in buckskin or bottle underneath thy cabin; but has paid all that was in thy purse away, worn out thy boots and thy garments, so that there is nothing good about them but the pockets, and thy patience is likened unto thy garments; and at last thou shalt hire thy body out to make thy board and save thy bacon.

III

Thou shalt not go prospecting before thy claim gives out. Neither shalt thou take thy money, nor thy gold dust, nor thy good name, to the gaming table in vain; for monte, twenty-one, roulette, faro, lansquenet and poker will prove to thee that the more thou puttest down the less thou shalt take up; and when thou thinkest of thy wife and children, thou shalt not hold thyself guiltless, but—insane.

IV

Thou shalt not remember what thy friends do at home on the Sabbath day, lest the remembrance may not compare favorably with what thou doest here. Six days thou mayest dig or pick all that thy body can stand under, but the other day is Sunday; yet thou washest all thy dirty shirts, darnest all thy stockings, tap thy boots, mend thy clothing, chop thy whole week's fire-wood, make up and bake thy bread and boil thy pork and beans that thou wait not when thou returnest from thy long-tom weary. For in six days' labor only thou canst not work enough to wear out thy body in two years; but if thou workest hard on Sunday also, thou canst do it in six month; and thou and thy son and thy daughter, thy male and thy female friend, thy morals and thy conscience be none the less better for it, but reproach thee shouldst thou ever return to thy mother's fireside; and thou strive to justify thyself because the trader and the blacksmith, the carpenter and the merchants, the tailors, Jews and Buccaneers defy God and civilization by keeping not the

Sabbath day, nor wish for a day of rest, such as memory of youth and home made hallowed.

V

Thou shalt not think more of all thy gold, nor how thou canst make it fastest, than how thou will enjoy it after thou hast ridden rough-shod over thy good old parents' precepts and examples, that thou mayest have nothing to reproach and sting thee when thou art left alone in the land where thy father's blessing and thy mother's love hath sent thee.

VI

Thy shalt not kill thy body by working in the rain, even though thou shalt make enough to buy physic and attendance with. Neither shalt thou kill thy neighbor's body in a duel, for by keeping cool thou canst save his life and thy conscience. Neither shalt thou destroy thyself by getting "tight," nor "slewed," nor "high," nor "corned," nor "half-seas over," nor "three sheets in the wind," by drinking smoothly down "brandy slings," "gin cock-tails," "whisky punches," "rum toddies" nor "egg nogs." Neither shalt thou suck "mint-juleps" nor "sherry cobblers" through a straw, nor gurgle from a bottle the raw material, nor take it neat from a decanter, for while thou art swallowing down thy purse and thy coat from off thy back, thou art burning the coat from off thy stomach; and if thou couldst see the houses and lands, and gold dust, and home comforts already lying there—a huge pile—thou shouldst feel a choking in thy throat; and when to that thou add'st thy crooked walking and hiccupping; of lodging in the gutter, of broiling in the sun, of prospect holes half full of water, and of shafts and ditches from which thou hast emerged like a drowning rat, thou wilt feel disgusted with thyself, and inquire, "Is thy servant a dog that he doeth these things?" Verily, I will say, farewell old bottle; I will kiss thy gurgling lips no more; and thou, slings, cock-tails, punches, smashes, cobblers, nogs, toddies, sangarees and juleps, forever, farewell. Thy remembrance shames me; henceforth I will cut thy acquaintance; and headaches, tremblings, heart-burnings, blue-devils, and all the unholy catalogue of evils which follow in thy train. My wife's smiles and my children's merry-hearted laugh shall charm and reward me for having the manly firmness and courage to say: "No! I wish thee an eternal farewell!"

VII

Thou shalt not grow discouraged, nor think of going home before thou hast made thy "pile," because thou hast not "struck a lead" nor found a rich "crevice" nor sunk a hole upon a "pocket," lest in going home thou leave four dollars a day and go to work ashamed at fifty cents a day, and serve thee right; for thou knowest by staying here thou mightest strike a lead and fifty dollars a day, and keep thy manly self-respect, and then go home with enough to make thyself and others happy.

VIII

Thou shalt not steal a pick, or a pan, or a shovel, from thy fellow miner, nor take away his tools without his leave; nor borrow those he cannot spare; nor return them broken; nor trouble him to fetch them back again; nor talk to him while his water rent is running on; nor remove his stake to enlarge thy claim; nor undermine his claim in following a lead; nor pan out gold from his riffle-box; nor wash the tailings from the mouth of his sluices. Neither shalt thou pick out specimens from the company's pan to put in thy mouth or in thy purse; nor cheat thy partner of his share; nor steal from thy cabin-mate his gold dust to add to thine, for he will be sure to discover what thou hast done, and will straightway call his fellow miners together, and if the law hinder them not they will hang thee, or give thee fifty lashes, or shave thy head and brand thee like a horse thief with "R" upon thy cheek, to be known and of all men Californians in particular.

IX

Thou shalt not tell any false tales about "good diggings in the mountains" to thy neighbor, that thou mayest benefit a friend who hath mules, and provisions, and tools, and blankets he cannot sell; lest in deceiving thy neighbor when he returns through the snow, with naught but his riffle, he shall present thee with the contents thereof, and like a dog thou shalt fall down and die.

X

Thou shalt not commit unsuitable matrimony, nor covet "single blessedness," nor forget absent maidens, nor neglect thy first love; but thou shalt consider how faithfully and patiently she waiteth thy return; yea, and covereth each epistle that thou sendest with kisses of kindly welcome until she hath thyself. Neither shalt thou covet thy neighbor's wife, nor trifle with the affections of his daughter; yet, if thy heart be free, and thou love and covet each other, thou shalt "pop the question" like a man, lest another more manly than thou art should step in before thee, and thou lovest her in vain, and, in the anguish of thy heart's disappointment, thou shalt quote the language of the great, and say, "sich is life;" and thy future lot be that of a poor, lonely, despised and comfortless bachelor.

A new commandment give I unto you. If thou hast a wife and little ones, that thou lovest dearer than thy life, that thou keep them continually before you to cheer and urge thee onward until thou canst say, "I have enough; God bless them; I will return." Then as thou journiest towards thy much loved home, with open arms, shall they come forth to welcome thee, and falling on thy neck, weep tears of unutterable joy that thou art come; then in the fullness of thy heart's gratitude thou shalt kneel before thy Heavenly Father together, to thank Him for thy safe return. Amen. So mote it be.

LANGTON, SAMUEL W. DOWNIEVILLE, CALIFORNIA

PLATE 42 Publisher of Britton & Rey's "View of Goodyears Bar," and Justh, Quirot & Company's "View of Downieville"—reproduced in *America on Stone* as Plate 80.

LAPHAM, J. M. SAN FRANCISCO

PLATE 30 The artist of Britton & Rey's "Mammoth Arbor Vitæ."

LAUFFER & STOLP BUDAPEST

"Los Angeles. Kalifornia. Föutcza és templom. Lauffer & Stolp tulajdona. Rajz. Xántus J.2/7 57. Nyomva, Rohn, Pesten 1857. Xántus János Levelei Éjszakamerikából. Pesten, Lauffer és Stolp Kiadó Könyvkereskedése tulajdona. (1857)"

Translated, this reads: "Los Angeles, California. Main Street and church. Property of Lauffer & Stolp. Drawing. Xántus J.2/7 57. Printed by Rohn in Pest [now Budapest] 1857. The letters of János Xántus from North America. Pest, Lauffer & Stolp, book publishers and book dealers. (1857)"

DRAWN BY EDWARD VISCHER

NAGEL, FISHBOURNE & KUCHEL, LITHOGRAPHERS, S.F.

THE MAMMOTH TREE GROVE, CALAVERAS CO. CALIFORNIA, AND ITS AVENUES.

No. 1. The HORSEBACKRIDE, a hollow trunk, Distance through 70 feet, 12 feet in the clear.
" 2. EAGLES WING, the root of a fallen tree, near Old Dominion, not named before.
" 3. PIONEER'S CABIN, 33 feet in diameter, 150 feet high, the top being broken off.
" 4. MINER'S CABIN, as standing 1855, 80 feet circumference, 290 feet high.
" 5. The tops of OLD DOMINION and UNCLE TOM'S CABIN and clusters of other trees, as seen from the base, lying under their shade.

No. 6. MINER'S CABIN, overthrown and uprooted in the November gale 1860.
" 7. A WALK THROUGH THE FOREST; a combination, representing the following:
STUMP and LOG of the original "BIG TREE", Dimensions below; HORSEBACKRIDE, THE MOTHER OF THE FOREST, stripped of its bark 1855 and its skeleton 1861.
Dimensions: 90 feet in circum. at the base, 84 feet without the bark; height 321 feet, the bark taken off 116 feet high 1854.
The PRIDE OF THE FOREST, height 275, circum. 60 feet, and
THE THREE GRACES, height 295 feet, together 92 feet circum.

No. 8. The FATHER OF THE FOREST, the largest specimen of the Grove; though prostrate and half buried in the ground; 300 feet from the root, where broken off by striking against another large tree, measures 18 feet in diameter.
" 9. MOTHER AND SON, Dimensions: height 315 & 302 feet, united circumference 93 feet.
" 10. The ORIGINAL "BIG TREE" Stump and Log, felled in 1852. Its Size, when standing, was 302 feet height, 96 feet in circumference, Stump 7 feet high; thickness of bark from 15 to 18 inches.
" 11. The TWO GUARDSMEN by the roadside at the entrance of the clearing; height 300 feet each; the respective circumference 65 & 69 feet.

No. 12. The MAMMOTH GROVE HOTEL, grounds and general view of the forest, from a sketch taken in September 1861 on the occasion of the first imported Bactrian Camels crossing the Sierra Nevada by the Big Tree Route.

Centrepiece above: VIEW OF THE SIERRA NEVADA from the Carson Route.
Middle space below: SPERRY'S HOTEL AT MURPHYS. The Suspension flume, Deep Cut and Union Aqueduct, as Monuments of the Mining Enterprise of the inhabitants of "Murphys Camp".

This Grove is situated in a small valley near the headwaters of the San Antonio, one of the largest streams in Central Calaveras and five miles east of the Falls on said stream. Daily lines of stages run from Sacramento and Stockton, passing through San Andreas, Angels and Vallecito, and arriving at Murphys in the evening. Murphys is 15 miles from the Grove; and here the traveler may take a coach at Sperry's Hotel, at 6 o'clock next morning. Leaving Murphys by an excellent carriage road, and gradually ascending, winding through a splendid forest of pine, cedar and firs, intermixed with various kinds of oaks, mostly in sight of the magnificent Aqueduct of the Union Water Company, the Mammoth Grove Hotel is reached after a drive of from three to three and a half hours. The distance from Sacramento to Murphys though longer by Stageroute, is only 80 miles. From Stockton, on a good road for private conveyance, it does not exceed 50 miles. From Sonora it is 14 miles, from Columbia 11 miles, and from Copperopolis 11 miles. Woodfords, at the mouth of Carson Cañon beyond the Sierra Nevada, is only 65 miles from the Grove; and the „Big Tree Route" from Murphys to Genoa opened by the enterprising citizens of Murphys, (an excellent natural road following up undulating ridges and descending through fertile valleys), becomes more and more appreciated. The Alpine Scenery on this the southern route is truly magnificent. The Valley contains something over 160 acres of land. It is 4000 feet above the level of the Sea. Ninety three trees of the Mammoth Species (not including those of one, two and three years growth), are now standing, and are all found within an area of 50 acres of the valley. They are evidently a gigantic species of Cedar, as indicated by the growth, bark and leaf; according to Botanists however, they belong to the family of Taxodia, and have been justly named Washingtonia Gigantea. They are beyond doubt the most stupendous vegetable products upon earth. They were discovered in the spring of 1850, by Mr A. T. Dowd, whilst on a hunt for deer, whose account to his companions of what he had seen, upon returning to camp, was considered fabulous and utterly discredited until proved by actual measurement. The valley enjoys a splendid climate during the spring, summer and autumn months, being exempt from the heat of the lower country and from the cold of the higher mountains. Vegetation remains fresh and green until the middle of October and the water is always pure and cold. Snow falls usually about the middle of December, often accumulating to a depth of four or five feet, and entirely disappears by the middle of April. The vicinity offers every inducement to sportsmen; all kinds of game common to the country abound, while the adjacent streams afford excellent Trout fishing. Delightful horseback or buggy rides conduct the visitor to many interesting points of scenery or objects of curiosity, among wich may be mentioned the Falls of the San Antonio, and the Basaltic Cliff on the North Fork of the Stanislaus river.

It is only justice to the Proprietors of the Grove to add, that the newly constructed fine and spacious Hotel at the Mammoth Grove vies with the one at Murphys in excellence of accommodations and that every comfort is provided for. E. V.

EMPIRE
EXCHANGE BUILDINGS
Montgomery
H.M.LEWIS
Clay
Kearny
PUBLISHED BY MARVIN & HITCHCOCK
PIONEER BOOK STORE SAN FRANCISCO
Lith of Geo. F. Nesbitt N.Y
THOMPSON & HITCHCOCK
MANAGERS AND AGENTS OF
EGORY'S CALIFORNIA EXPRESS
149 PEARL ST COR. WALL ST N Y
San Francisco February 1860

HONEST VOTERS TRYING TO ELECT THEIR OFFICERS
In front of the house

BALLOT BOX STUFFERS, ELECTING THEIR MEN
behind the house.

NOISY CARRIERS 64 & 66. Long Wharf

VIEW OF SAN FRANCISCO FROM TELEGRAPH HILL.

Published by Cooke & Le Count

September 1850

87

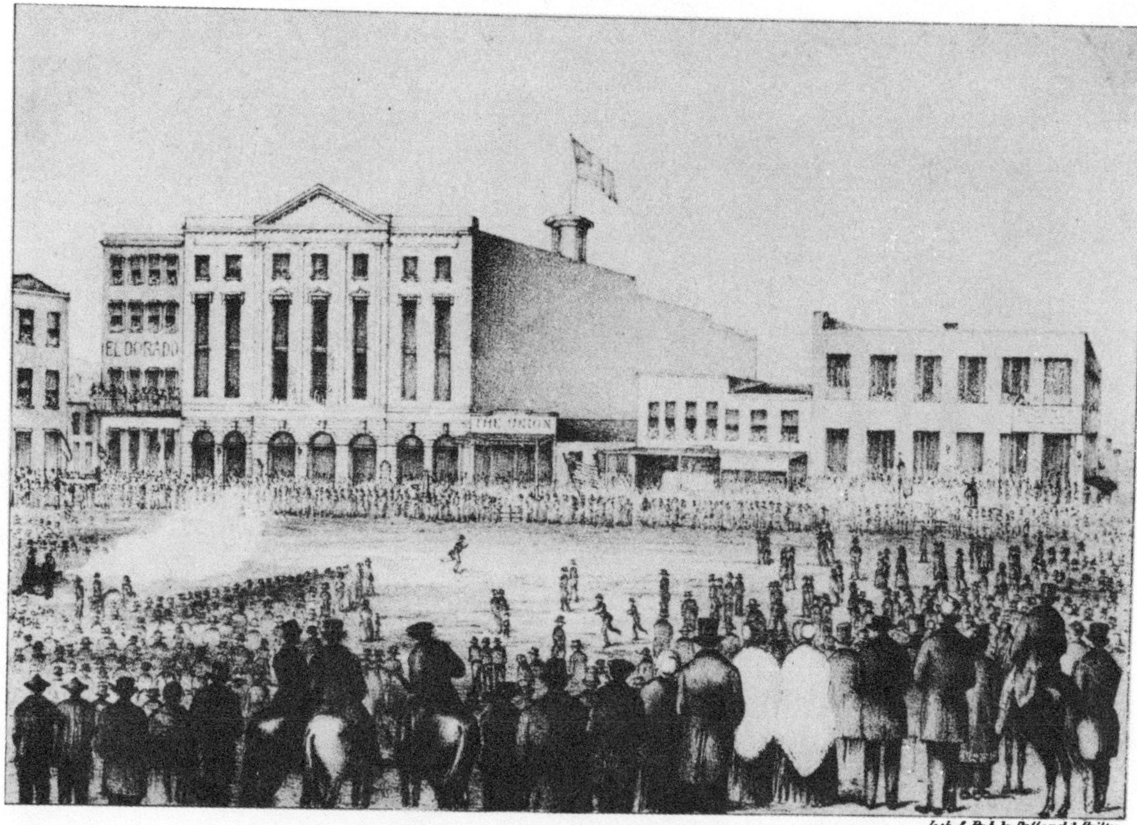

Lith & Pub. by Pollard & Britton

„ *CELEBRATION of WASHINGTON'S Birth Day* "

——— *San Francisco Feby. 23d 1852* ———

Pub. by Cooke & Le Count

88

G.H. Goddard del. Entered according to act of Congress in the year 1852 by G.H. Goddard in the Clerks Office of the Dist. Court of the Northern Dist. of California. Pollard & Britton's Lith. Merchant St.

COLUMBIA

JANUARY, 1852.

SONORA
January, 1852.

Mr John Smith takes final leave of Mrs John Smith.
John Smith, being short of Cash, turns porter to the Elephant House.
John Smith has struck a lead.
John Smith having made a pile leaves for Sacramento on a "bust."
John Smith bets his pile on the Jack.
OREGON
HUMBOLDT
John Smith dead broke.
HAY & C
GROCERY & HOTEL.
John Smith resolves to reform.
Fortune favors John Smith & he invests his dust in a "Ranch."
Published by Lovegrove & Murray Sacramento City.
John Smith arrives safe home with his
Lith. of Pollard & Peregoy

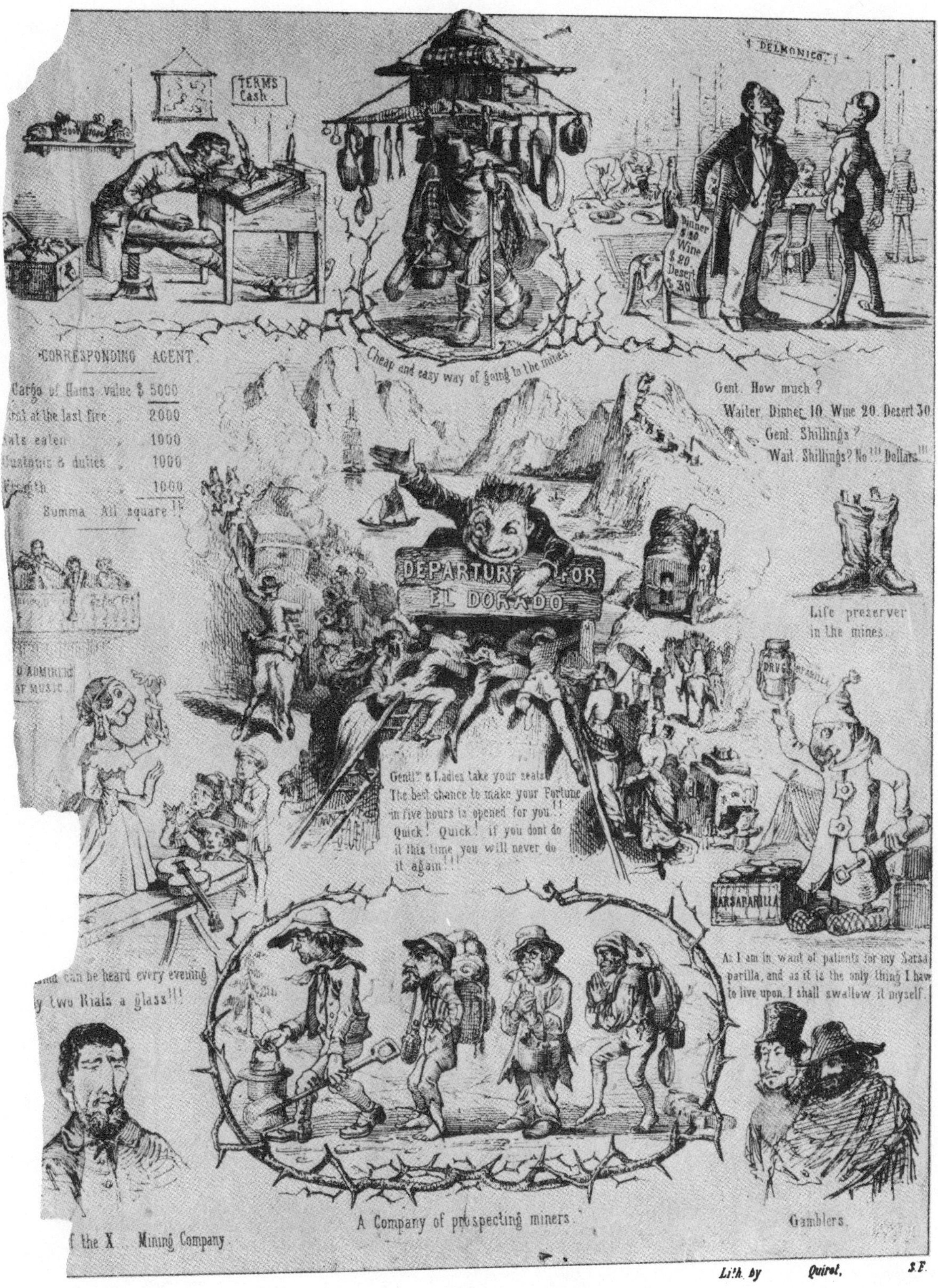
TERMS Cash.
DELMONICO
Dinner $ 10 Wine $ 20 Desert $ 30
CORRESPONDING AGENT.
Cargo of Hams value $ 5000
urnt at the last fire 2000
Rats eaten 1000
Customs & duties 1000
Freigth 1000
Summa All square!!
Cheap and easy way of going to the mines.
Gent. How much?
Waiter. Dinner 10. Wine 20. Desert 30.
Gent. Shillings?
Wait. Shillings? No!!! Dollars!!!
DEPARTURE FOR EL DORADO
Life preserver in the mines.
DRUGS
O ADMIRERS OF MUSIC
Gentl.^m & Ladies take your seats
The best chance to make your Fortune
in five hours is opened for you!!
Quick! Quick! if you dont do
it this time you will never do
it again!!!
SARSAPARILLA
As I am in want of patients for my Sarsa
parilla, and as it is the only thing I have
to live upon, I shall swallow it myself.
can be heard every evening
y two Rials a glass!!!
f the X ... Mining Company.
A Company of prospecting miners.
Gamblers.
Lith. by Quirot, S.F.

"San Gabriel Missio á keleti oldaról. Déli-Kalifornia. Lauffer & Stolp tulajdona. Term. után rajz. Xántus J.2/7 57. Ny. Rohn; Pesten 1858. Xántus János Levelei Éjszakamerikából Pesten, Lauffer és Stolp Kiadó Könyvkereskedése tulajdona. (1857)

Translated, this reads: "San Gabriel Mission, Southern California, looking from the west. Property of Lauffer & Stolp. Drawn from nature. Xántus J. 2/7 57. Printed by Rohn in Pest [now Budapest] 1858. The letters of János Xántus from North America. Pest, Lauffer & Stolp, book publishers and book dealers. (1857)"

LEARY, A. J. SAN FRANCISCO

I have seen only one thing from this man: a stock certificate, small, n.d.. for the "Silver Hill Mining Company."

LE BRETON, L. PARIS

"San-Francisco, Vue prise d'un point élevé du côté Sud. (Californie) 45" PLATE 111
and "Ville de Sacramento (Californie) 46," both: "Dess. et Lith. par L. Le Breton, Paris. Imp. par Auguste Bry, 142, r. du Bac. Paris. E. Savary et Cie edit. 10 Place du Louvre. London, Gambart et Co. 25 Berners St. Oxford St."—both medium, n.d. See William Endicott & Company's "Sacramento City."

LE COUNT BROTHERS SAN FRANCISCO

See Cooke & Le Count.

LE COUNT, JOSIAH J. SAN FRANCISCO

See Cooke & Le Count.

LEFEVRE, L. M. LONDON

Lefevre lithographed two of the plates in "California: A History of Upper and Lower California. By Alexander Forbes, Esq. London: Smith, Elder & Company. Cornhill. 1839." The other plates were done by Day & Haghe (*q.v.*). Those by Lefevre are:

"Californian Mode of Catching Cattle, With a Distant View of the Mission of St. Joseph. Drawn by Captn. Smyth, R.N."

"Santa Barbara—Upper California. Drawn by J. A. Pinto from a Sketch by I. Hall, Esqr."

LEMERCIER PARIS

"San Francisco. From California Street. Drawn from a Daguerretype, the property of Eng. Delessert, Esqre. Imp. Lemercier, Paris. Copyright 1855 by M. Knoedler."—large.

L'ENFANT LONDON

"To the West, From the Entertainment of the 'Far West or the Emigrants Progress.' The poetry written by Charles Mackay, L.L.D. The music dedicated with great respect to Mrs. Herbert Ingram, by her friend Henry Russell. London. Published at Webb's Royal Music Harmonium & Piano Forte Salon, 33, Soho Square & At His Branch Establishment 15, Southampton St. Covent Garden and where may be had all Mr. Henry Russell's Compositions. Ent. Sta. Hall. L'Enfant Lith. 12, Rathbone Pl."—music sheet, n.d.

LEWIS (EDWARD) & BÖHM (G.) UNKNOWN

From "California and its Resources" by Ernest Seyd, London, 1858, the following plates, all 7″ x 4″:

"The Yo-Hamite Falls"
"Suspension Flume across Brandy Gulch"
"A Ditch for the Conveyance of Water to the Dry Diggings"
"Mining by Hydraulic Power"
"City of San Francisco in 1857"
"View of Clear Lake"
"The Yo-Hamite Valley"
"The Mother of the Forest"
"The Father of the Forest, Fallen"
"Farming Scene in Napa Valley"
"California River Steamer"
"California Steam-ship on the Pacific Ocean"

MACLURE, MACDONALD & MACGREGOR LONDON

"San Francisco in 1848. In 1865 the Fourth Commercial City in America. Population 160,000. Maclure, Macdonald & Macgregor, litho. 37, Walbrook, London"—small, n.d. This appeared as an illustration in "The Resources and Prospects of America ascertained during a visit to the States in the autumn of 1865," by Sir S. Morton Peto, Bart. London & New York, 1866, Alexander Strahan, publisher.

MADELEY, G. E. LONDON

A music sheet from this English lithographer is:

"The Good Time's Come at Last, or The Race To California. A Comic Song Written to a Golden Measure and Dedicated to the Master of the Mint by One of the Golden Fleece. Desg. & Lith. by G. E. Madeley, 3 Wellington St. Strand. Entd. at Sta. Hall. Price 1/6. London, Leoni Lee & Coxhead, Music Sellers to Her Majesty Queen Victoria"—n.d. The effect, in England, of the Gold Rush fever is shown in the words of the song:

Oh the good time is come at last, and each succeeding day Sir
Inventions, Curiosities—new novelties display Sir
But power of Steam, and light of Gas, and Electricity Sir
Are nought to California's wealth that great and last discovery.

(*Chorus:*) Gold, Gold, Gold.
Ev'ry body's running after Gold, Gold, Gold.

Ten thousand Ships they're building now to cross the wide Atlantic
And all are on their way to reach those golden shores romantic
Butchers Bakers leave their work Coblers and "Navvies" too Sir
And even Lawyers Emigrate Oh dear what shall we do Sir.

The Miser looks with wistful eye, the Spendthrift hails with glee Sir
This golden scheme now set afloat by many a Company Sir
In breathless haste they all set off and like the Gilpin chase Sir
All Nations for the Ingots rare to California race Sir.

Some travel by the aid of Steam, some tramp upon their feet Sir
And some in Ships—some in Balloons their voyages complete Sir
But all go with the same intent, the hope of gaining wealth Sir
Nor do they stop to eat or drink—regardless of their health Sir.

Soldiers desert, no wonder, since the means of getting rich Sir
Is open to the Poorest Man by scraping in a Ditch Sir
Their Officers now make their beds, and cook their meals we hear Sir
But soon they must betake themselves to scrape THERE too we fear Sir.

'Tis time we have a SILVER STREET and a GOLDEN SQUARE Sir
But still we must remember they've Golden Mountains THERE Sir
Now doubtless they will build their Towns of Gold or such like stuff Sir
And as we all are going THERE, they'll soon have "BRICKS" enough Sir.

Oh the glorious time has come at last deny it who's so bold Sir
A pound of baked potatoes now, will bring its weight in gold Sir
While blankets, brandy, Lucifers, and shoes and boots "WORN OUT" Sir
Will rise, that every "SOUL" will wish, a "HEALING" time no doubt Sir.

Instead of drinking Pump water, or even HALF AND HALF Sir
We all will live like jolly souls and Port and Sherry quaff Sir
In "SPIRITS" we will keep ourselves,—The Mettle's coming in Sir
And not a man will now be found who'll say he wants for "TIN" Sir.

Oh the Good Time has come at last, we need no more complain Sir
The Rich can live in luxury, and the Poor can do the same Sir
For the Good Time has come at last, and as we all are told Sir
We shall be Rich at once now, with, California Gold Sir.

MAGNUS (CHARLES) & COMPANY NEW YORK

1858–1865 12 Frankfort Street

An Eastern lithographer, listed in *America on Stone,* who did many letterheads and views. The only California item I have seen is a lovely, colored letterhead, "Panorama of San Francisco. Sold by Charles Magnus, 12 Frankfort Street, New-York"—n.d. This is one of the very few colored letterheads.

MANSFIELD, H. NEW HAVEN, CONN.

Publisher of Baker's "View of the Town and Harbour of San Francisco."

MARQUIER, L. HAVANA, CUBA

"Tipos Californianos. No. 2. (Augusto Ferran) Augusto Ferran lo Litografió. Litogra. de L. Marquier Ce. de Lamparilla. No. 96. Posiciones Cómodas.—Comfort"—small, n.d.

"Tipos Californianos. No. 4. (Augusto Ferran) Augusto Ferran lo Litografió. Litogra. de L. Marquier Ce. de Lamparilla No. 96. Un Protector de las artes.—A Protector of Arts"—small, n.d.

"Tipos Californianos. No. 5. (Augusto Ferran) Augusto Ferran lo Litografió. Litogra. de L. Marquier Ce. de la Lamparilla. No. 96. Un Buen Flete.—A good freight"—small, n.d.

"Tipos Californianos. No. 8. (Augusto Ferran) Augusto Ferran lo Litografió. Litogra. de L. Marquier, Ce. de Lamparilla. No. 96. Una ligera indisposición. —A light Indisposition"—small, n.d.

"Tipos Californianos. No. 10. (Jose Baturone) Jose Baturone lo Litografió. Litogra. de L. Marquier Ce. de Lamparilla. No. 96. Argumentos sólidos. —Solid Arguments."—small, n.d.

MARRYAT, SAMUEL FRANCIS (FRANK) LONDON

This very fine English artist, who usually called himself "Frank" Marryat, was born in 1826, the son of the celebrated novelist, Frederick Marryat, and died in London in 1855. He was in California from 1850 to 1853. He drew one of M. & N. Hanhart's 1851 views of San Francisco.

Perhaps his most interesting California work is "Mountains and Molehills, or recollections of a burnt journal. By Frank Marryat. With illustrations by the Author. Longmans, Brown, Green and Longmans. New York and London. 1855." The London edition had eight plates lithographed by J. Brandard, (*q.v.*).

The following drawings by Marryat were exhibited in New York City in 1930. They were in the J. S. Drum Collection:

Original Watercolor Drawing of a general View of San Francisco and the Bay. Signed and dated, 1850. Small.

Original Watercolor Drawing of the Great Fire in San Francisco. Signed and dated, 1850. Small.

Original Watercolor Drawing of Bay Place, San Francisco. Signed 1850. Small.

Original Watercolor Drawing of Fremont Hotel, San Francisco. Signed and dated, 1850. Small.

Original Watercolor Drawing of San Francisco Fire. Signed and dated, 1850. Small.

Original Watercolor Drawing of Sansome Street, San Francisco. Signed and dated, 1850. Small.

Original Watercolor Drawing of Fremont Hotel San Francisco, California. Signed (1850). Small.

MASSETT, STEPHEN C. SAN FRANCISCO

See Boyd.

A noted composer, actor, lecturer, and singer. He landed in San Francisco in 1849 and is said to have given the first theatrical performance there, on June 22nd of that year.

MATHEWS, A. E. CINCINNATI AND NEW YORK

As a member of a regiment of Ohio volunteer infantry, Mathews drew Civil War scenes for several Cincinnati firms, and later did a few Western views, only two of which enter our story:

"California Golden City, Looking East. Sketched by A. E. Mathews"—small, n.d.

See also Britton & Rey's "Oceanic Steamship Company's Steamers."

MAYER & KORFF NEW YORK

Lithographed four maps, all small, in "Route from The Gulf of Mexico and the Lower Mississippi Valley to California and the Pacific Ocean. By Robert Creuzbaur, 1849. Published by H. Long & Bro. N. Y. 1849." Mayer & Korff are mentioned in *America on Stone* under Ferdinand Mayer, *et al.*

McDOUGAL, W. H. WASHINGTON

See W. H. Dougal.

McFARLANE, W. H. EDINBURGH, SCOTLAND

The only thing of his I have seen is "Sequoia Wellingtonia. The Two Guardsmen. From a photograph"—small, n.d..

McILVAINE, WILLIAM, JR. PHILADELPHIA

McIlvaine was the author and artist of "Sketches of Scenery And Notes of Personal Adventure, in California And Mexico. Containing Sixteen Lithographic Plates. By William M'Ilvaine, Jr. Philadelphia: 1850":

"California And Mexico" (frontispiece); "San Francisco. Drawn June 1849"; "Sacramento City"; "Sutters Fort"; "Sütters Mill"; "Stockton"; "Prairie"; "Woods Creek"; "Kanaka Creek"; "Cañon on the Towalumne"; "Acapulco"; "Ruins of Convent at Acapulco"; "Chapultepec"; "Belen Gate"; "City of Mexico"; and "St. Juan d'Ulloa"

These plates are of unusually fine workmanship.

McLELLAN, DAVID — NEW YORK

"Map of the United States, Canada, Mexico and the West Indies with Central America. Showing all the routes to California with a table of distances. New York. Ensign, Bridgman & Fanning, 156 William St. cor. of Ann St. 1854. D. McLellan, Lithogr. 26 Spruce St. N.Y."—large.

He also did important Eastern views. See *America on Stone.*

McMURTRIE, WILLIAM B. — SAN FRANCISCO

See Butler's "Elephant & Prospector." Also N. Currier's "View of San Francisco." PLATE 58

METCHIM & COMPANY — LONDON

1850 Adam Street, Strand

Lithographed three of the plates, all "W. R. Ryan del. On stone by R. J. Hamerton," in "Personal Adventures in Upper and Lower California in 1848–9; with the Author's Experiences at the Mines. By William Redmond Ryan. London: William Shoberl, Publisher, 1850":

"The Stanislaus Mine"; "Sacramento City"; and "The Principal Street of San Francisco"

MICHELIN, FRANCIS — BOSTON AND NEW YORK

One of the important Eastern lithographers, noted chiefly for his large group of views. His work is fully listed in *America on Stone.* Two California items are:

"City of San Francisco, Cala. From Daguerreotypes taken on the spot. Lithographed & printed in tints by F. Michelin, 225 Fulton St. N.Y. Published by Marvin & Hitchcock, Booksellers & Stationers, San Francisco"—medium, n.d. (c.1852).

"View of Proposed Trinity Church. San Francisco, California. On stone by G. W. Burton. Printed by Michelin"—small, n.d.

MILLER (PETER) & COMPANY NEW YORK

A company which seems to have made maps and plans only. They worked from 1834 through to 1869, at various addresses, fully listed in *America on Stone*.

The only California print of theirs seems to be: "San Francisco. From Actual Surveys. 1850. Millers Lith. 140 Pearl Street, N. Y."—small, n.d. (c.1850)

MOLLHAUSEN, H. B. UNKNOWN

Drew many of the originals, lithographed by Sarony, Major & Knapp, for "The Pacific Railroad Reports and Surveys." He was a geologist and worked on the explorations. Later in Germany he wrote a book on his travels in the West.

MONMONIER, WILLIAM B. CALIFORNIA

1856	Montecristo
1858	Downieville
Unknown	Goodyears Bar

See Britton & Rey's "View of Goodyears Bar & Goodyears Creek" and
PLATE 42 "View of Minnesota," and their two letterheads, "View of Goodyears Bar" and "View of Montecristo."

Monmonier, one of the fine artists of the period, evidently moved about the gold region frequently, for each of his lithographs gives his address in a different one of the mining towns.

MOODY, EDWIN UNKNOWN

PLATE 47 Drew two shipwreck views for Bufford, and Peirce & Pollard's "View of
PLATE 87 San Francisco, from Telegraph Hill."

MURDOCH, JOHN SAN FRANCISCO

PLATE 29 "Lady Vernon. San Francisco, Cala., August 1855. Painted by John Murdoch. Lithy. of Britton & Rey S. F. Entered . . . 1855"—large. There is only one copy known of this print—the one herein reproduced. Here we have, also, the only trotting print for California, and since none has been found by the other lithographers, it may well be called the first real sporting print of the Pacific. In the margin, to the left, are records of Lady Vernon's races at Cambridge Park Course, Boston, and Union Course, Long Island. To the right, her races on Pioneer Course, San Francisco, in 1854, both of which she won, beating Lady Mac and Daniel Webster in April and May, for purses of $3,000.

There is a story in one of the old sporting papers confirming the title on the print. It was the first race in San Francisco. The paper further stated that Lady Vernon and her sulky had been part of one of the wagon trains from the East, she having crossed the continent on her own feet before participating in the race.

NAGEL (LOUIS), *ET AL.* NEW YORK AND SAN FRANCISCO

New York:

1844–1845	Louis Nagel, 74 Fulton Street
1846	Nagel & Mayer, 74 Fulton Street
1847–1848	Louis Nagel, 74 Fulton Street
1849–1854	Nagel & Weingaertner (Adam), 74 Fulton Street
1854–1857	Nagel & Weingaertner, 143 Fulton Street (and 1855: Nagel & Lewis, 122 Fulton Street)

San Francisco: (Louis Nagel)

1856	unknown
1858	133 Clay Street
1859–1860	151 Clay Street
1861	543 Clay Street
1862	529 Clay Street; also Nagel, Fishbourne & Kuchel, corner Clay and Leidesdorff Streets, and 529 Clay Street
1863–1864	529 Clay Street
1864–1865	611 Clay Street
1866	lithographer, residence, King Street
1867–1869	lithographer, residence, 6 Malvina Place
1870	lithographer, residence, 4 Malvina Place
1871–1873	lithographer, residence, 4 Ewer Place
Unknown	Nagel & Schwartz, 58 Montgomery Street

In the East, Nagel's most important work was done in the association with Weingaertner, a firm that turned out a considerable mass of very important and interesting lithographs. Their work is quite fully listed in *America on Stone.*

But four California prints of theirs have come to light:

Nagel & Weingaertner lithographed the plates, all "on stone by C. Gildemeister," in "Illustrated Notes of an Expedition Through Mexico and California. By J. W. Audubon. New-York: J. W. Audubon, 34 Liberty Street. 1852":

> "Fourth of July Camp"; "The Night Watch"; "Canon, Jesus Maria"; and "Jesus Maria"

At the time *America on Stone* was published, I understood that Nagel had not gone to San Francisco before 1858, but since then I have seen a print, the "Private Signals," reproduced in colors, copyrighted in 1856 and printed "by L. Nagel, San Francisco." Since then, too, the combination of Nagel & Schwartz has been discovered, although just when this association was formed is not known.

From Nagel alone, in San Francisco, the following prints have turned up:

PLATE 112 "Bay-View-Park Galop. Composed by P. R. Nicholls, San-Francisco. Dedicated to W. F. Williamson. C. B. Gifford, Del. L. Nagel, Print."—music sheet, n.d. One of the three sporting prints.

"Camano Island. Puget Sound. Grennan & Cranney's Mills. C. B. Gifford, lith. Print. by L. Nagel"—medium, n.d.

"The Exhibition Fair. New Song as Sung by Mr. S. A. Wells. Composed and dedicated to the members of the San-Francisco Mechanics' Institute by P. R. Nicholls. Published by A. Kohler, 178 Washington Street and 276 Stockton Street. Lith. Print. by Louis Nagel, No. 133 Clay Street. San Francisco"—music sheet, n.d.

"First Annual Encampment of the Second Brigade C. M. Brigadier General Ellis, Commander. Reviewed by His Excellency Govr. Stanford. Brigade Drill and Sham Fight, Octr. 14th 1863. From nature & on stone by T. Grob. Printed by L. Nagel. Entered . . . 1864"—medium.

"First Annual Encampment, Of The Second Brigade, California Militia. Camp Allen. Encinal Alameda. October 1863. Brigadier General John S. Ellis Commanding. Printed by L. Nagel, S. F. C. B. Gifford, Lith."—medium, n.d. This differs from the Grob view above.

"Hayes' Valley, San Francisco. C. B. Gifford del. et lith. Printed by L. Nagel, S. F."—medium, n.d. Shows one of the early Market Street railroad trains. A note below the copy at the Pioneer Society dates it as 1862. PLATE 79

"L. & A. B. Burr's, North Beach, San Francisco. C. B. Gifford, del. L. Nagel, Print."—small, n.d. (c.1860). A view of a famous roadhouse at the entrance to the Bay.

"Lombard, North Point and Greenwich Docks, San Francisco. Ships Great Republic, Hurricane and Zenobia Discharging. On stone by H. Eastman & A. Nahl. Drawn from nature by C. B. Gifford. [L. Nagel, Print.]"—medium, n.d. PLATE 80

"Map of the Country 40 Miles Around San Francisco. Exhibiting the County Lines and correct plats of all the Ranchos and the Public Land. Compiled from U. S. Surveys by Leander Ransom. Lith. of L. Nagel, 151 Clay St. S. F. Entered . . . 1860"—medium.

"Private Signals of the Merchants of New York and San Francisco. Respectfully Dedicated to the Merchants of San Francisco by Charles B. Gifford. Lith. Print in colors by L. Nagel, San Francisco. Entered . . . 1856"—large. These were the signals used to send word into the city as to what ships were about to enter the harbor of San Francisco. It must be realized that until about 1855 California had no telegraph system, nor was the delivery of mail from the East any too rapid. A shipping company's agent was informed on each ship's arrival what the nature of the cargo would likely be on the next voyage. There was a lookout tower high on the hill above the Cliff House at the outside entrance to the Bay. There these signals were displayed as the ships hove into view far out in the Pacific, and the message of the signal flags relayed in to the tower atop Telegraph Hill. From there the agents in the city could tell of the approaching arrival and assemble the necessary stevedores on the wharf. Often a good share of the population would also see the signal and go en masse to meet the ship. PLATE 81

"San Francisco. Bird's Eye View. Drawn & Lithographed by C. B. Gifford. Printed by L. Nagel, S.F. Published by Snow & Roos, San Francisco. Entered 1864"—large. This view was also published by Robinson & Snow.

"San Francisco. Panoramic View of San Francisco, from Russian Hill, 1862. Painted and lithographed by C. B. Gifford. Printed by L. Nagel, San Francisco and published by A. Rosenfield, S.F., copyrighted, 1862." The print is divided into five sections, each measuring 12½ x 20½, is mounted and joined on linen in a decorated clothbound folder, and has on inside of cover: "A Printed Historical Sketch of California." The blue paper cover mount is decorated in gold with title and picture of an early railroad train. A note in the folder reads:

" 'The accompanying Panoramic View' was taken from the top of Russian Hill, which is (with one exception) the highest eminence in San Francisco. Its elevation is three hundred and sixty feet.

"From its summit we overlook nearly the whole city, and of the bay we have an uninterrupted view, from the Golden Gate to its southern extremity.

"The 'View' embraces the entire circle, commencing at the Golden Gate and ending at the place of beginning, in five sections, as follows:

Section No. 1—Looking West. Showing Point Lobos, Telegraph, City Water Works, Greenwich St. School, etc.

Section No. 2—Looking North. Showing Jones St., Taylor St., Pfeiffer's Castle, etc.

Section No. 3—Looking East. Showing Telegraph Hill, Vallejo St., Jackson St. Wharf, Jewish Synagogue, etc.

Section No. 4—Looking East and South. Showing Broadway, Second St., Steamboat Point, etc.

Section No. 5—Looking South and West. Showing Mission Bay, Jobson Observatory, Calvary Cemetery, etc.

"The light and shade are so arranged that every house is plainly shown, and all the prominent buildings are numbered and the names given beneath. Not only the city but the surrounding land and water are visible."

This important, rare panorama is also found with an 1863 copyright date.

PLATE 82 "Steamer Day in San Francisco. [Signed on stone:] E. Jump. Published by Snow & Roos, San Francisco. L. Nagel Print. Entered . . . 1866"—medium. Steamer Day in San Francisco came on the 13th and 28th of each month, two days before the sailing dates of the steamers to Panama. Collections were always made on these days, so that the remittances could be sent to firms in the East. Steamer Day became such a firmly established tradition that even after the coming of the railroads the custom was maintained for some thirty years. Greenbacks were unknown in San Francisco in those days, all transactions being made in so-called "hard money"—gold or silver; hence the money bags in the hands of the figures in the picture. This lithograph has been seen with a key written in the lower margin. Among the figures named are Frank C. Snow, Joseph Roos, and Fred M. Marriott.

"U. S. Navy-Yard. Mare Island, and City of Vallejo, Solano Co. Cal. C. B. Gifford, del. et lith. Print. L. Nagel, S. F."—medium, n.d.

See also: Gray & Gifford's "Birds Eye View of San Jose"; Kuchel & Dresel's "The Great Yosemite Fall," "Shasta Butte & Shasta Valley," "View of That Portion of the City," and "Views of the New Ditch"; Nahl's "Abraham's Daughter," "Agricultural . . . Society," "An Hour at the Cliff," "Constitutional Amendment," "General View of the Great Yosemite Valley," "In Memoriam" (reproduced in *America on Stone*), "Mission Dolores," and "Society of California Volunteers." PLATE 76

From Nagel, Fishbourne & Kuchel are the following:

"The Mammoth Tree Grove, Calaveras Co. California, And Its Avenues. Drawn by Edward Vischer. Nagel, Fishbourne & Kuchel, Lithographers, S. F. Entered . . . 1862"—large. The center view in this print (Plate IX of Vischer's Mammoth Tree Grove Portfolio) shows the train of imported Bactrian Camels crossing the Sierra Nevadas by the Big Tree Route—one of our really curious records. PLATE 84

General Edward F. Beale, while once exploring Death Valley with the famous Kit Carson, happened to carry in his pack a book on travels in China and Tartary. Reading of the use of camels in those countries, he became convinced of their usefulness as a means of transportation over deserts. Feeling that they would have military value in the southwestern parts of the United States, he went to Jefferson Davis, then Secretary of War, and interested him in the idea. A Navy ship was outfitted and sent to the Near East, returning to Texas in 1856 with thirty-three camels. Very soon afterwards forty-four more were imported. Beale set out on an expedition with a train of them, and in a report to the Secretary of War says: "For Indian Scouts with infantry companies in countries as badly supplied with water as Texas and New Mexico they would prove an invaluable aid." He comments on the camels' ability to carry huge loads, to get along on food which mules would reject, such as greasewood, the toughness of their unshod feet, their indifference to heat, etc. He also reported, however, a difficulty in obtaining drivers who understood the proper care of the animals. He then quoted the statement which had appeared in a Los Angeles newspaper for January 21, 1858:

> General Beale and about fourteen camels stalked into town last Friday week and gave our streets quite an Oriental aspect. It looks odd indeed to see, outside of a menagerie, a herd of huge, ungainly, awkward but docile animals move about in our midst with people riding them like horses and bringing up weird and far-off associations to the Eastern traveller, whether by book or otherwise, of the lands of the mosque, crescent or turban, of the pilgrim mufti and dervish with visions of the great shrines of the world, Mecca and Jerusalem, and the toiling throngs that have for centuries wended thither, of the burning sands of Arabia and Sahara where the desert is boundless as the ocean and the camel is the ship thereof. These camels under charge of Gen. Beale are all grown and serviceable and most of them are well broken to the saddle and are very gentle. All belong to the one hump species. These animals are admirably adapted to the travel across our continent and their introduction was a brilliant idea the result of which is beginning most happily.

In spite of all Beale's hopes, the experiment proved unsuccessful, and the War Department decided the camels would be impractical for military use. They were sold off in California, and from then on kept turning up in the most unexpected places. Some were bought for use in the mining country.

The camels are mentioned in Newmark's "Sixty Years in Southern California" as follows:

> On September 21st, Captain W. S. Hancock, who first came to Los Angeles in connection with the expedition against the Mojave Indians in 1859, sought to establish a new kind of express between Los Angeles and Fort Mojave, and sent out a camel in charge of Greek George to make the trial trip. When they had been gone two and a half days, the regular express messenger bound for Los Angeles met them at Lane's Crossing, apparently in none too promising a condition; which later give rise to a report that the camel had died on the desert. This occasioned numerous newspaper squibs apropos of both the speed and the staying powers of the camel as contrasted with those of the burro; and finally, in October, the following announcement appeared placarded throughout the town:

By Poulterer, De Ro & Eldridge

Office and Salesroom, Corner California &
Front Streets, San Francisco

Peremptory Sale
of
Bactrian Camels
Imported from the Amoor River
Ex Caroline E. Foote.

On Wednesday, Oct. 10, 1860,
We will Sell at Public Auction
In Lots to Suit Purchasers,
for Cash,
13 Bactrian Camels,

From a cold and mountainous country, comprising 6 males and 7 females, (5 being with young,) all in fine health and condition.

***For further particulars, inquire of the Auctioneers.

Frederic L. Paxson in his "History of the American Frontier, 1763–1893" speaks of them as follows:

> Salt was freighted across the Sierras until prospectors developed many and extensive deposits. The first efforts to bring salt from beyond the forty-mile desert was remarkable on account of the animals used. The owners of the salt deposit sent to Asia and obtained in good condition nine Bactrian camels in the spring of 1861, and used them for a year or two. Each one carried about five hundred pounds, or twice as much as a pack mule did. They ate nearly every kind of desert vegetation, particularly the harsh "greasewood." On the other hand, they suffered greatly from the alkali, and their drivers despised and neglected them in every conceivable manner, so that the experiment never had a fair trial. In the end some of them died, some were used to carry ore in Arizona, and some escaped and have been reported at intervals by frightened cowboys or astonished tourists in the mountains of northern Arizona and New Mexico.

"Panorama of the Washoe Region, From the Summit of Mount Davidson. From nature by Edward Vischer. Lith. & Print. of Nagel, Fishbourne &

Kuchel, Cor. Clay & Leidesdorff Sts. San Francisco. Entered . . . 1862"—medium. One of Vischer's Washoe Mining District series. A curious circular panorama in the center, with six views and two tabulations of lodes and mills at the sides.

PLATE 15 "Puget Mill Co's Mills. Teekalet W.T. Talbot & Co. San Francisco, California. From Nature & on Stone by T. Grob. Nagel, Fishbourne & Kuchel, 529 Clay Street, San Francisco, California"—large, n.d.

From Nagel & Schwartz but one print has been found:

PLATE 83 "San Juan Del Norte, or Greytown. Nagel & Schwartz Lithographers, 58, Montgomery St., Sn. Franco."—small, n.d.

NAHL BROTHERS — SAN FRANCISCO

1852–1853	Charles Nahl, corner Kearny and Sacramento streets
1854	C. Nahl & A. Wenderoth, daguerreotype artists, 79 Broadway
1856–1858	C. Nahl & Bro. (Arthur), artists, 79 Broadway
1859	Nahl Bros. (Charles & Otto), artists, 79 Clay Street
1860–1862	Nahl & Bro. (Charles & Arthur), Broadway
1863–1865	Nahl Brothers (Arthur & Charles), artists, 611 Clay Street
1866	same, 121 Montgomery Street
1867–1871	Nahl Brothers (H. W. Arthur & Charles), art & photographic gallery, 121 Montgomery; in 1867 as Nahl Brothers & Dickman
1872	Nahl, H. W. Arthur, artist, 12 Montgomery Street
1873	Nahl, Charles, artist, 12 Montgomery Street; also H.W. Arthur Nahl, landscape painter

The Nahls were best known as painters, but we find their names on several California lithographs as artists or lithographers.

A. Nahl did, in 1863, a portrait of Thomas O. Larkin, one of the early American settlers who served as United States Consul to California from 1844
PLATE 80 to 1846. With H. Eastman, A. Nahl drew on stone Nagel's "Lombard North Point."

Charles Nahl drew, with A. Wenderoth, Butler's "Miners Cabin" and "A Miner Prospecting." Alone, he drew Britton & Rey's certificate of membership in the Committee of Vigilance, and drew and lithographed "In Memoriam.

THE

CALIFORNIA PIONEERS

a Song

Lith & del. by Quirot & Co. cornr. Califa. & Montgomery Sts. S-F.

RESPECTFULLY INSCRIBED TO

MRS. J. EMERSON SWEETSER.

Words & Music

BY

Dr. M. A. RICHTER

Published & Sold by ATWILL & Co. in San-Francisco.

N.B. The First Piece of Music Pubd. in Cala.

Entered according to the act of Congress in the Year 1852 by Sweeny & Baugh, in the Clerks office for the Northern district of Califa. July 29th

Lith. by Quirot & Co. corner California & Montgomery Sts. S. F.

Length 140 Ft

INTERIOR VIEW OF MERCHANTS EXCHANGE, SAN FRANCISCO, CAL.
As Draperied on the occasion of the Obsequies of the Hon. Henry Clay 1852
SWEENY & BAUGH, PROPRIETORS

94

Healy del

Lith. of Quirot & Co. corner of Montgy. Califa. Sts. S. Francisc

VIEW OF SHASTA CITY.
Published by Geo. W. King Shasta.

95

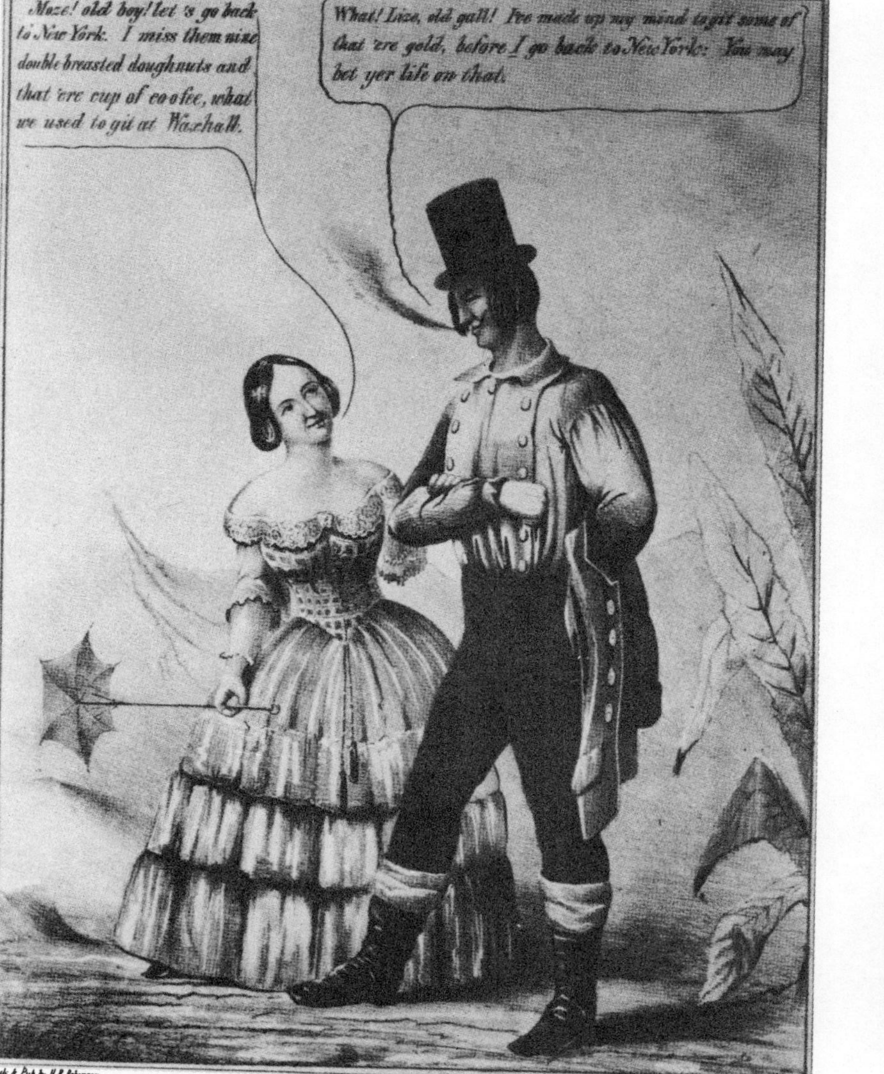
Moze! old boy! let 's go back to New York. I miss them nize double breasted doughnuts and that 're cup of co-fee, what we used to git at Waxhall.
What! Lize, old gall! I've made up my mind to git some of that 're gold, before I go back to New York: You may bet yer life on that.
Lith. & Pub. by H.R. Robinson,
31 Park Row N.Y.

MOSE AND LIZE IN CALIFORNIA.

96

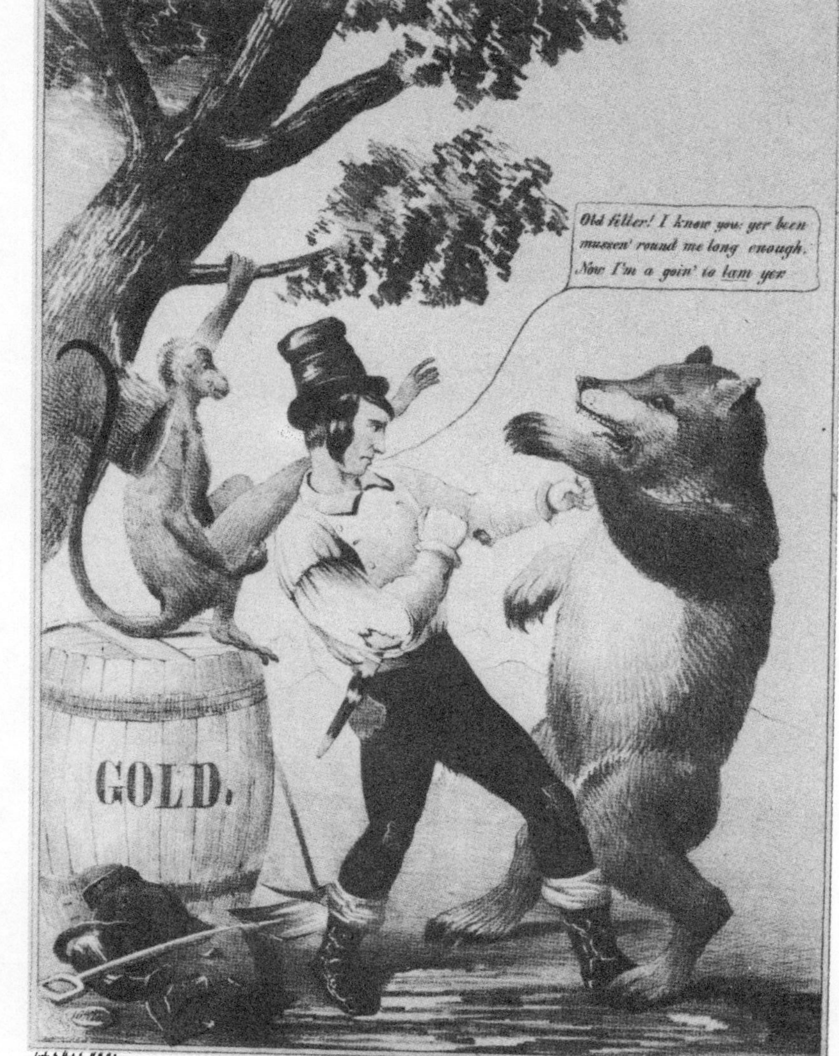
Old feller! I know you: yer been mussen' round me long enough. Now I'm a goin' to lam yer
GOLD.
Lith. & Pub. by H.R. Robinson,
31 Park Row N.Y.

MOSE IN CALIFORNIA.

Set-to with a ***BEAR.***

97

ONE OF THE CALIFORNIAN BO HOYS TAKING LEAVE OF HIS GAL.

J. STREET, FROM THE LEVEE.

K, STREET, FROM THE LEVEE.

INUNDATION OF THE STATE CAPITOL.

City of Sacramento, 1862.

Published by A ROSENFIELD, San Francisco

LOSS OF THE GOLDEN GATE BY FIRE

ON THE 27TH JULY 1862 15 MILES FROM MANZANILLO,

Sketched by an Eye Witness, Published by A. Rosenfield

TERRIBLE LOSS OF LIFE.

338 Persons on board, 228 Lost and Missing.

On Sunday July 27th, about quarter to 5 P. M. while the first cabin passengers were at dinner, word was brought to Captain Hudson that the ship was on fire. So soon as the Captain saw that the alarm was not a false one, the passengers were ordered forward and the ship headed for the shore, which was 3 or 4 miles distant.

About 100 of the passengers had succeeded in reaching the forecastle, when the flames bursting out amid-ships cut off all communication between the fore and after part of the ship. The sea was calm, but the westerly wind hurled the flames aft, and soon many who were in that part of the vessel leaped early into the sea and were drowned. There appear to have been plenty of life-preservers on board, but they were in the boats and not easily reached. The pumps were manned, the male passengers vieing with the crew to work them, but the flames burst out so rapidly that they soon had to be deserted.

There was a terrible panic among the passengers on the forecastle; yet no more than might have been expected. A few leaped into the sea and a very few of them provided with life preservers. Others clung to the deck till the fire compelled them to leap or endure a more horrible death. Others whose garments were on fire had to be thrust overboard as the desperate chance of life. The hurricane deck fell with a crash while the vessel was still under way. Several ropes were made fast to the sides of the ship and thrown overboard. Passengers descended by these to the water but they were soon so much loaded that those who first went down by them were crowded off and drowned. One of these ropes burned off and all who were on it sank together.

Life-preservers, spars, everything that would float was thrown overboard by those who could reach them, and the survivors availed themselves of their aid. Of the ten boats on board but five could be reached. One of these was capsized and sunk on being launched. The other four were but partly filled when launched, but many of those who were found swimming were taken on board. They could not land though the surf, and instantly steered off for Manzanillo.

The ship struck when about 300 yards from the beach, where a heavy surf was rolling. By the shock many who still clung to the bows were thrown overboard. The last to leave the ship were Captains Hudson and Pearson, who dropped from the bowsprit after the vessel beached, and with great difficulty made their way to the beach.

Many were washed up by the surf, more dead than alive. Those who were in a better condition labored faithfully to draw them out of the surf. By 6 o'clock the vessel, except her huge machinery, had entirely disappeared, the fire having burned all the woodwork to the water's edge. The living on shore counted some 80—and there were many dead. These were carefully conveyed to the upper beach, and as night drew on, the sad survivors prepared as they might to pass the night. They almost buried themselves in the dry sand both for warmth, for as the night proceeded it grew quite cold, and for protection from the mosquitoes and sand-flies which very much tormented them.

Early next morning, the living took such thin boards as they could find on the beach and with them excavated a grave for each of the 16 dead, whose bodies had been washed ashore.—[San Francisco Evening Bulletin.]

BAYARD TAYLOR

LITH. OF SARONY & MAJOR. N.Y.

SAN FRANCISCO IN NOVEMBER 1849.

NEW YORK. GEO P PUTNAM

SAN-FRANCISCO

1849.

DRAWN ON THE SPOT BY HENRY FIRKS, FOR

W. H. JONES, ESQ.

OF SAN-FRANCISCO U.C.

102

A full color reproduction of this plate appears in the color section in this book.

LITH OF SARONY & MAJOR NEW YORK.

A VIEW OF SUTTER'S MILL & CULLOMA VALLEY.

ON THE SOUTH FORK OF THE AMERICAN LINE, ALTA CALIFORNIA.

Respectfully dedicated to Capt. John A. Sutter,

by his obedient Servant John T. Little

103

A full color reproduction of this plate appears in the color section in this book.

MISSION DOLORES

SAN FRANCISCO

Presented to subscribers of Puck, the Pacific Pictorial. L. Nagel, print."—large, n.d. Both of these were reproduced in *America on Stone*.

From Nahl Brothers we have:

"Abraham's Daughter, as sung by Ben Cotton; arranged by F.H.H. Oldfield. San Francisco, published by M. Gray, 613 Clay Street; E. L. Ripley & Co., Sacramento; E. G. Randall, Portland, O. (1862)"—a music sheet. The lithograph is by Nahl Bros., from a photo. by Bryan & Johnston, L. Nagel, Print.

"The Agricultural, Horticultural and Mechanics Society, Of The Northern District Of California Award This Diploma To . . . Exhibited At The Annual Fair At Marysville. Nahl Brothers. L. Nagel. Print. S. F."—medium, n.d. Five rural scenes around border of print.

"An Hour at the Cliff. Published by M. Gray. L. Nagel, print."—music sheet, n.d.

Certificate of membership in the "Society of California Pioneers"—large, n.d. (c.1880). (Reproduced in *America on Stone*.)

Certificate of membership in the "Society of California Volunteers. Organized April 25, 1868. L. Nagel, print"—large, n.d.

"Constitutional Amendment Abolishing Slavery. L. Nagel, print. Entered . . . 1866"—large.

"General View of the Great Yo-Semite Valley. Mariposa County, California. T. A. Ayres, del. L. Nagel, print. Published by Hutchings & Rosenfield. Entered . . . 1859"—medium. This was sketched by Ayres in 1855.

"Mission Dolores. San Francisco, 1860. From the Potrero Nuevo. Drawn from nature by C. B. Gifford. Printed & Published by L. Nagel, 151 Clay St. S.F. Nahl Bros."—medium. This is a very attractive view of the famous mission.

"Instructions in Gymnastics By Arthur and Charles Nahl: Illustrated with Fifty-three Plates . . . Designed and Engraved By The Authors . . . San Francisco: Published by A. Rosenfield, 1863." All the plates in this volume were lithographed. The frontispiece is an especially beautiful piece of work.

NEAL, DAVID D. SAN FRANCISCO

Painter of good portraits that were lithographed, including "Captain John Paty." He was born at Lowell, Mass., in 1838, became well known for historical paintings and portraits, and died in 1915.

NESBITT, GEORGE F. NEW YORK

PLATE 85 "San Francisco. Lith. of Geo. F. Nesbitt—N.Y"—small, n.d. In the margin is stamped: "Published by Marvin & Hitchcock, Pioneer Book Store, San Francisco. Thompson & Hitchcock, Managers and Agents of Egory's California Express, 149 Pearl St. Cor Wall St. N. Y." Written in ink on the print is: "February 1860," although the lithograph was apparently copied from a Le Breton daguerreotype view of San Francisco in the early fifties.

NEWS LETTER, THE SAN FRANCISCO

The San Francisco *News Letter* was established in 1856 by Fred M. Marriott, an Englishman, born in 1805, who came to San Francisco in 1850 after founding a number of English papers, including the present *Illustrated London News*. Arriving in San Francisco, Marriott found that mail to and from the East cost five dollars the half-ounce, whereupon he conceived his novel weekly, most aptly named the *News Letter*. It was a digest of city and state news, issued in such form as could be sent through the mails at minimum cost. Printed on very thin, dull blue paper, its first two pages contained news and advertisements, the third page was left blank for letter writing, and the fourth for addressing. It was immediately successful. Bret Harte and Mark Twain were among its early contributors, and later Jack London, Gertrude Atherton, and other noted authors wrote for it. The paper carried many illustrations, a few of them lithographs, here listed under Britton & Rey, *et al.*, and one under Korbel & Brothers, the original owners of the *Wasp* (*q.v.*).

Marriott knew both Britton and Rey, and at one time they were mutually interested in the promotion of an early flying machine. Nagel's "Steamer Day"
PLATE 82 shows a caricature of Marriott—a tall, silk-hatted gentleman trying to collect from Messrs. Snow and Roos (*q.v.*) in front of their shop.

He died in 1884, and his son, Fred M. Marriott, Jr., took over the *News Letter*. It passed into the third generation's hands in 1925 when F. A. Marriott became owner, and was continued until 1928. In that year it combined with the *Wasp*, and the two are now being published in San Francisco as the *News Letter-Wasp: A Weekly Journal of Illustration and Comment*.

NOÉ, AMÉDÉE DE PARIS

This famous French caricaturist who drew under the name of "Cham" was born in Paris and died there. 1818–1879.

"Actualités. '1851 otant le bandeau que 1850 avait mis sur les yeux des actionnaires Californiens.' Chez Aubert & Cie. Pl. de la Bourse. 29 Paris. Imp. de Me. Ve. Aubert, 5 r. de l'Abbaye, Paris"—small (1851).

"Famille En Californie. 'Ah! mon Dieu voilà déjà nos domestiques qui nous abandonnent pour courir aux mines! Faudrait peut-être leur promettre une petite augmentation de gages!' Chez Aubert Pl. de la Bourse. Imp. Aubert & Cie."—small, n.d.

NOISY CARRIERS — SAN FRANCISCO

Noisy Carrier's Publishing Hall (Charles P. Kimball, Proprietor):

1852 — 77 Long Wharf

Noisy Carrier's Book & Stationery Company:

1856 — unknown

Noisy Carriers:

Unknown — 64 & 66 Long Wharf

Most of the work published or sold by the Noisy Carriers consisted of woodcuts, but their imprint appears on a few lithographs. Reproduced as an illustration is their "Honest Voters Trying to Elect Their Officers, in front of the house. Ballot Box Stuffers, Electing Their Men, behind the house"—small, n.d. PLATE 86

See also Britton & Rey's letterhead "Fort Vigilant," Pollard & Britton's "Sonora January, 1852," Butler's "Infancy," Fishbourne's "Map of the Mining Region," Cooke & Le Count's "Stockton," and De Vere's "Sixth Great Conflagration in San Francisco." PLATE 90 PLATE 54 PLATE 57

OGILBY, R. E. — SAN FRANCISCO

The artist of Britton & Rey's letterhead, "Grass Valley, Nevada County, California," of their "View of Ham's Mammoth Aqueduct," and of J. J. Le Count's "View of Grass Valley." PLATE 28

O'GRADY, W. H. — SAN FRANCISCO

1854 — artist, California Street and Buena Vista

1856–1857 — artist, 18 Court Block, Clay Street

Drew on stone the Justh, Quirot & Company "View of Downieville" reproduced in *America on Stone* as Plate 80.

I have seen no other lithographs by him.

OTIS, F. N. UNKNOWN

See Endicott & Company's "City of San Francisco."

PALMER, F. NEW YORK

PLATE 58 Drew on stone the McMurtrie view of San Francisco listed under N. Currier. See *Currier & Ives: Printmakers to the American People, Vol. I.*

PARSONS, C. NEW YORK

Parsons's story has been fully written in *Currier & Ives: Printmakers to the American People,* Volume I. Only two California prints of his have turned up, but see the Britton & Rey biographical sketch for mention of him. He and Joseph Britton were close friends as young men.

Parsons lithographed the Endicott & Company "City of San Francisco. From Rincon Point." He drew the large, 1878 Currier & Ives "City of San Francisco," possibly during his visit in San Francisco with Britton and Rey.

PAYOT, UPHAM & COMPANY SAN FRANCISCO

"Chart of the Comstock Mines and Sutro Tunnel. By Payot, Upham & Co. 204 Sansome Street, San Francisco"—large, n.d., with a border of views.

PEIRCE (JOSHUA H.), *ET AL.* NEW YORK AND SAN FRANCISCO

San Francisco:

1850 artist, Montgomery & Commercial Street

1854 lithographer, 110 Montgomery Street

1858 19 Court Block, Yerba Buena near Clay Street

Peirce did portraits, about 1841, for G. W. Lewis in New York.

From Peirce & Pollard, which association was formed sometime about
PLATE 87 1850, is "View of San Francisco, from Telegraph Hill. [Signed on stone:] Moody del. from a sketch by Swan. Lith. of Peirce & Pollard, San Francisco. Published by Cooke & Le Count"—letterhead, n.d. Written in ink on margin: "September 1850."

For other work by Peirce, see: Butler's "Grace Church," "Infancy," "James Evrard," "Jenny Lind Theatre," "Miss Cathrine Hayes"; Cooke & Le Count's "San Francisco in 1851"; Peregoy's "View of the Steam-boat Landing"; Pollard's "San Francisco from Rincon Point."

PEREGOY, CHARLES E. SAN FRANCISCO

See Pollard & Peregoy; also Cooke & Le Count's "San Francisco in 1851."

From Peregoy:

"View of The Steam-Boat Landing Sacramento City, from K Street. J. H. Peirce del. Printed by Chas. Peregoy"—and—"L Street—M Street. J. H. Peirce del. Printed by Chs. Peregoy. Published by Conner & Forrest, Stationers 2nd St. between J & K"—two separate views on one lettersheet.

The following interesting letter, dated San Francisco, Jan. 23rd, 1851, is appended to the view:

Dear Parents, Sisters, Brother &c.

I yesterday received two letters Dated the 21st & 25th of Novr. by which I was informed of Catharines severe sickness. Now if I was at home & the two celebrated physicians Drs. Mitchell & Armsby failed in effecting her perfect restoration to health the poor common miner himself would bet his life he could accomplish it. The latest news from the Southern mines is in relation to the rising of the Indians who have killed over 75 men who were engaged in mining on Rattlesnake creek, the miners are arming & intend to retaliate. My old partner Abbott is at Burn's diggings & in the very heart of the disturbed district. This mornings paper—says the U S troops in California are ordered against the Indians. Tell Mrs. Hance that I have seen her husband a number of times the past summer & fall. he is on Carsons creek engaged in a company to grind quartz, he also keeps a store. he is in good health & so are all the Albany boys. Some fool wrote home that Maggy Lenvereas husband Tim Knower was dead, but it is not so for he is still alive & kicking & mining on the Middle Fork of the American river at last accounts. Mr. Darrow was well at last accounts & Mr. Geo Trumbell is in town in good health & spirits. I am sorry to hear by your letters that Bill Vosburgh has taken to drinking merely on account of the loss of a few dollars, but before I would take it so hard I'd work with my feet when my hands would not hold out & strive to recover, but I have lost my all & think of it only at times I may be home in 2 or 3 months & it maybe the same number of years I love the climate of this country & could live here contented if you were all here. Another steam boat burst her boiler this morning in the harbor she was called the Major Tompkins & a number of lives were lost. You complain of my not writing but I will explain it all one of these days & now I dont think you will complain again as this is my 3rd or 4th letter since I came down Billy will arrive before this reaches you remember me to him The hombre that gave such a description of me must have seen me pretty often, as it is true I am as red as an Indian & my hair hangs down on my shoulders & back to say nothing of a few tufts of down on my face here & there. Tell Anthony to look out or I shall have a good opportunity to run him on whiskers & mustachios. I am in good health & spirits as I can make my board & clothing besides have some left while hundreds in town cannot do the first alone, but I know the ropes & know on which *line to pull.* The mail closes in a few minutes & I must hurry. Now for my sake don't worry about me for I never was in as good health as I have been since September. headache does not trouble me anymore & I weigh only 158 lbs ha ha ha what think you of that Give my love to all enquiring friends & do not forget Maria Phillips in particular for she is a good girl no mistake. Tell Ma to remember her last words to me & she need have no fears but what she said will come to pass Love to All & I remain your

Affectionate Son & Brother
John D. Mitchell

P. S. I will write by every mail until I start for home—John and Charlie well. JDM—

PLECKER, D. A. **UNKNOWN**

Drew Fishbourne's "A Correct View of the Mammoth Tree Grove."

POLLARD (C. J.), *ET AL.* **SAN FRANCISCO**

1850 C. J. Pollard, Lithographer, Montgomery & Clay Streets
Unknown Peirce & Pollard
Unknown Pollard & Peregoy
1852 Pollard & Britton, Merchant Street

See Peirce & Pollard.

Pollard was among the pioneer lithographers of California. From him is probably one of the earliest lithographs made in San Francisco:

"View of San Francisco February 1850. C. J. Pollard's Lith. San Francisco. Drawn on Stone for J. P. Bogardus"—letterhead, n.d. This view has a

Gold Rush look. It seems hurriedly drawn, as if to meet the popular demand for a picture of the town, to send back home.

He issued at the same time, or possibly shortly after, the companion view:

"San Francisco from Rincon Point. C. J. Pollard's Lith. Pub. by J. P. Bogardus. J. H. Peirce del."—letterhead, n.d. This title was taken from an impression used by an early pioneer, who emigrated from Massachusetts to California soon after the discovery of gold, having apparently been attracted by stories of the fabulous wealth of the gold mines to be found in that country. The letter which is penned below the view, and which is addressed to his wife, Mrs. Charles A. Wood, Neponset, Mass., is of interest, as showing that the view is earlier than March 28, 1850, the date of the letter. This letter, which is written from San Francisco, is a description of the view with references and numbers, as to the places of interest in it. The writer states that "You have above a picture of the place where I am now writing." The view is one looking towards Telegraph Hill, showing a scanty settlement, sailing vessels and steamboats in the harbor. In the foreground are tents of settlers. A copy has been seen lithographed in gold.

From Pollard & Peregoy is "John Smith. Published by Lovegrove & Murray Sacramento City. Lith. of Pollard & Peregoy San Francisco"—letterhead, n.d., with nine views: PLATE 91

"Mr. John Smith takes final leave of Mrs. John Smith"; "John Smith, being short of cash, turns porter to the Elephant House"; "John Smith has struck a Lead"; "John Smith having made a pile leaves for Sacramento on a bust"; "John Smith bets his pile on the Jack"; "John Smith dead broke"; "John Smith resolves to reform"; "Fortune favors John Smith & he invests his dust in a 'Ranch' "; and "John Smith arrives safe home with his pile"

From the very interesting early alignment of Pollard & Britton we have:

"Celebration of Washington's Birth Day—San Francisco Feby. 23rd, 1852 Pub. by Cooke & Le Count"—letterhead, n.d. PLATE 88

"Columbia, Stanislaus County, in 1852. G. H. Goddard del. Entered . . . 1852"—small. A short-lived mining town. It was famed as a gambling center, having as many as one hundred and forty-three gambling houses. The diggings were dry but with much gold, principally in the form of nuggets.

PLATE 89 "Columbia January, 1852. G. H. Goddard del. Entered . . . 1852"—letterhead. The only known copy of this rare letterhead is the one reproduced, on which appears the following letter:

San francisco July 28th 1852

Dear father,

I received your letter dated in May 1852 and was very sorrow to hear of your ilness, but knowing that you are generaly accoustom to such ill turns I have evry reason to hope that you will soon recover and be able to attend to business again. I wish that I was at home so that I would be able to render you some assistance. however I hope that we shall be able to see each other before longe. I think that we shall by next April if our lives are spared. I have left the mines now and arrived in this citty with the intention of taking a voyage to sea. I expect to sail for Perue the first of the month. I have seen Mr. Ware and received a degurrean type and a letter from you it look so natural that I fancied that it was your self in person when I opened it I said to myself (how do yo do father.) I could fancy that I had you by the hand. but alass we are not so near together. Mr. Ware said that he enjoyed himself very well at home. I have seen several from Dorchester since my arrival in this citty Stephen Guliver Amasa Bird and Mr. Severns. today I see Mrs Howard Josephine schoolmarm. She has been unwell the most part of her time. but she says that she likes the country very well. Joseph Ware is working up to Benecia I have writen a letter to James Wiggenton and requested him to send me some things which was sent by him for me. but I have not had even an answer, from him yet. you stated in your letter that he was on Spanish Bar but you did not mension what river it was on. pleas not write any more letters until you hear from me again and I remain your affectionate so

[Signed] FRANK.

N B you may look for me home by next April if nothing happens.

"San Francisco. Published by Cooke & Le Count. [Signed on stone]: Britton. Entered . . . 1852"—letterhead.

"San Francisco, January 1852. On stone by J. Britton. Sketched by H. Eastman"—medium, n.d.

"Sonora January, 1852. Entered . . . 1852 by G. H. Goddard [Stamped in margin]: Noisy Carriers Publishing Hall 77 Long Wharf San Francisco Charles P. Kimball Propr[i]etor"—letterhead. PLATE 90

PRANG (LOUIS) & COMPANY BOSTON

This firm, which was considered in *America on Stone*, published a set of chromo-lithographs of California views in 1873. They were "after John R. Key," size about 7″ x 14″:

"The Golden Gate, Looking West"
"Cliff House"
"Mt. Diablo, San Joaquin Valley"
"Lake Tahoe, Looking Southwest"
"Sacramento Valley"
"Redwood Trees, Santa Cruz Mts."
"Big Trees, Calaveras Grove"
"Yosemite Valley, Looking East from the Mariposa"
"The Domes of the Yosemite"
"Bridal Veil Fall, Yosemite Valley"

PRENDERGAST, J. SAN FRANCISCO

"Montgomery Street, San Francisco. Prendergast Del."—small, n.d., is the only thing of his alone I have seen.

See also Zakreski & Hartman. PLATE 110

PREVOST, V. UNKNOWN

See Sarony & Major.

This is probably Victor Prevost, who did a portrait printed by Nagel in Philadelphia.

QUIROT & COMPANY SAN FRANCISCO

See Justh, Quirot, *et al.*

REY, JACQUES JOSEPH SAN FRANCISCO

See Britton & Rey.

Also see Butler's "San Francisco Quadrilles," signed on the stone: "Rey."

RIEHN, C. UNKNOWN

See Quirot & Company's "View of Agua Fria Valley."

RINGGOLD, CADWALADER WASHINGTON

Ringgold was a commander in the United States navy who was the author of and drew some of the plates in "A Series of Charts, with Sailing Directions, State of California," listed here under W. H. Dougal. See also the charts listed under Curtis B. Graham.

ROBINSON, ALFRED UNKNOWN

PLATE 59 The artist of some of the plates in "Life in California," listed under G. & W. Endicott.

Alfred Robinson arrived first in California in 1829 as supercargo on the ship *Brookline,* of Boston, and made several trips in that capacity on various other ships. In 1842 he was the agent on the maiden voyage of the *California,* the first steamer sent out by the Pacific Mail Steamship Company. He married a Spanish girl in California and settled there, becoming known as "Don Alfredo Robinson." In 1889 William Heath Davis speaks of him as one of the few surviving pre-Gold Rush settlers. Davis, in addition to being noted here as the author of the interesting "Seventy-Five Years in California" (see Teschmaker), was one of the pioneers who corrected the last known issue of the Firks view.

ROBINSON, HENRY R. NEW YORK

1833–1834	carver & gilder, 52 Cortlandt Street
1835	Fleetwood & Robinson, corner of Nassau and Spruce Streets
1836–1837	caricaturist, 52 & 48 Cortlandt Street
1837–1842	caricaturist, 52 Cortlandt Street (and 1839–1841: 2 Wall Street)
1842–1843	caricaturist, 58 Cortlandt Street
1843–1848	lithographer, 142 Nassau Street
1848–1849	lithographer, print and caricature publisher, 142 Nassau Street and 31 Park Row.
1849–1850	lithographer, 31 Park Row
1850–1851	lithographer, 11 Theater Alley

Robinson also had an office on Pennsylvania Avenue, Washington, D. C. Robinson was one of the major Eastern lithographers, noted particularly for his cartoons and caricatures. For the full story of him, see *America on Stone.*

The only California items of his we have found are four comics:

"A Gold Hunter on his Way to California, via, St. Louis. Published by H. R. Robinson, 31 Park Row N.York"—small, n.d. This was issued, with a different background, by N. Currier and by Kelloggs & Comstock, as "The Independent Gold Hunter on his Way to California." It has also been seen, with this title, "Verlag v. F. A. Behrens." The Robinson version carries at the top the words, "I am sorry I did not follow the advice of Granny and go round the Horn, through the Straits, or by Chagres." The issue reproduced is by Kelloggs & Comstock.

"Mose and Lize in California. Lith. & Pub. by H. R. Robinson, 31 Park Row N.Y."—small, n.d. PLATE 96

"Mose in California. Set-to with a Bear. Lith. & Pub. by H. R. Robinson, 31 Park Row, N.Y. Entered . . . 1849"—small. PLATE 97

"One of the Californian Bo-Hoys Taking Leave of His Gal. [Signed on stone:] E. W. C. Lith. of H. R. Robinson 142 Nassau St. N.Y. Entered . . . 1846"—small. "E. W. C." is Edward W. Clay, the brilliant satirist. PLATE 98

ROSENFIELD, A. SAN FRANCISCO

See Hutchings & Rosenfield; Thomas Armstrong; Nagel's "San Francisco. Panoramic View"; and Nahl's "Instructions in Gymnastics."

Rosenfield also published the following two letterheads:

"Inundation of the State Capitol, City of Sacramento, 1862. J, Street, from the Levee. K, Street, from the Levee"—n.d., two views on one sheet. PLATE 99

"Loss of the Golden Gate by Fire on the 27th July 1862 15 Miles from Manzanillo, Sketched by an Eye Witness. [Signed on stone:] A.N."—n.d., with text: "Terrible Loss of Life," an account of the disaster. PLATE 100

According to dates on his work, Rosenfield evidently carried on after the firm of Hutchings & Rosenfield was terminated, for their work was done previous to 1859.

ROWE, E. R. BENICIA

1850 Benicia

"Plan of Benicia City. Founded by R. Semple and T. O. Larkin Esqrs, 18 . . . Drawn by E. R. Rowe in this City of Benicia, February 1850. Joseph O'Farrell, C.F. San Francisco"—size unknown. Date obliterated on the copy from which this title was taken. It was probably "1847."

RYAN, WILLIAM REDMOND LONDON

The author and artist of "Personal Adventures in Upper and Lower California," listed under Metchim & Company.

SARONY, MAJOR, *ET AL.* NEW YORK

1843–1844	James P. Major, engraver, 10 Watts Street
1845–1846	Henry B. Major, 10 Watts Street
1846–1847	Sarony (Napoleon) & Major (Henry B.), 99 Nassau Street and 117 Fulton Street
1847–1857	Sarony & Major, 117 Fulton Street
1853–1857	Sarony & Company, 117 Fulton Street
1856–1857	Joseph F. Knapp, 42 Ann Street
1857–1860	Sarony, Major & Knapp, 449 Broadway
1860–1865	Sarony, Major & Knapp, 449 Broadway and 26 Mercer Street
1865–1867	Sarony, Major & Knapp, 449 Broadway
1867–1868	Sarony, Napoleon, photographic materials, 543 Broadway; Major & Knapp, engraving, manufacturing, and lithograph company, 71 Broadway
1871	Major & Knapp, 56 & 58 Park Place

The stories of all these various firms are given fully in *America on Stone*, and there is a narrative of Napoleon Sarony's life in *Currier & Ives: Printmakers to the American People*, Volume I. They were among the most prolific of the Eastern firms, and produced quite a number of California views.

From Napoleon Sarony alone:

"View of Sacramento City, as it appeared during the Great Inundation in January 1850. Drawn by Geo. W. Casilear and Henry Bainbridge. Lithographed by Sarony, New York, 1850. Attested as a true picture, in facsimile, by Capt. Sutter and Alcade J. L. Thomas"—large, n.d. This is a rare view.

From Sarony & Major:

The eight plates in "Eldorado," by Bayard Taylor. New York, 1850. The first was drawn by J. C. Ward, the others by Taylor (*q.v.*):

"San Francisco in November 1848"; "Lower Bar Mokelumne River"; "Monterey"; "The Volcano Diggings"; "San Francisco in November 1849"; "Sacramento City from the South"; "Portsmouth Square, San Francisco"; and "Mazatlan" PLATE 101

"San Francisco In 1846"—small, n.d. (c.1850). Frontispiece to Coltons, "Deck and Port," N.Y., 1850. A charming little lithotint view of the peaceful and sylvan settlement of San Francisco before the deluge of Forty-niners. A view of the Bay is pictured, with one ship, and about thirty-five houses on the land. When the view was made, the population of all of California was about three thousand settlers. In the first two months of 1849 about eleven thousand people sailed for California. About fifty thousand prepared to go by land and thousands more from other parts of the world. This beautiful port-of-call of an occasional whaler for water, this sunny land of mission bells suddenly became a melting pot of world races caused by the discovery of a flake of gold.

"San Francisco Upper California in 1847. Drawn on stone by V. Prevost. Entered by Robert Wells . . . 1849"—small. Below the view is a plan of the city. At the top, an eagle with shield displayed, floreted scrolls.

"San Francisco Upper California in January 1849. Drawn on stone by V. Prevost. New-York. Published by Goupil Vibert & Co., 289 Broadway. Entered . . . 1849"—small. Does not have top description as the preceding.

"View Of Cunningham Wharf, San Francisco. Depth Of Water Outside Of T, At Low Tide, 25 Feet Depth Of Water Inside Of T, At Low Tide, 21 Feet Length Of Wharf, 300 Feet Length Of T, 350 Feet Charles Minturn, Agent Shipping and Commission Merchant References: Edward Minturn, New York"—small, n.d. The view shows the wharf and an animated scene of unloading goods from the side-wheelers "Senator" and "New World." Two sailing vessels and a frigate are anchored offshore.

"View of San Francisco. Taken from the Western Hill at the Foot of Telegraph Hill, looking toward Rincon Point and Mission Valley. Drawn from nature by Henry Bainbridge & Geo. W. Casilear. Published by Geo. W. Casilear,

New York City, and by Atwill, San Francisco, California. Entered . . . 1851" —large. In the lower margin is a description of the city.

PLATE 103 "A View of Sutter's Mill & Culloma Valley. On the south fork of the American Line [River], Alta California. Respectfully dedicated to Capt. John A. Sutter, by his obedient servant, John T. Little"—large, n.d. This is a very beautiful view of the first scene of the great drama, made very early. A Sarony & Major of the first importance.

From Sarony & Company:

"General Map of a Survey in California in connection with examinations for railroad routes to the Pacific ocean made by order of the war department, by lieut. R. S. Williamson. Drawn by Charles Preuss. New York, lith. of Sarony & co. 1855"—large.

"San Francisco in 1854. From the head of Sacramento Street"—small, n.d. Identical with Britton & Rey's letterhead, "San Francisco, 1854."

From Sarony, Major & Knapp:

Plates, all 1853, small, in "Report Of A Geological Reconnaissance In California: Made in Connection with the Expedition to Survey Routes in California, to Connect with the Surveys of Routes for a Railroad From the Mississippi River to the Pacific Ocean, under the Command of Lieut. R. S. Williamson, Corps Top. Eng'rs, in 1853. By William P. Blake, Geologist and Mineralogist of the Expedition. New York: H. Bailliere, 290 Broadway":

"Vicinity Of Fort Miller. Drawn by Charles Koppel"

"U. S. Military Post Benicia. Drawn by Charles Koppel"

"Crossing of Chowchillas River. Drawn by Charles Koppel"

"Great Basin From The Summit Of Tejon Pass. Drawn by Charles Koppel"

"Mission And Plain Of San Fernando. Drawn by Charles Koppel"

"Mirage On The Colorado Desert. Drawn by W. P. Blake"

"Metamorphic Rocks—Borders Of the Desert. Drawn by Charles Koppel"

Two large folded maps at the back of the book are:

"Map of the Geological Sections Of The Bernardino Pass (1853)"

"Map of the Sections Of The Colorado Desert. Explored by Lieut. R. S. Williamson Corps Top. Engrs. in 1853. Prepared in the Office of Pacific

Rail Road Exploration and Survey War Department. By William P. Blake."

"Las Mariposas Estate Mariposas County California"—large map in a book gotten out by "The Mariposa Company. 34 Wall Street, New York. Published in New York by Wm. C. Bryant & Co., 1863."

Several colored lithographic views, after sketches by J. M. Stanley and Gustavus Sohon, for Stevens's "Report of The Pacific Railroad Exploration," Washington 1860. Among these are some of the earliest Western views.

SCHENCK, F. EDINBURGH, SCOTLAND

Lithographed "Sequoia Wellingtonia, Mariposa Grove, South California. From a photograph"—small, n.d. I have seen no other work by him.

SCHILE, H. NEW YORK

Though often bearing titles in foreign languages, for the convenience of immigrants, and invariably outrageously crude in conception, Schile's prints are undoubtedly American in spirit. They are all late. For fuller information concerning him, see *America on Stone.*

But one of his views concerns our story: "Across the Continent. Passing the Humboldt River [title repeated in German]. 1870"—large. (Reproduced in *America on Stone.*)

SCHLESINGER, LELAND F. UNKNOWN

Published "Monetary Panic in California!!!" printed by F. Kuhl. PLATE 78

SCHMIDT, MAX SAN FRANCISCO

Although Schmidt's work was all very late, I have considered him rather fully because he was one of the few California lithographers of whom it was possible to obtain much exact knowledge. The following information comes from "Max Schmidt; the Log of a Cabin Boy," by Elford Eddy, 1922.

Max Schmidt was born in Schönbaum, near Danzig, in 1850. After seven years of sailing the seven seas, he left Hamburg in 1871 for San Francisco. At first he worked for a while in a restaurant. Soon after he got a job on the *Daily Stock Report* as a transfer man, after explaining to the editor that he had already worked as a transfer man in a restaurant! He learned very quickly, and by 1872 was doing fine engraving.

At this time in San Francisco "there was a colored man who had a lithograph establishment at 520 Clay Street. He did business under the name of G. T. Brown & Co. Otto Schoering was his lithographer. Otto conceived a liking for Max and gave him a stone to conjure with. Max proved apt at lithography."

After three months with the colored man, Max went to work for Korbel Brothers, who manufactured cigar boxes, labels, and bands. After a while with Korbel Brothers, he set himself up in a room at 535 Clay Street, as M. Schmidt & Company. The business was successful, and years later he established a branch in Los Angeles. In 1922 the firm was still going under the original name, and Schmidt himself is still living in San Francisco.

Schmidt issued, in 1886, the Firks view of "San Francisco, 1849" (*q.v.*). His other work is also late:

"Gen'l John A. Sutter's Saw Mill At Coloma (On The American River) Where Gold Was First Discovered In California Jan. 18, 1848. By James W. Marshall. Pub. by Schmidt Label & Lith. Co. Lith. for Fleehart, Amador City, Cal."—medium, n.d.

"The Weekly Call map of California and Nevada. 1878. San Francisco, lith. by M. Schmidt & co."—large, n.d.

"The Weekly Call map of California and Nevada. 1882. San Francisco, lith. M. Schmidt & co."—large, n.d.

"A Year Of Plenty. California—What shall I do with this bounteous harvest of fruit and grain? My barns verily burst with plenty and my cup runs over. Would that the Nicaragua Canal were completed, and then I might find a market for my surplus. Schmidt, L. & Litho. Co. S. F."—medium, n.d. Shows Miss California surrounded by a massive load of farm products. A railroad to the right and steamship to the left. One of the numerous cartoons appearing in the *Wasp*.

SCHWARTZ, A. SAN FRANCISCO

He is probably the Schwartz of Nagel & Schwartz.

PLATE 104 "Mission Dolores San Francisco. A. Schwartz Lithographer 51 Montgomery Str. S. Franco"—medium, n.d., is the only work of his I have seen. The real name of this Mission was Mission de San Francisco de Asis. It was often called Mission San Francisco Dolores, to distinguish it from San Francisco de Solano Mission at Sonoma, and usually shortened to Mission Dolores.

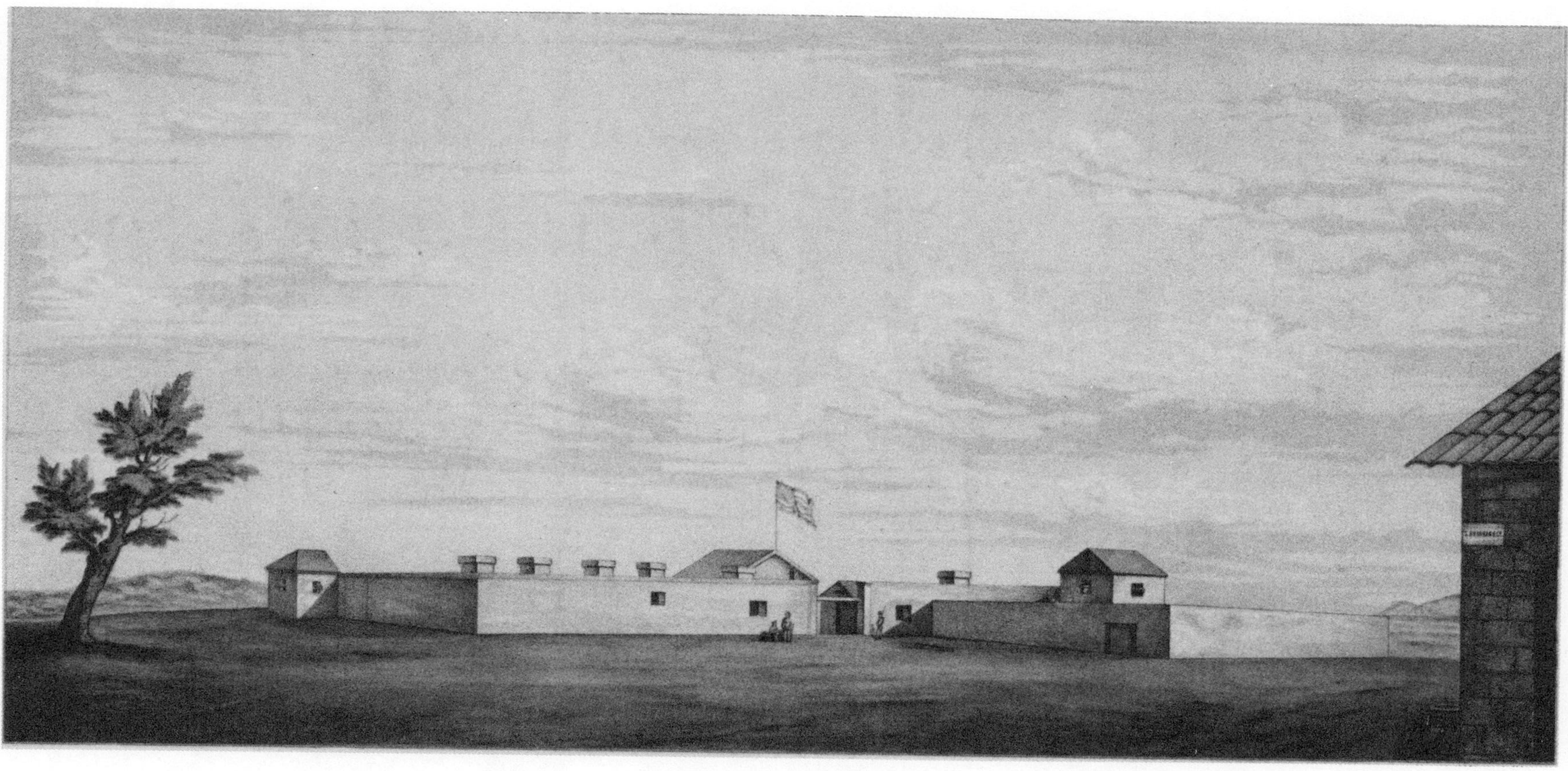

SUTTER'S FORT, SACRAMENTO, CALIFORNIA 1847.

105

A full color reproduction of this plate appears in the color section in this book.

APOLLO WAREHOUSE
APOLLO WAREHOUSE
H.D. BEACH & Co
APOLLO
SUN LITHOGRAPHIC ESTABLISHMENT
THE APOLLO WAREHOUSES, SAN FRANCISCO, CALIFORNIA.
Advantageously located at the foot of Sacramento street, and connected by strong bridges to the well known Central Wharf, The Apollo Warehouses offer uncommon advantages for storage of all descriptions. They are approachable for lighters at nearly all tides, while for commodiousness, business convenience and safety from fire and all other risks, they are truly unsurpassed.
Storage of every description taken upon the most moderate terms.
Trunks and Chests safely stored; Lumber stored; Goods received and delivered on Central Wharf, when desired.
Liberal advances made on all kinds of saleable Merchandise.
Goods received on consignment.
Ships discharged, and prompt attention to orders for lighterage.
Open policies for the Insurance of Merchandise, when desired.
H. D. BEACH & CO.
APOLLO WAREHOUSES,
J. P. BEACH San Francisco, Cal

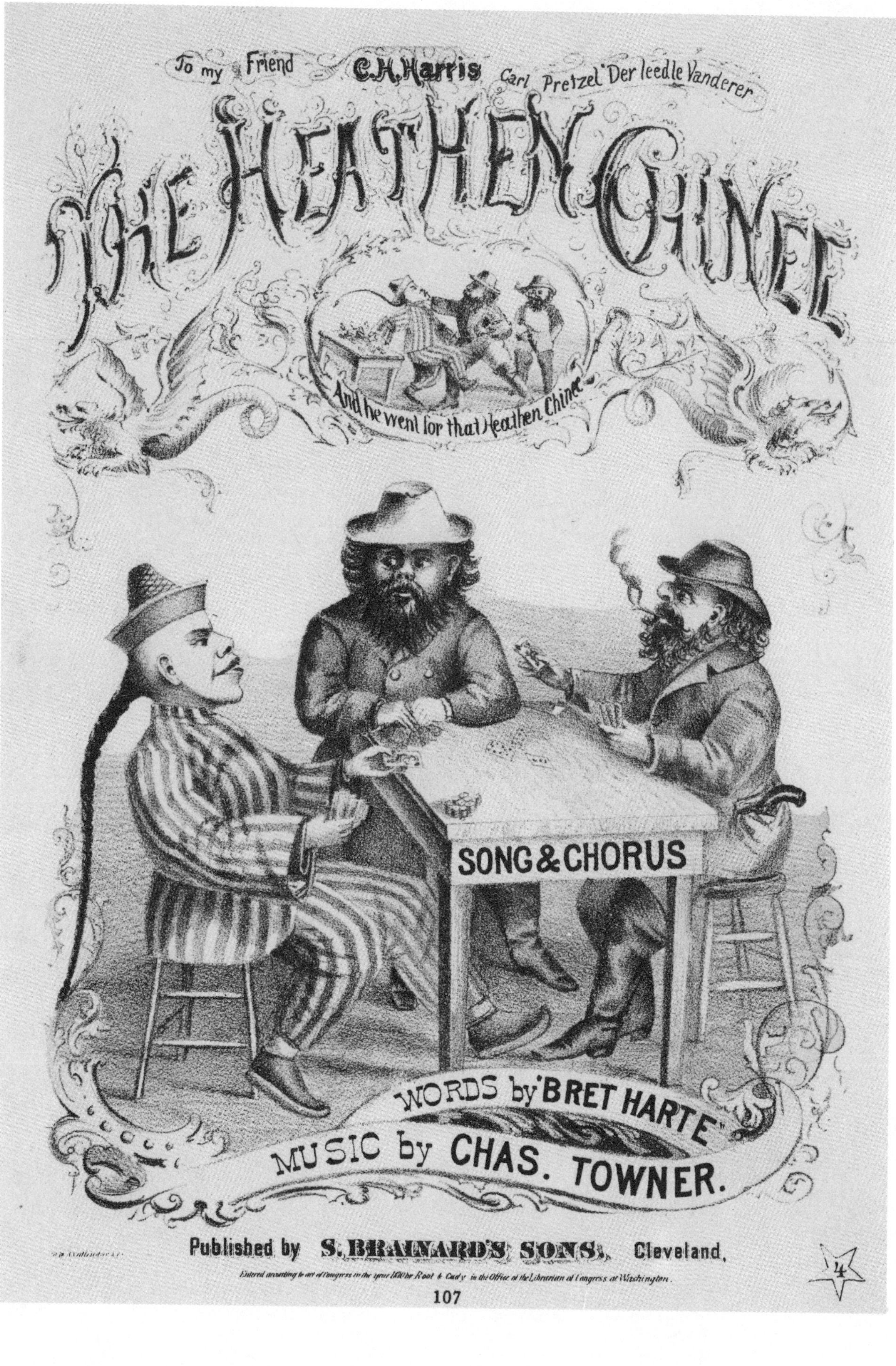

To my Friend C. H. Harris Carl Pretzel "Der leedle Vanderer"
The Heathen Chinee
And he went for that Heathen Chinee
SONG & CHORUS
WORDS by "BRET HARTE"
MUSIC by CHAS. TOWNER.
Published by S. BRAINARD'S SONS, Cleveland,
Entered according to act of Congress in the year 1870 by Root & Cady in the Office of the Librarian of Congress at Washington.
4

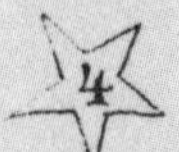

OVERLAND MAIL COMPANY
USM
B&S
THIS IS THE ONLY
STAGE LINE
ning to all points in New Mexico and the
San Juan Mining District in Southern Colo-
connection with the
DENVER & RIO GRANDE,
KANSAS PACIFIC, AND
ATCHISON TOPEKA & SANTA FE
RAILWAYS.
OVERLAND MAIL COMPANY
BRADLEY BARLOW & J. L. SANDERSON, PROPRIETORS.
VIEW OF UNCOMPAHGRE MOUNTAIN 14,430 FT ABOVE THE SEA ON OVERLAND STAGE ROUTE
THIS IS THE ONLY
STAGE LINE
Making Direct Connections with the CEN-
TRAL PACIFIC and O. & C. RAILROADS
at Redding and Roseburg, to and from
PORTLAND, Oregon.

The only correct & fully complete Map of
SAN FRANCISCO.
Compiled from the Original Map & the recent Surveys.
Containing all the latest extensions & improvements.
Respectfully dedicated to the
CITY AUTHORITIES.
BY ALEX: ZAKRESKI,
1853.
PART OF THE WESTERN ADDITION
Government Reserve.
San Jose P.
Lagoon
ADDITION of MISSION DOLORES
Pasturage
PLAZA
PLAZA
PLAZA
PLAZA
Channel
MISSION
Street
Rincon P.
Clarks P.
BAY OF SAN FRANCISCO
Explanation
Places of Worship
Scale

VIEW OF THE PROCESSION
in celebration of the **ADMISSION of CALIFORNIA,** *Oct. 29th 1850.*
crossing the Plaza of San Fransisco.

Dessiné et Lithog. par L. Le Breton.

45.

Paris, Imp. par Auguste Bry, r. du Bac.

SAN-FRANCISCO,

Vue prise d'un point élevé du côté Sud.

(CALIFORNIE)

Paris, E. SAVARY et Cie édit. 10, Place du Louvre

London, Published by E. GAMBART et Cie

111

Bay-View-Park Galop.
COMPOSED BY
F.R. NICHOLLS.
SAN-FRANCISCO.
C.B. Gifford, Del.
L. Nagel Print.
DEDICATED TO
W. F. WILLIAMSON

SERRELL & PERKINS NEW YORK

1849–1852 75 Nassau Street

Publishers of Elton's "A California Gold Hunter Meeting a Settler." PLATE 68

SHAW, S. W. UNKNOWN

Painted Kuchel & Dresel's view of "Lachryma Montis."

SHEARD (CHARLES) & COMPANY LONDON

A music sheet, showing the interest in the California Gold Rush which existed abroad, is:

"Pull Away Cheerily! (The Gold Digger's Song.) Written and Sung by Harry Lee Carter, in his Entertainment of 'The Two Lands of Gold.' Also sung by George Henry Russell, in Mr. Payne's popular entertainment, 'A Night in the Lands of Gold.' Music composed by Henry Russell. London. Printed & Published by Chas. Sheard & Co. Music Publishers & Printers, 192, High Holborn, W.C. Telegraph Address 'Musical Boquet,'—London"—n.d. (c.1853).

The words of the song are amusing:

Pull away cheerily, Not slow or wearily,
Rocking your cradles, boys, fast to and fro;
Working the hand about, Sifting the sand about,
Seeking for treasures that lie hid below.
Rocking your cradles, boys, fast to and fro,
Working the hand about, Sifting the sand about,
Seeking for treasures that lie hid below.

Here's a brave nugget! like children we hug it!
Courage! my lads, fortune favours the bold!
What are our thoughts about, Knocking the quartz about?
Thoughts that we'll soon send our parents some gold!
So pull away cheerily, ha! ha! ha! ha! ha! ha!
Pull away cheerily, fast to and fro;
Working the hand about, ha! ha! ha! ha! ha! ha!
Seeking for treasures that lie hid below.

There's Dick a young digger, Works a cradle much bigger,
Than his own little self, While Sally she must
Add her mite to the store, by collecting the ore,
And filling her apron with bright yellow dust.
Rocking your cradles, boys, fast to and fro,
Working the hand about, Sifting the sand about,
Seeking for treasures that lie hid below.

Here's a mere mannikin, bringing a panakin,
He scarcely can grasp in his small tiny hand,
While tilting his dish up, We merrily fish up,
Another supply of the glittering sand;
So pull away cherrily, ha! ha! ha! ha! ha! ha!
Pull away cherrily, fast to and fro;
Working the hand about, ha! ha! ha! ha! ha! ha!
Seeking for treasures that lie hid below.

SHELTON, C. A. SAN FRANCISCO

Published the two excellent lithographs, painted and drawn on stone by Charles Nahl and A. Wenderoth, "Miners Cabin" and "A Miner Prospecting." They will be found listed under B. F. Butler, the lithographer.

SINCLAIR, THOMAS S. PHILADELPHIA

Sinclair was a lithographer who had, to a certain degree, the news sense of Nathaniel Currier. His work is interesting, and is fully covered in *America on Stone.*

I have seen the following California views issued by him:

"Adams & Co.s Express 'Polka' Composed Expressly For Adams & Co. And Respectfully Dedicated To E. S. Sanford Esq. By Frances Weiland"—music sheet, n.d. On the building: "Adams & Co.s Express"—"Edward S. Sanford & Co's Foreign Express." In the street, one-horse express wagons—"Adams & Co." and "California Express."

"All's Not Gold That Glitters"—small. Frontispiece to "All's Not Gold That Glitters or The Young Californian," New-York, D. Appleton & Co. 1853. Title within circle surrounded by illuminated rectangular border; below, a colorful composition of a miner at work.

"Entrance of Livermore's Pass"—small, n.d.

"San Francisco, 1849. Drawn on the spot by Henry Firks for W. H. Jones, Esq. of San Francisco, U.C. On stone by Ibbotson. T. Sinclair's Lith. 101 Chestnut St. Phila. Entered . . . 1849"—large. See Firks. Following are the marginal references on this view, which is reproduced: PLATE 102

1. Am. Sh. Huntress. 2. Br. B. Asenath. 3. Dan. B. Neptunas. 4. Fr. B. Staoeuil. 5. Fr. Sh. Chateaubriand. 6. Mer. Sh. Victoria. 7. Am. Sh. Forrester. 8. Am. B. Oberon. 9. Am. B. Superior. 10. Am. Shr. Philadelphia burnt. June 24th. 11. Ch. B. Carmen. 12. Haiv. B. Mary Frances. 12. Am. Sh. Edwin. 14. Fr. Sh. Ronald. 15. Dan Sh. Adelia. 16. Am. Sh. Grey Eagle. 17. Br. B. John Ritson. 18. Am. B. Col. Fremont. 19. Ch. Sh. Virginia. 20. Am. Sh. Sea Queen. 21. Ch. B. Maria Louisa. 22. Ch. B. Romano. 23. Am. Sh. Thomas. 24. Am. B. Quito. 25. Am. B. Louisiana. 26. Am. Sh. Greyhound. 27. Ch. Sh. California Dorado. 28. Am. Steamer. Panama. 29. Am. Br. Col. Benton. 30. Am. Sh. Massachusetts. 31. Am. B. Lucy Penniman. 32. Fr. B. Limanienne. 33. Ch. Sh. Gen Ferrias. 34. Am. Schoon. Honolulu. 35. Fr. B. Olympa. 36. Am. Sh. Heber. 37. Am. Steamer Oregon. 38. U.S.S. Warren. 39. U.S.S. Southhampton. 40. Quartm. P. Invincible. 41. H.B.M. Inconstant. 42. Launch for Stockton (Emily & Jane). 43. Customhouse. 44. Golden Gate. 45. Parkers Hotel Isld. Yerba Buena.

"San Francisco. 1851. Published for the History of the World, by Henry Bill. New York. Entered . . . 1851"—small. Views in 1850, 1852, 1854, 1855, 1856 and 1857 were also issued, all copyrighted by Henry Bill, and all, save 1851, from the same plate.

"View of Benecia from the West. Chas. Koppel."—small, n.d. This was one of the plates in the "U. S. Postal Rail Road Expedition & Survey" (see Anonymous). Benecia was the state capital from 1853 to 1854.

Plates, all 1853, small, in "Report Of A Geological Reconnaisance In California: Made in Connection with the Expedition to Survey Routes in California, to Connect with the Surveys of Routes for a Railroad from the Mississippi River to the Pacific Ocean, under the Command of Lieut. R. S. Williamson, Corps Top. Eng'rs, in 1853. By William P. Blake, Geologist and Mineralogist of the Expedition. New York: H. Bailliere, 290 Broadway":

"Water Line And Shores Of The Ancient Lake. (Colorado Desert). From a sketch by W. P. Blake"

"Point Of Rocks Covered With A Calcareous Incrustation. Ancient Lake, Colorado Desert. Chs. Koppel"

"Geological Map Of The Vicinity of San Francisco. Prepared in Office of P. R. R. Exp. & Surveys by William P. Blake"

"Geological Map Of The Tejon Pass & Canada De Las Uvas And The Vicinity. Including The Pass Of San Francisquito & Williamsons Pass"

"Mammoth Tree. 'Beauty Of The Forest.' Sequoia gigantea, Torrey. Height 325 Feet. W. P. Blake"

Two large folded maps at the back of book are:

"Map of the Geological Section Of The Coast Mountains And Sierra Nevada Explored by Lieut. R. S. Williamson, U. S. Top. Engrs. in 1853 From San Francisco To The Great Basin Prepared in Office of P. R. R. Exp. & Surveys by W. P. Blake. Scale of 2 Miles to 1 Inch. (1853)."

"Map of the Geological Section Of The Bernardino Sierra Explored by Lieut. R. S. Williamson, U. S. Top. Engrs. in 1853 From The Great Basin To The Pacific Ocean At San Pedro. Prepared in the Office of Pacific Rail Road Explorations & Surveys War Department. by William P. Blake. (1853)."

SMITH (C. L.) & COMPANY — OAKLAND

"Bird's Eye View of California and Nevada. Published by C. L. Smith & Co. Oakland, Cal. 1879"—large.

See also Wallace W. Elliott, *et al.*

SMYTH, CAPTAIN WILLIAM, R.N. — UNKNOWN

See Day & Haghe; also Lefevre.

Captain William Smyth, R. N., was an officer on H. M. S. *Blossom,* a British warship which visited the California coast in 1826.

SNOW, *ET AL.* — SAN FRANCISCO

Not many prints have come from the various alignments of Snow, *et al.*, and their dates and addresses are not known completely.

Robinson & Snow seem to have come first, publishing in 1864 Nagel's "San Francisco. Birds Eye View." This was also published by Snow & Roos in 1864, indicating a new alignment in that year.

In 1866 Snow & Roos published Nagel's "Steamer Day" (*q.v.*). In that view is shown the store of "Snow & Roos Artists Materials," and the key to the print labels the short, silk-hatted man in front of it "Frank C. Snow," and the taller man with no hat "Joseph Roos"—also sometimes called "Gustav" Roos. They are talking to Fred Marriott, the owner of the San Francisco *News Letter* (*q.v.*). PLATE 82

In 1868 Snow & Roos published Britton & Rey's "Birds Eye View of San Francisco and Surrounding Country." This was reissued in 1875 by Snow & May, from 21 Kearny Street, and was lithographed by Britton, Rey & Company. This second issue was again "Re-published in 1880 by Snow & Company, 20 Post Street, S.F.," making in all three editions of the view by three different alignments of lithographers and publishers.

Snow & Company also published the frequently issued Firks view (*q.v.*).

SNYDER & BLACK NEW YORK

1850–1851 138 William Street and 87 Fulton Street

1852–1854 87 Fulton Street

There were other alignments of this firm. See *America on Stone*.

Two California prints by them are:

"Sutter's Fort, Sacramento, California 1847"—large, n.d. Captain John A. Sutter, in 1839, with a small band of companions, settled a few miles above what is now Sacramento and built a post called Fort Sutter. In 1841 the Mexican government, then ruling over California, gave him a land grant which became known as New Helvetia. As emigrants from "The States" began to trickle through the Sierra Nevadas, Sutter's Fort became an important settlement. The American flag was raised there in July, 1846. It was at Sutter's Mill, a few miles away, that gold was discovered in 1847. (See "Captain Sutter's account" under Britton & Rey). The inrushing flood of prospectors that followed swept over Sutter's land, forcing him to abandon the Fort. Sacramento City was established by the Forty-niners a few miles from there. Sutter's claim to the land was disputed when California became a state, and to this day litigation over this dispute is being carried on by the Sutter estate. PLATE 105

"View of The Burnt District, San Francisco. Lithographed by Snyder & Black. 1850"—medium. Scarce.

SOHON, GUSTAVUS UNKNOWN

Sohon drew some of the sketches for Stevens's "Report of the Pacific Railroad Exploration," mentioned under Sarony, Major & Knapp. He was a private soldier in the 4th Infantry, and was an artist of considerable talent.

STANLEY, J. M. UNKNOWN

Stanley was an artist detailed to some of the government surveying parties. He was a fine artist and made many of the drawings for Sarony, Major & Knapp's plates in Stevens's "Report of the Pacific Railroad Exploration." Stanley in later life was well known as a painter of Indian scenes and portraits.

STEIN, A. UNKNOWN

PLATE 21 Drew on the stone Britton & Rey's "California & Oregon Stage Company."

STEINEGGER, HENRY SAN FRANCISCO

1856 lithographer with Britton & Rey
1859–1866 member, Britton & Company
1867–1880 member, Britton, Rey & Company

PLATE 43 He drew Britton & Rey's "Ulysses S. Grant"; Britton, Rey & Company's
PLATE 17 "Territorial Pioneers" certificate; and Becherer's "May & Turnfest."

STRINGER & TOWNSEND NEW YORK

1850 222 Broadway

PLATE 60 This firm published the fine William Endicott & Company view of Sacramento (*q.v.*).

They also published:

"View of the Chagres. Lorenzo Castle. Indian Village of Chagres. Corect map of Chagres River with distances. West Chagres or American Side. Taken on the spot June 16th 1850 by George P. Clarke. Entered . . . 1850"—large, with thirteen references. One view at top, another at bottom, with the map in the middle.

STUART, FREDERICK D. UNKNOWN

See the charts listed under Curtis B. Graham.

SUN LITHOGRAPHIC ESTABLISHMENT NEW YORK

Two lithographs have turned up from this firm:

"The Apollo Warehouses, San Francisco, California. Sun Lithographic Establishment. 128 Fulton St. N.Y."—small, n.d. The ship *Apollo* was sent around the Horn from New York in 1849 to San Francisco. There it was beached and converted into a store, restaurant, and warehouse. This was the fate of many ships in those days, when whole crews would often desert ship and rush to the gold fields. It was also profitable to the owners to beach a vessel and turn it to just such uses as the *Apollo,* for San Francisco was largely a city of tents, with few buildings either for homes or storage for the thousands of newcomers. PLATE 106

"Map of Vera Cruz, Alvarado & Hautubco. Shewing the new route of the steamer for San Francisco from the gulf of Mexico to the Pacific. 1850. New York, sun lith. establishment, (1850)"—large.

I have seen an 1851 lithograph, showing America's superiority at the great World's Fair, published by "Perkins Sun Lithographic Establishment, 128 Fulton Street (Upstairs) New York." The workmanship in this print is similar to that in "The Apollo Warehouses," and in all probability the two firms were one and the same.

SWASEY, CAPTAIN WILLIAM F. SAN FRANCISCO

See Bosqui's "View of San Francisco, formerly Yerba Buena, in 1846–7."

SWINTON, F. NEW YORK AND ALBANY

Drew on stone some of the plates in "Life in California," listed under G. & W. Endicott. He did other work for them, but this is all that pertains to California. PLATE 59

TAPPAN & BRADFORD BOSTON

This firm's largest output was in maps and plans, views, etc. Their work is described in *America on Stone*. Only a few California items have come to light:

"E. S. Holden & Co. Importers, Wholesalers and Retail Dealers in Drugs & Medicines, and Chemicals. Stockton and Sonora, California. Tappan & Bradford Lith."—small, n.d.

Series of designs for the Custom House in San Francisco, all dated 1851, large.

TAVERNIER, JULES SAN FRANCISCO

The artist of Bosqui's "Hotel Del Monte." Tavernier was a painter of some distinction, and an early member of the Bohemian Club in San Francisco, of which Bosqui was a founder.

TAYLOR, BAYARD NEW YORK

The interest of the early books on California, illustrated by lithographs, is evidenced in a volume I happen to have before me at the moment: "Eldorado, or, Adventures in the Path of Empire: comprising a voyage to California, via Panama; life in San Francisco and Monterey; pictures of the gold region, and experiences of Mexican travel, by Bayard Taylor, author of 'Views A-foot,' 'Rhymes of travel,' etc., with illustrations by the author. New York: George P. Putnam, 155 Broadway. London: Richard Bentley. 1850." This edition is in two volumes, octavo. There were later English and American editions, and translations into other languages. There are eight colored lithographs as illustrations: "San Francisco in November, 1848," "Lower Bar, Mokelumne River,"
PLATE 101 "Monterey," "The Volcano Diggings," "San Francisco in 1849," "Sacramento City," "Portsmouth Square, San Francisco," and "Mazatlan." The first is "From a sketch by J. C. Ward, Esq.," the others are by Bayard Taylor, and all are lithographed by Sarony & Major.

On June 28, 1849, Bayard Taylor, a twenty-four-year-old Pennsylvanian of German and Quaker ancestry, sailed from New York for Chagres, bound for California, and commissioned by the New York *Tribune* to write a series of articles on the Gold Rush. Five years before, he had gone to Europe, wandered about on foot for two years, and written a series of articles and a book, "Views A-foot," that had proved his abilities as a traveler and as a reporter. The California journey was no less successful. "Eldorado," made up only in part of the *Tribune* articles, is a most lively and entertaining record, full of action, of concrete details shrewdly observed and carefully selected, and of illuminating comment. Like the first-class reporter that he was, Taylor went to all the interesting places, the gold mines, San Francisco, Monterey, Sacramento, and other towns and cities as they were springing up at incredible speed, talked with everyone he could find who could tell him something interesting, and except that what he sought was impressions rather than gold, had, himself, most of the experiences of a typical Forty-niner. Also, he observed the drafting and signing of the state constitution at Monterey, and met such notable early Californians as General Castro and Captain Sutter. On his way home, he toured Mexico.

Taylor's later life is interesting. On his return, he married, and his wife died two months later. He experimented with country journalism, returned to his first enthusiasm, poetry, and obtained an interest in the *Tribune*. Most of the rest of his life was spent in travel, in Europe, the Near East, and the Orient. In 1853 he took part in Perry's expedition to Japan. He married again in 1857, and in 1861 settled at his birthplace, Kennett Square, Pennsylvania, but the following year went to St. Petersburg as the secretary to the American legation. In 1870 and 1871 he published the work by which he is now chiefly known, the metrical translation of Goethe's "Faust." He lectured widely in the United States, published more than a score of books of travel, poetry, and fiction, and was for a time professor of German at Cornell. In 1878 he was appointed ambassador to Germany, but in Berlin, the same year, he died. To me, the lecturer, the writer of rhetorical poetry, the scholar, and the ambassador are less exciting than the young man bound for California with a notebook and pencil in 1849.

TESCHMAKER, F. UNKNOWN

Drew "View of the Place of Anchorage at Yerba Buena," one of the plates in "Life in California," listed under G. & W. Endicott.

This is undoubtedly H.F. Teschemacher, who is listed in 1846 as "clerk to Henry Mellus' bark 'Tasso,' and afterwards agent for the same vessel" in William Heath Davis's "Seventy-Five Years in California" (San Francisco: John Howell, 1929). He and Alfred Robinson were friends.

THOMPSON & WEST OAKLAND

Published and lithographed the plates in the following county histories:

"History of Nevada County, California. 1880"
"History of San Luis Obispo County, California. 1883"
"History of Sutter County, California. 1879"

VALLENDAR (A.) & COMPANY UNKNOWN

The only thing by this firm I have seen is the rare and amusing music sheet, reproduced here: "The Heathen Chinee. Words by 'Bret Harte.' Music by Chas. Towner. To my friend, C. H. Harris, Carl Pretzel Der leedle Vanderer. Lith. by A. Vallendar & Co. Published by S. Brainard's Sons. Cleveland. Entered . . . 1870." PLATE 107

VANCE, R. H. SAN FRANCISCO

1856–1857 daguerreotype artist, Montgomery & Sacramento streets

PLATE 26 His name appears on Britton & Rey's letterhead "Fort Vigilant."

VIOGET, JOHN J. SAN FRANCISCO

PLATE 14 See George Holbrook Baker's "Yerba Buena (now San Francisco) in the spring of 1837."

William Heath Davis speaks frequently of Vioget in "Seventy-Five Years in California." In 1835 and for a few years following Vioget was captain of a coast trading bark, the *Delmira,* from Ecuador and Peru. 1838 finds him as a civil engineer employed in the survey of the Sutter lands, and in 1839 he drew the first plan of San Francisco—then still Yerba Buena. In 1841 he was the owner of a saloon and billiard hall, which was about the only public "resort for captains, supercargoes, merchants and clerks of the town": and in "San Francisco: A Pageant," Charles C. Dobie says that "here his map of Yerba Buena was hung for want of a more official location"—a graphic pair of comments on the village that was soon to become the San Francisco of Forty-nine.

Vioget has been variously called "Jean Jacques Vioget, a Swiss," and "J.J. Vioget, the first permanent French settler in Yerba Buena." Davis includes him in an 1846 directory as "John Vioget, Maria Montero, his wife, two children, and one servant," which looks as though he had been one more "gringo" settler who married into a Spanish don's family.

Davis describes Vioget as a large man, a huge eater, and fine violinist. Once during his years as a sea captain he was jokingly referred to as "Blucher" by his close friend, Captain Steel of the bark *Kent,* from Boston, and Vioget was afterwards known up and down the coast by this nickname.

VISCHER, EDWARD SAN FRANCISCO

1850	merchant, California Street between Kearny Street & Montgomery Street
1852–1853	107 Montgomery Street
1854	real estate agent, 105 Montgomery Street
1856–1858	agent, 159 Jackson Street
Later	unknown

(For biographical material on Vischer we are particularly indebted to "Edward Vischer: His Pictorial of California," by Francis P. Farquhar. San Francisco, 1932.)

Edward Vischer was born in Bavaria April 6, 1809, of a family that counted an artist and craftsman among its ancestors. At nineteen years of age, he went to Mexico as an employee of a firm whose work took him all over that part of the world. Once, in Valparaiso, Charles Darwin, then on his voyage on the *Beagle,* stayed with him as a guest. He lived in Mexico for fourteen years, at one time being American consul at Acapulco.

Vischer went first to California in 1842 on business for his firm, and while in Monterey was among those imprisoned when Commander Jones prematurely seized that town in the name of the United States. In 1855 or 1856 Vischer sailed for China, which he eventually reached after being shipwrecked off the Philippines. From China he went around the Cape of Good Hope to Philadelphia, then back to England and Germany on business. He returned to Mexico in 1847 in time to learn of the Gold Rush in California, and went to San Francisco, settling as a merchant and agent for foreign companies. For some time he acted as Austrian consul in San Francisco.

In 1852 he married an English girl he had met on his European trip, and their home became a gathering place for many distinguished and interesting people.

Vischer made his start at sketching as a result of the interest one of his friends, Captain J. W. Osborne, took in a set of charts he had compiled on his voyages. Impressed by his draftsmanship on these charts, Osborne asked him to make a drawing of the Osborne Ranch, house and grounds. Vischer felt he could not possibly do it, but Osborne insisted, Mrs. Vischer added her encouragement, and when she agreed to read a history of Napoleon to him while he drew, he finally consented. The buildings he drew easily, and when he ran into difficulty with figures and backgrounds he would skillfully cut out the unsatisfactory parts and insert revised attempts. These views of the Osborne Ranch were so successful that he took to sketching wherever he went. On his travels he would make rough drafts on whatever material was at hand, make notes, and then finish the sketch in detail later.

In 1861 he visited the Calaveras Big Trees, where he saw the Bactrian camels, as shown in the Nagel, Fishbourne & Kuchel view. In 1862 he pub- PLATE 84
lished a portfolio of a dozen lithographed plates of sketches made on his trip, the Mammoth Tree Grove Series listed below. Dissatisfied with the lithographic process because he felt it did not adequately reproduce the quality of his work, he later had this series, (1), photographed from his sketches and mounted on cards or in albums, and most of his subsequent work was so issued.

His outstanding work was the "Pictorial of California," (2), a set of more than one hundred and fifty views with a text descriptive of life in California in the sixties and historical notes, issued in 1870. In the "Pictorial" were a number of views of the Missions, in which he had become interested on his first trip to California in 1842. These were also issued in a separate volume.

In 1862 he issued a set of sketches of the Washoe Mining District, (3), accompanied by a descriptive pamphlet. One of this set, "Panorama of the Washoe Region," was lithographed. In this series were a number of views showing the Bactrian camel. Vischer, in the pamphlet, states that animals shown in the views were all sketched on the spot, and adds:

> We must, however, account for the recurrence of camels, in sketches relating to the Big Tree Route, by the circumstance of our having travelled over that route, for the sake of studying their habits, with a little caravan of nine Bactrian camels, taken over the Sierra Nevada to Washoe in 1861.

(A story of this experiment in the use of camels is included under Nagel.)

A very interesting pamphlet is "Camels in the Sketches of Edward Vischer," by Francis P. Farquhar. Reprinted from the *California Historical Society Quarterly,* San Francisco, for December, 1930.

At General Vallejo's suggestion, Vischer later gathered data on and made drawings of the early Presidios of California to supplement the Mission series, but as far as I know these were never published.

Vischer died in 1879.

The three Vischer publications mentioned above are:

(1) "The Forest Trees of California. Sequoia Gigantea. Calaveras Mammoth Tree Grove. Photographs, from the original drawings from Edward Vischer, with contributions from various sources. Edward Vischer, 515 Jackson Street, above Montgomery, San Francisco. 1864"

(2) "Vischer's Pictorial of California. Landscape, Trees and Forest Scenes. Grand Features of California Scenery, Life, Traffic and Customs. In Five Series of Twelve Numbers Each, With A Supplement, and Contributions from Reliable Sources. San Francisco, April, 1870. Printed by Joseph Winterburn & Company, No. 417 Clay Street, between Sansome and Battery Streets"

(3) "Sketches of Washoe Mining Region: Photographs, reduced from origi-

nals, twenty-five numbers. By Edward Vischer. San Francisco: Valentine & Co.: Commercial Steamprinting Office, Nos. 517 Clay and 514 Commercial Streets. 1862"

The following Vischer views have been ascertained as lithographs:

C. C. Kuchel's "View of the Mammoth Tree Grove"; Nagel, Fishbourne & Kuchel's "Mammoth Tree Grove," and "Panorama of the Washoe Region"

Plates in his Mammoth Tree Grove Series:

I "The Approaches of the Grove. Views of the Mining Town of Murphy's, the Starting Place for the Grove: Suspension Flume at Murphy's, 1859—Sperry's Hotel at Murphy's—the Deep Cut at Murphy's, 1859. Views from the Murphy or Big Tree Route over the Sierra Nevada: Mud Springs—First Glimpse of the Sierra Nevada from the Ridge on the Carson Road—Cascade at Woodford's."

II "Entrance to the Grove, Arriving from Murphy's"

III Six "Views of Individual Trees." The "cabins" are hollowed tree trunks: "The Horseback Ride—Eagle's Wing—Pioneer's Cabin —Miner's Cabin, 1855—Old Dominion and Uncle Tom's Cabin—Miner's Cabin, 1860"

IV "Mother of the Forest, (1855 and 1861), and other groups"

V "The Three Graces. [Signed on stone:] C. C. Kuchel"

VI "Mother and Son. From a photograph"

VII Two views: "Stump and Log of the Original Big Tree, 1855. From photographs—The Father of the Forest. Partially buried in the ground. Circumference at the root 112 feet. Estimated height, before its downfall 450 feet"

VIII "The Two Guardsmen at the Entrance of the Grove, 1861"

IX "The Mammoth Grove Hotel, Grounds and General View of the Forest"—This is the center view in the Nagel, Fishbourne & Kuchel print.

X "The Fallen Hercules of the Grove. Dimensions: Height while standing, 320 feet; Circumference at the base, 95 feet. Swept down by the December Gale, 1861"

XI "Hermit. Height 318 feet; Circumference at the base, 60 feet." In the foreground: "The Burnt Tree," a charred trunk. Signed on stone: "C. C. Kuchel"

XII "The Orphans. At the Entrance of the Grove from the Sierra Nevada. [Signed on stone:] C. C. Kuchel"

All of the above plates were small, and entered in 1862.

WAGNER & McGUIGAN PHILADELPHIA

This firm, in various alignments, worked in Philadelphia from 1840 to 1865. Wagner was best known as a map engraver. Their work is listed in *America on Stone*. Only one California lithograph has been seen:

"Map of the City of San Francisco Compiled from Records & Surveys by R. P. Bridgers, C. E. Respectfully dedicated to the citizens by the publisher, M. Bixby, 1854. Lith. of Friend & Aub, 80 Walnut St. Phila. Wagner & McGuigan's Lith. & Steam-press, Phila. Entered . . . 1854"—large.

WARD, J. C. UNKNOWN

See Sarony & Major's "San Francisco in November 1848."

WASP, THE SAN FRANCISCO

The *Wasp* was founded in 1877, the first cartoon paper in colors ever published in America. It was famous for the excellent quality of its caricatures. Korbel Brothers (*q.v.*) were the original proprietors of the paper. Lithographed cartoons from the *Wasp* will be found listed under Anonymous and Schmidt. See also Britton & Rey's "Haverley's Theatre"; and "The News Letter."

WEBER (EDWARD) & COMPANY BALTIMORE

1835–c.1838 20 Gay Street

c.1842– 1854 Baltimore & Light streets

Weber's work is listed in *America on Stone*. Their California prints are:

"Map of Oregon and Upper California. From the Surveys of John Charles Fremont and Other Authorities. Drawn by Charles Preuss under the Order of the Senate of the United States, Washington City 1848. Lithy. by E. Weber & Co., Balto."—large, n.d.

"Pass in the Sierra Nevada of California. Lith. by E. Weber & Co. Baltimore" —small, n.d.

E. Weber & Co. lithographed the plates in:

"Notes of a Military Reconnoissance, from Fort Leavenworth, in Missouri, to San Diego, California, Including Parts of the Arkansas, Del Norte, and Gila Rivers. By W. H. Emory, Brevet Major, Corps Topographical Engineers. Made in 1846–7, With the Advanced Guard of the 'Army of the West.' Washington: Wendell and Van Benthuysen, Printers." Most of these plates are of the early part of the trip, through New Mexico and Arizona, but a few of them add to our story of California:

"Junction of the Gila & Colorado Rivers"—This is the site of Yuma, pictured in the George H. Baker view reproduced as Plate 10.

"Sketch of the Actions Fought at San Pasqual in Upper California Between the Americans and Mexicans Dec. 6th & 7th 1846"

"Sketch of the Passage of the Rio San Gabriel Upper California by the Americans—discomfiting the opposing Mexican Forces January 8th 1847"

"Sketch of the Battle of Los Angeles Upper California. Fought between the Americans and Mexicans Jany. 9th 1847"

"San Diego."

At the back of book, a large folded map entitled:

"Military Reconnaisance of The Arkansas Rio Del Norte and Rio Gila by W. H. Emory, Lieut. Top. Engrs. Assisted from Fort Leavenworth to Santa Fe by Lieuts. J. W. Albert and W. G. Peck, and from Santa Fe to San Diego on the Pacific by Lieut. W. H. Warner and Mr. Norman Bestor, Made in 1846–7, with the advance guard of the 'Army of the West.' Under Command Of Brig. Gen. Stephn. W. Kearny Constructed under the orders of Col. J. J. Abert Ch. Corps Top. Engrs. 1847 Drawn by Joseph Welch"

WELLS, G. S. SONORA, CALIFORNIA

G. S. Wells, of Sonora, published and copyrighted the two Britton & Rey letterheads, "Sonora from the North" and "Springfield, Tuolumne County."

WENDEROTH, A. SAN FRANCISCO

1854 C. Nahl & A. Wenderoth, daguerreotype artist, 79 Broadway.

Wenderoth seems to have been a lithographer of unusual ability. With Charles Nahl he drew on stone B. F. Butler's "Miners Cabin" and "A Miner

Prospecting." Also drew on stone "Calvary Presbyterian Church, San Francisco" listed under Britton & Rey.

WHEELER, PHELAN & COMPANY — SAN FRANCISCO

The only work of theirs I have seen is a stock certificate of the "Chapman Mill and Mining Co. Lith. Wheeler, Phelan & Co. San Francisco"—small, n.d.

WILEY, T., JR. — BOSTON

Published Bufford's "Map of the Valley of the Sacremento."

WILLIAMS, B. — LONDON

"California. Miscellaneous Series of Songs No. 164. Written, composed & sung by W. H. C. West. Pr. threepence. London. B. Williams, 11, Paternoster Row & 170, Gt. Dover Rd. Where may be had at the same price Jenny Lind's Mania, Things That Won't Wash, The Monkey's Wedding, Caudle's Second, Wedding, O 'Tis Love, [etc., etc.]"—music sheet, n.d.

WINCKELMANN & SÖHNE — BERLIN

"Strasse In St. Francisco. Guckkastenbilder No. 136—by Winckelmann & Söhne in Berlin"—small, n.d. A colored *vue d'optique.* The title, as well as the view, is reversed. The scene shown is a view looking up California Street from Montgomery. The composition is the same as that used in the Hildebrandt view.

WITHINGTON, E. G. — UNKNOWN

Sketched B. F. Butler's "View of the Conflagration of Nevada City."

WOODWARD, TIERNAN & HALE — ST. LOUIS

No more work by this company has turned up since the publication of
PLATE 108 *America on Stone,* the only lithograph of theirs I have seen being "Overland Mail Company. Bradley Barlow & J. L. Sanderson, Proprietors. View of Uncompahgre Mountain 14,400 Ft. above the Sea on Overland Stage Route. [Signed on Stone:] Holdertine"—large, n.d., with advertisements for the stage in the margin. On the baggage are the names of Kit Carson, S. B. Maxwell, and Col. Bent. This print so resembles Britton & Company's "California Stage Company," (*q.v.*) especially in the foreground, that it is likely both were done

by the same artist. This one is usually found colored, the other in black and white. Both are scarce, and extremely interesting "Deadwood Coach" views.

WORTH, L. W. UNKNOWN

The artist of Britton & Rey's letterhead "Petaluma, Sonoma Cy. Cal."

ZAKRESKI (ALEXANDER), *ET AL.* SAN FRANCISCO

c.1850	Zakreski & Hartman, unknown
1850	Alexander Zakreski, Clay Street between Dupont and Kearny
1851–1854	"& Company," corner Montgomery & Washington Streets; 1854, 152 Washington Street
1856–1857	"& Company," lithography & topographical drawing, 100 Merchant Street
1858	draughtsman, U. S. Surveyor General's Office, 133 Clay Street

The only work I have seen by Zakreski & Hartman is:

"View of the Procession in Celebration of the Admission of California, Oct. 29th, 1850, Crossing the Plaza of San Francisco. J. Prendergast del. On stone by Coquardon"—medium, n.d. When California was admitted to the Union on September 9, 1850, a special flag was made up in New York, sent to Panama, and there forwarded to California on the mail steamer *Oregon*. The news reached San Francisco on October 18th, when the *Oregon* entered the Bay with the streamer flying from her masthead and fired the prearranged signal guns. Eleven days later the great celebration was held which is shown in this view. California still celebrates Admission Day, making September 9th an official holiday throughout the state. PLATE 110

From Zakreski, and Zakreski & Company:

Certificate of membership in "The Committee of Vigilance of the City of San Francisco. Organized 9th June, 1851, for the mutual protection of life & property, rendered insecure by the general insufficiency of the laws and their mal-administration. Lith. by Alex. Zakreski & Co. Corner of Montgomery and Washington Streets"—small, n.d.

"The only correct & fully complete Map of San Francisco. Compiled from the Original Map & the recent Surveys . . . Respectfully Dedicated to the City Authorities. By Alex: Zakreski, 1853. Drawn & Lith by Alex: Zakreski, Cor PLATE 109

Washington & Montgomery Streets, at his Topographical Office"—small, n.d. This was also issued in 1852 and in 1854, the latter having marginal views of public buildings.

"Plan of Marysville Compiled from The Original Map Respectfully dedicated to the Citizens of Marysville 1852. Published by Eddy, Broths. Stationers Marysville. Cal. Lith. by Alex: Zakreski at his Topographical Office. Cor. Washington & Montgomery. up stairs"—small, n.d.

"A Topographical and Complete Map of San Francisco. Compiled from the original map, from the recent survey of W. M. Eddy, County Surveyor. Entered . . . 1853"—small.

ACKNOWLEDGMENTS

In acknowledging the help given me on this book I must first thank my friend, Mr. Harry MacNeill Bland, who gave generously of his time and knowledge in reading the manuscript and making additions and suggestions.

On the work done in California I am indebted particularly to Mrs. Mae Gibson Foster, formerly curator of the Society of California Pioneers, and to Mrs. Helen Putnam Van Sicklen, the librarian. Without their help in suggesting leads our difficulties in picking up the trails of the lithographers would have been infinitely greater. The society was also kind in permitting us to reproduce many of the lithographs from their fine collection.

I am indebted for the use of reproductions and general help to the Henry E. Huntington Library in San Marino, California, the California State Library at Sacramento, California, and the California Historical Society and the M. H. de Young Memorial Museum of San Francisco, California.

Mr. Roger D. Lapham, Mr. John Howell, Mr. Edwin Grabhorn, Mr. Douglas S. Watson and Dr. William J. Haber, all of San Francisco, helped greatly in lending prints for reproduction and supplying much information.

The story of Britton & Rey could not have been written had it not been for the assistance of Miss Sylvia Rey and her sisters, Mrs. Sander and Mrs. Sproule, of Berkeley, and of Mr. Britton Rey, her nephew.

The story of George H. Baker has come from his daughter, Mrs. George Lilly, and the information on Edward Bosqui was given by his daughter, Mrs. Archie Treat.

From Mr. Francis P. Farquhar, of San Francisco, I obtained most of the story on Edward Vischer.

To the Misses McDevitt and Wright, of the Smithsonian Institution, Mr. Joseph M. Muller of the New York Public Library, and Mr. Malcolm N. Stone for material on the music sheets.

Mr. Ethan D. Alyea has very kindly lent several interesting and helpful books on California from his collection.

To William Murrell for information about Edward Jump, taken from the forthcoming Volume II of *American Graphic Humor*.

To Mr. Hirst Milhollen, of the Library of Congress, I am indebted for adding material to the text.

My friend, Mr. Harry M. Lockhart, gave me many helpful leads to his friends in California.

To A. E. Rueff for the information about George V. Cooper.

To Mr. John Marshall Phillips, of the Yale University School of Fine Arts, I am indebted for the use of one of the fine colored lithographs reproduced in this volume.

As usual, I have had much assistance from the Antiquarian Society at Worcester, Mass., and the New York Public Library.

And again I am indebted to Mr. Robert Fridenberg for the use of his records which produced additional material.

Kennedy & Company of New York were good enough to check over their stock and records and give me much additional material.

The Cadmus Book Shop gave me full access to their large collection of California material.

For her assistance during many long hours of proofreading, I am indebted to Miss Elizabeth F. Fuselman, of Sausalito, California.

To the American Art Association Anderson Galleries for the use of their California records.

To Maurice Sloog for the list of French caricatures relating to the Gold Rush.

I am grateful, too, for the help so freely given by many others in gathering the story of California on Stone.

SUBJECT INDEX

CONTENTS OF SUBJECT INDEX

Abbreviations used: *B&R*—Britton & Rey. *C&I*—Currier & Ives. *J, Q & Co.*—Justh, Quirot & Company. *K&D*—Kuchel & Dresel. *N.C.*—Nathaniel Currier. *S.F.*—San Francisco. *S,M&K*—Sarony, Major & Knapp. *V.*—View.

ADVERTISEMENTS

AMUSEMENTS

Gambling

Racing

Miscellaneous

ARCHITECTURAL PLANS

BOOK ILLUSTRATIONS

CARTOONS

CELEBRATIONS AND PARADES

CERTIFICATES

Membership

Stock

Miscellaneous

CHINESE

COMMANDMENTS

DRESS

EARTHQUAKES

ELEPHANT
(Symbol)

FIRE COMPANIES

FIRES

FORTS AND PRESIDIOS

HISTORICAL

INDIANS

LETTERHEADS

MAPS AND CHARTS

MILITARY

MINES AND MINING OPERATIONS

MINERS' LIFE

MISCELLANEOUS

MISSIONS

MUSIC SHEETS

PORTRAITS AND CARICATURES

Stage Coach

TREES, BIG

VESSELS

VIEWS

California: General

California Cities, Towns, Rivers, Etc.

San Francisco: General

San Francisco Bay

S.F. Buildings: Churches

S.F. Buildings: Commercial

S.F. Buildings: Fire Houses

S.F. Buildings: Hotels and Restaurants

S.F. Buildings: Miscellaneous

S.F. Buildings: Public

S.F. Buildings: Saloons

S.F. Buildings: Schools and Asylums

S.F. Buildings: Theatres

San Francisco: Miscellaneous

San Francisco Plaza

San Francisco Streets

San Francisco Wharves

VIEWS OUTSIDE CALIFORNIA

Mexico and Central America

Nevada, Oregon, and Washington Territories

Far West: General

VIGILANCE COMMITTEE

THIS BOOK

here first printed in an edition of 501 copies
of which 451 are for sale,
has been set on the monotype in Antique No. 98
and printed on Aurelian laid rag paper.
The illustrations have been printed by the Similetone Process
by Zeese-Wilkinson Company, Long Island City
Printing and binding by the Country Life Press, Long Island, N. Y.

This is No. 404

Because of its historical interest,
the publisher has retained
this original printing notice.
This notice does not contain
information for this Arno edition.

Houston Public Libraries
FOR LIBRARY USE ONLY